D1070715

CLOUT—

Womanpower and Politics

By Susan and Martin Tolchin

TO THE VICTOR—POLITICAL PATRONAGE
FROM THE CLUBHOUSE TO THE WHITE HOUSE

CLOUT—WOMANPOWER AND POLITICS

CLOUT ★★★

Womanpower and Politics

Susan and Martin Tolchin

Coward, McCann & Geoghegan, Inc.
New York

Portions of this book originally appeared in *Esquire,* The Magazine for Men, as "Getting Clout," by Susan and Martin Tolchin, published in July, 1973.

For permission to reprint copyrighted material the authors wish to thank the following:

The New York *Times* for "Mrs. Abzug's Image Shifts But Is She The Same Old Bella?" by M. Tolchin. Copyright © 1973 by The New York *Times* Company. Reprinted by permission.

SBN: 698-10600-8
Library of Congress Catalog Card Number: 74-79677
Printed in the United States of America

Endpaper montage by Judy Seifer, photographs used by permission of Wide World Photos, Inc. and United Press International.

To Charles and Karen

CONTENTS

ACKNOWLEDGMENTS

Once when our daughter Karen was about two and one-half years old, we rebuked her for some typically two-and-one-half-year-old peccadillo. "You can't talk to me like that," she said, drawing herself up to her full height, possibly three feet. "Why not?" we asked. "Because," she replied, "I'm a person."

We had just begun this book and took her remark as an omen. The female sex, even unto its youngest members, was asserting a new dignity, and it was nowhere more apparent than among those women who sought public office.

In the course of our research we relied on the advice and guidance of hundreds of politicians—both male and female—who helped us understand this phenomenon. Their experiences were recorded in taped interviews, some of which lasted many hours, and we gratefully acknowledge their help.

We would like to thank the women in Congress who spent so much time with us. Especially helpful were Bella Abzug and her aide Mim Kelber, Julia Butler Hansen, Yvonne Burke, Shirley Chisholm (whose staff contributed a great deal to our investigation of the fight to include domestics in the Minimum Wage bill), Ella Grasso, Edith Green, Martha Griffiths, Liz Holtzman, Margaret Heckler, Patsy Mink, Leonor Sullivan, and Pat Schroeder and her aide Mimi Barker.

For her insights and suggestions, we thank Gloria Steinem, who read portions of the manuscript. We would also like to thank Liz Carpenter, Jill Ruckelshaus, Esther Peterson, Jane and Bob Squier, and Karen De Crow.

Throughout the two years we spent researching and writing our book, we were ably assisted by the leaders and staff of the National Women's Political Caucus: Katie Herring, Jane McMichael, Doris Meissner, Sabina Parks and Fredrica Wechsler. Ronnie Feit and her assistant Carol Stuhrmer contributed to our understanding of the dynamics of money and politics.

Womanpower would never have materialized were it not for

the many women who worked hard through their parties and caucuses to convert an ideal to reality. Of those who spent many hours with us explaining the dynamics of their involvement, we owe special thanks to Nikki Beare, Gwen Cherry, Elaine Gordon and Monna Lighte of Florida; Martha McKay of North Carolina; Carol Gaddy and Jean Lambie of Arkansas; Donna Meyer of Oklahoma; Helen Cassidy, Sarah Weddington, Ginny Whitehill and Betsey Wright of Texas; Marilyn Kalbach of New Mexico; Bonnie Andrikopoulous of Colorado; Pat Vandershaaf and Mary Robinson of Tennessee; Colleen Alexander, Joanne Gardiner and Ruth Harper of Pennsylvania; Andrey Beck, Judy Pickering and Donna Brunstadt of Connecticut; Millicent Fenwick and Dr. Wynona Lipman of New Jersey; Joie Prevost, Geraldine Pleshaw, Marjorie Schiller, Katherine Kane and Caroline Chang of Massachusetts, Audrey Colum of Washington, D.C., and many others.

Two women exerted special efforts on our behalf: Lee Novick, who guided us through the intricacies of Connecticut politics, and Ann Lewis, who helped organize our trip to Boston.

The formidable task of unraveling the tangled strands of the 1972 Democratic convention was aided by George McGovern, Rick Stearns, Richard Dougherty, Shirley MacLaine, Ann Wexler and Jean Westwood. We are especially grateful to Sissy Farenthold, who devoted much time sharing her experiences with us.

We thank those who enlightened us on the role of women in New York politics: Ronnie Eldridge, Carol Greitzer, Ross Graham, Sara Kovner, Tom Morgan, Esther Newberg, Eleanor Holmes Norton, Susan Rennie, Priscilla Ryan, Susan Rosenfeld, Cathy Samuels and Howard Samuels.

For their generous efforts in helping us gather statistics, we thank Harriet Cipriani of the Democratic National Committee and Eleanor Oberwetter of the Republican National Committee. We also thank Mary Gereau and Dr. Irene Murphy for their help on ERA.

We are indebted to Jean Kidd, who performed the Herculean task of transcribing the tapes with clarity and precision, and to Nanette Lemmerman of Drew University for typing the manuscript in its final form, a task she completed with exceptional speed and accuracy. We also thank Drew University for providing us with secretarial help.

For her incisive criticisms and judgment, we thank our editor, Patricia Brehaut Soliman, whose careful editing helped shape our final product. Claire Moriarty meticulously copy edited the book.

We acknowledge a very personal debt to our agent, Don Congdon, for his constant encouragement, support and advice.

These were among the hundreds of people who gave us intellectual and moral support, and we thank them all. Our conclusions, of course, are our own, and we assume full responsibility for them.

Introduction

Getting Clout: Overcoming the Obstacles to Political Success

Look, Mr. President, I might sleep with them, but I'll be damned if I'll eat lunch with them.

—BILL LAWRENCE

"Women do the lickin' and the stickin' while men plan the strategy.

—MAYOR MOON LANDRIEU
of New Orleans

John Lindsay bounded up the City Hall steps as a woman television reporter and her camera crew struggled to keep pace alongside him. "Mr. Mayor," she asked, "why aren't there more women commissioners in your administration?" The mayor's eyes twinkled as he bolted for his office and tossed off a throwaway line, while the cameras were grinding away: "Honey, whatever women do, they do best after dark."

In many ways the Lindsay administration typified the locker-room quality of American politics—the tough, sweaty, combative bastion of the American male. Women are welcome as cheerleaders and water girls, to supply the glamor and perform the scut work, but are seldom accepted as members of the first team, or even the bench. No matter what their talents or accomplishments, traditionally "Women do the lickin' and the stickin'," says New Orleans Mayor Moon Landrieu, "while men plan the strategy."

The very texture of American politics—its folkways and

byways—militates against women's entry into the mainstream. The smoke-filled rooms, bourbon-and-branchwater rites, and all-night poker games exclude women from the fellowship and cronyism that seal the bonds of power. It is an exclusion practiced by Republicans and Democrats, reformers and regulars, liberals and conservatives. It crosses economic and social barriers, showing little distinction between rich women and poor, social lions, the upwardly mobile, and the disinherited. Nor do years of service, party loyalty, wisdom or experience provide women with a passport to those inner circles where priorities are set, careers advanced and strategies determined.

"Women are on the outside when the door to the smoke-filled room is closed," lamented Millicent Fenwick, an erudite Republican who served in the New Jersey legislature before her appointment as the state's Director of Consumer Affairs. Ms. Fenwick, an early and vigorous supporter of the gubernatorial candidacy of William Cahill, found that her credentials, hard work and long hours at campaign headquarters counted little. "When the campaign chairman and others came up for policy meetings, I was never invited to come in." One reason for the exclusion, in Ms. Fenwick's view, is that "women are new in politics; we come to it with some zeal and idealism. We think it's possible to have a brave new world. The result is that the political operators have a sense that we will not understand the political realities—and they are often right. Maybe it's not a female characteristic as much as an amateur characteristic. Maybe some day we'll lose our amateur standing." In the age of Watergate, however, this amateur standing has become a positive virtue at the polls.

Governor Cahill himself, when asked to explain why there were so few women in New Jersey's delegation to the Republican National Convention in 1972, replied, "Most women want to stay home and take care of their home and family. To ask them to do more is to ask them to do more than they are able."[1] His remarks fueled a running feud with women politicians in the state, some of whom seemed not overly upset when Mr. Cahill lost his bid for a second term.

Similarly, President Nixon advised Julie Darco, a thirteen-year-old who said she wanted to go into politics, "You're too pretty, you'll probably get married instead."[2]

There have been, to be sure, many great women in America's public life—the early abolitionists, the feminists, suffragists, muckrakers and socialists—but they were doomed, because of their oppression, to work outside the system. Other great women have derived power from their husbands or families, but seldom wielded it in their own right, and ultimately discovered that real power was nontransferable. Eleanor Roosevelt proved a notable exception, retaining her derivative power after her husband's death, and using that power to help create a reform movement in New York City. In the nation's long, turbulent political history, however, few women have enjoyed great careers in mainstream politics. Few have begun at the grass roots, and amassed power slowly, inexorably, and irrevocably as have male politicians within the two-party system.

This barring of women from mainstream politics and the councils of government is now being challenged by increasing numbers of women who have sought and won elective posts in city halls and statehouses, and begun to build their own political bases. They are the cutting edge of an unusual middle-class revolution, initiated by well-heeled, well-educated, well-dressed, and well-spoken women. Its leaders are not high school dropouts but college professors, lawyers, writers, physicians and business-women. They live in neat suburban homes and comfortable apartments. They enjoy good health, good contacts, good organizational abilities, and a record of personal achievement in fields outside politics.

It has been a quiet revolution, and one that has gone virtually unnoticed both by hard-nosed pols and the predominantly male press. In the past two years the representation of women in state legislatures has increased by 50 percent, from 282 to 437. Although the number of women in state legislatures still remains puny—only 7 percent of all legislators—their power is clearly on the rise. The biggest increases began in the 1972 elections. In Illinois, which previously had four women in the entire legislature, there are now eight in the House and three in the Senate. In New Jersey, where there was previously one in the

Senate and three in the House, there are now two in the Senate and six in the House. In North Carolina the number of women in the House quadrupled, from two to eight. In Florida Paula Hawkins, a Republican, was the first woman in the state's history (and the third Republican) elected to statewide office. In Connecticut women won ten mayoralties, sweeping the towns along the eastern corridor, where many became the first Democratic mayors in their towns' histories. In Connecticut, too, Representative Ella Grasso became the first woman in the state to win the gubernatorial nomination of a major party. In Rochester, New York, a woman led the field in the City Council race, while another New York woman became a candidate for lieutenant governor. In Texas Frances "Sissy" Farenthold, who confounded politicians by edging out two front-runners to qualify for a runoff in the 1972 gubernatorial race, ran again in the spring of 1974 in the gubernatorial primary.

Indeed, women from all walks of life seemed to be running for office, including Beverly Harrell—operator of a brothel in one of two Nevada counties where prostitution is legal—who filed for state Assembly.

Women's heightened political clout was also reflected by Congress' passage of the Equal Rights Amendment and by a rash of settlements of sex-discrimination cases in the spring and summer of 1974. American Telephone and Telegraph weighed in with $15 million in back pay and $23 million in raises to women and a relatively small number of minority males, with another $30 million later negotiated for 25,000 managerial employees, most of them women. In San Francisco, the Bank of America awarded a $10 million settlement to 54,000 employees, 73 percent of whom were women. Experts characterized as unprecedented a part of the settlement under which the bank agreed to establish a $3.75 million trust fund exclusively for women employees at all levels of the bank's operations, to be used for education, training, travel and other so-called self-development programs. Rutgers University in New Jersey awarded a $375,000 settlement to 210 women. These settlements were no doubt hastened by a United States Supreme Court decision in May, 1974, that upheld the principle that men and women doing equal work must be paid equal wages;

that decision itself was heralded as both a reflection of women's increased political power and a catalyst for greater power in the future. The following month HEW handed down regulations barring sex discrimination practices in public schools on all levels, and in all graduate schools receiving federal contracts.

Statistically, their exclusion from government is particularly acute on the national level. There are no women in the Senate, and only 16 among the House's 435 members, three fewer than the high of 19 during 1961–1963. There have only been three women governors, all stand-ins for their husbands: Miriam "Ma" Ferguson, in Texas; Nellie Tayloe Ross, Wyoming; and more recently, Lurleen Wallace, Alabama. "Ma" Ferguson ran with the campaign slogan, "Me for Ma, and I ain't got a durn thing against Pa."

Ironically, women constitute 52 percent of the population and 53 percent of the voting population, a comfortable majority in the political ledger, but one that merely underscores a further measure of their failure to date—the fact that women constitute only 3 percent of the country's elected officials.

No women hold Cabinet posts, although President Nixon had more than doubled the number of women in high executive posts. The Supreme Court has never seated a woman justice, although here, too, strong pressures have been brought to bear to break that precedent. There are no women governors. On the state and local levels, however, the picture is rapidly changing. Twenty-seven women mayors preside over small-to-medium-sized cities (cities having a population over 30,000), including Oklahoma City (Patience Latting) and New Brunswick, New Jersey (Pat Sheehan). None of the large cities has a woman mayor, although Diane Feinstein was a serious contender in the last mayoralty race in San Francisco.

Perhaps the greatest strides toward increased representation were made by the Democrats and Republicans at their 1972 conventions. Women made up 40 percent of the Democratic delegates, compared with 13 percent in 1968, and 30 percent of the Republican delegates, compared with 17 percent in 1968. Here, too, the locker room remained a presence, and many women delegates complained that male delegates failed to grasp the historic aspects of the female presence and treated the women as a carnal convenience. "You have no conception of how gross some of the men were," recalls Lee Novick, a Connecticut Democrat describing her experiences at the Miami Beach convention. "They'd walk over to you on the floor of the convention and say, 'Hey, you want to get laid?' They were absolute Neanderthals."

The conventions were historic, however, in involving women in the highest councils of Republican and Democratic decision making. Many women returned home dissatisfied with their former roles, and gave up the "lickin' and the stickin'" in favor of campaigns for city attorney, county sheriff and state legislator —local races in which their initial successes portend a gradual redistribution of mayoralties, governorships and Congressional seats.

But they have not yet ascended to the higher echelons, or penetrated the locker room, where women are valued more for their sexual contributions than their political ones. "If there's a kind of semiattractive woman around a candidate, the assumption is that she's there to sleep with him—and the assumption is usually correct," says Richard Reeves, a journalist who has logged more campaign miles than he cares to remember. Charles Goodell, a former Republican Senator from New York, describing the sexual atmosphere of big-time campaigns, says, "When people are embarked on a sort of exciting adventure, and they're uprooted, moving from place to place, it tends to generate liaisons." And Myra MacPherson, who covered national campaigns for the Washington *Post,* conveys the tenor of those months on the road by recalling that her biggest problem was in becoming what she calls "one of the boys," which she said meant reassuring the politicians, their aides and the traveling press that she wasn't going to tell their wives what went on during the road trips.

Women who work in campaigns—especially single women —often find the criterion for their acceptance rests on sexuality rather than on intellect or ability. Esther Newberg, one of the "Boiler Room Girls" in Senator Robert F. Kennedy's office, who served as Muskie's campaign manager in New York State, says of the local politicians, "They told me I had better legs than

Crangle's. They relate to us sexually. It has to be worse for a single woman. They assume that the reason you're in politics is for sex." Even now, in her post as executive director of the state Democratic Committee, Ms. Newberg finds she has to field sexual innuendos from many of the men in her political circle. "I just had a guy on the phone ask me if I was going to Washington tonight, where was I going to stay, and that sort of thing," she said. "I don't mind, though. If there has to be fifteen seconds of bullshit, okay. It makes them bigger men. They are products of their background."

Party politics, elective office, and high-ranking government jobs are not the only areas in which women lose out: They suffer—as women's issues suffer—from being part of a society whose priorities are set by male-dominated governments, Republican and Democratic, which find the money to wage wars and support mammoth military establishments while hunger and poverty continue unabated.

Women have ruefully come to realize, moreover, that their exclusion has helped shape the character of the game—to their disadvantage. Although they have not responded to the traditional incentives offered male politicians—money, jobs and contracts—they have been energized by social issues long ignored by male pols. Their rallying cries have focused on peace, women's rights, abortion reform, day-care centers, and greater sensitivity to the disenfranchised—children, minorities and the poor.

Women whose issue-oriented careers illuminate the humanist tradition of the women's movement include the late Jeannette Rankin of Montana, a pacifist who was the only member of Congress to vote against America's entry into both World Wars; Margaret Chase Smith, the first Senator to attack Joseph McCarthy; and Margaret Heckler, a Massachusetts Republican who led the 1972 convention fight for a day-care plank and has tried to organize a Women's Caucus in the House. In Texas Sissy Farenthold, while a member of the legislature, initiated reforms that shook the state Democratic leadership, as did her strong showing in a gubernatorial race, in which she had been opposed by party leaders. Bella Abzug and Shirley Chisholm were among the earliest opponents of the Vietnam War and, along with Gloria

Steinem, politicized countless women in the process. This humanist tradition more than outweighs those relatively few women politicians who have been indifferent to social concerns, or such women as Phyllis Schlafly, who is leading the fight against the Equal Rights Amendment.

If women constituted a significant input into its policy-making apparatus, would the Nixon administration have been able to preside over a priority system that paid billions in cost overruns on the C-5A while at the same time cutting back school lunch programs and milk money in its budget? Would the same administration have vetoed the day-care bill with such strong language—comparing day care to the start of a communal life-style—if a woman had lent her perspective to the Cabinet? Defense contracts in the city of Charleston alone total $66,900,000 annually, while several hundred million dollars of federal appropriations were withdrawn in 1972 from the state of New York—an act that forced working mothers who were the sole support of their children to go on welfare.

Nevertheless, many women, knowledgeable, compassionate and resourceful women who seek to change these priorities, find they cannot surmount the obstacles to running for office, or move from the periphery into the centers of power, where they find such politicians as Queens Democratic leader Councilman Matthew J. Troy, Jr., the genial Peck's Bad Boy of New York City politicians. Some politicians merely send Christmas cards. Others send whiskey. Mr. Troy outdoes them all. He hosts an all-night party at a motel. The motel is a law client of Mr. Troy's, as are the divorceés whom he invites to entertain the politicians and newsmen. Some of the merrymakers stumble back to their jobs days later. No women politicians have ever been invited, nor, undoubtedly, would they accept such an invitation.

A more serious omission, however, has until recently barred women from attending the annual political lampoons produced by political reporters in Washington, Albany and New York. The shows are not merely glittering, full-dress social gatherings. They provide access to public officials who are otherwise unavailable, and spectacular opportunities to renew old acquaintances and transact political deals. Indeed, politicians line up near the governor's table and the mayor's table in both New York and Albany for rare moments alone with the political leader and his aides—without benefit of appointment—to plead their cases. Many a political career has been advanced at these festivities.

Washington's resolutely all-male Gridiron Club (the other clubs have finally admitted women to membership), which hosts the President, members of Congress and the Cabinet, and leading politicians and lobbyists at its annual lampoon, has admitted women to the audience only reluctantly and sparingly. Last year tradition was broken and invitations were sent to 19 prominent women, of whom only 8 accepted, out of 500 guests.

"President Kennedy was one of those who thought women should have full rights and privileges in our club, and he never let up the pressure on me to see to it that they were admitted," recalled the late Bill Lawrence, a newsman who had been the club's president, in his book *Six Presidents, Too Many Wars.* "But I was as direct and blunt in saying no to Kennedy, who was my friend, as I would have been to any other member of the Press Club, President of the United States or not. . . . One day we were flying with Kennedy aboard Air Force One . . . and . . . Kennedy again called on me to exert my leadership as a past president to get them admitted. 'Look, Mr. President,' I responded, 'I might sleep with them, but I'll be damned if I'll eat lunch with them.' "[3]

Indeed, many newsmen who cover politics are genuinely as discriminatory as the politicians they cover, from whom they often derive their identity. It is extraordinary to see political reporters elevate seniority, for example, into the absolute virtue it has become for veteran politicians, who, like veteran reporters, benefit from the seniority system. Then, too, the media are blinded by the prejudices of society at large, recalling political consultant Joe Napolitan's comment that "I don't know who discovered the ocean, but I'm sure it wasn't a fish."[4]

Complaints are legion. "The media does not concentrate on the blue-haired lady in pearls testifying on behalf of the Equal Employment Opportunities Bill," said Representative Shirley Chisholm, the first black woman elected to Congress. "It trains its eyes on a young girl, shaking her fists and screaming some obscenities at an abortion rally."

Karen De Crow, who ran as the Liberal party candidate for mayor of Syracuse, recalled with rancor the media's attitude toward her. "I was given hilarious treatment," she said. "The day I announced I was going to run, the photo that the morning paper ran was from the legs up—you know, I had been sitting on a couch in this press club, and he [the photographer] just took it—all leggy. The political columnist from a Syracuse newspaper called to ask for my measurements." Ms. De Crow, an articulate and committed young woman, was elected president of the National Organization for Women (NOW) in the late spring of 1974.

Often the press fails to take a serious woman candidate seriously, forcing her to run her campaign virtually without coverage. Massachusetts Representative Margaret Heckler, who won an upset victory over former Speaker Joe Martin in the 1966 primary, said the only time she was mentioned in the press before the election was in the Sunday edition in a story that said: "Margaret Heckler is a candidate, but is not going to win."

"It was the only mention in the whole campaign," said Representative Heckler emphatically, "except for the professional advertisements that I paid for."

The press also tends to report what its journalists want to see, charge some critics, who would like to see women covered with more accuracy. Gloria Steinem reports that when the Manhattan Women's Political Caucus was founded, there were 600 women at a daylong meeting. "About a third of them were black and Puerto Rican. It actually represented the city. It is the only political meeting I have ever been to in my life which racially represented the city. And the press reported it as mostly white middle class. They do not go into the NDC [New Democratic Coalition] and report that as mostly white middle class. It is a way of disqualifying them by saying, 'See, you are not as noble as you say.'"

Why this hostility to women in politics? It is undoubtedly true that many men enter its time-consuming, all-engrossing world to escape their home lives, and for such men, the last thing in the world they would seem to want would be a meaningful relationship with a woman. Not merely on a romantic level, but also on a business or professional level.

For many politicians it provides male companionship from breakfast through a nightcap. Meade Esposito, the powerful Brooklyn Democratic leader, meets with his key male aides every weekday morning at Garfield's cafeteria. He has a luncheon ritual, eating with politicians at Foffe's restaurant in Brooklyn Heights, and often ends his day with them during the wee hours of the morning with a nightcap at a Coney Island bar.

The big-time politician inhabits a surreal world without clocks or geographic locations, families or outside interests. The surreality is heightened during political campaigns, when politicians wake up in unfamiliar cities, in unfamiliar hotel rooms with unfamiliar bed partners. These campaigns exude an air of sexuality, reflecting the anxieties of those involved, from anxious staffers to insecure candidates. The gratification received from a triumphant tour seems interchangeable with that received from a sexual encounter. "The real definition of a politician is that if he wakes up happy in the morning, he can't remember if he's had a good crowd or a good lay the night before," says Robert Squier, a political television consultant.

Nor should a politician's one-night stands be considered a sexual relationship, Myra MacPherson argues. "A sexual relationship involves two people. A one-night stand, in which two people frantically jump into bed and frenetically engage in sex, is more like masturbation. There is no relationship."

"It's the pressures and the tension," Ms. MacPherson added. "It's their need and their drive. The aides arrange the one-night stands in the background."

Power is an aphrodisiac, concluded Robert Redford, the actor, who studied politicians while preparing to make the film *The Candidate.* "When I got into it, I couldn't believe how male it all was," he is reported as saying. "Women are just for sex. The [political] groupie thing is unbelievable. More so than in my business—the power must attract. There are so many bad marriages. They don't have anything at home and the wives —they're never as good looking as they seem in the magazines —they're just hanging on."[5]

Even when more "protected" women take part in a campaign, they often find themselves in secondary and degraded roles, regardless of their official standing within the organization. Jane

Squier, who is her husband's partner in the television consultant firm that worked for both Muskie and Humphrey, recalled that she has been an invisible person in the eyes of some politicians. "I was literally introduced to Hubert Humphrey twenty-six times, and he always reacted as if it was the first time," she said. As for the Muskie campaign, "I got shunted to Jane Muskie quite a bit." Senators Eagleton and Haskell were exceptions, she added, both accepting her creative contributions without assuming she merely did her husband's secretarial work.

The lack of physical facilities for women is also an index of their alienation. In New York's City Hall there *is* no women's rest room, except in the basement. Women in Congress bemoan the restricted hours for use of the swimming pool and other athletic facilities. When they enter Congress newly elected, they are given men's hairbrushes as part of their routine office equipment.

These are but symbolic of the more pervasive double standard that expects women to work endlessly without claiming rewards that would ordinarily be given to men who performed the same services. They are excluded from the Godfather structure of politics—a ladder that reaches from the clubhouse to the White House, whose rungs include ward heelers, district captains, district leaders, county leaders, state leaders, city councilmen, judges, state legislators, members of Congress, governors and Presidents. Each person on the ladder receives rewards from the person above him, whom he has helped elect to office, and disburses rewards to those beneath him, who sustain him in office. It is a system in which loyalties are repaid many times over: A district leader will obtain a judgeship from a county leader whom he has helped to elect, and the county leader will in turn receive courthouse patronage in the form of receiverships, guardianships, etc., back from his beneficiary. Through this system, a Mayor Daley can reach directly into the state legislature, the halls of Congress and the White House to bring back rewards that will strengthen him in office. Through this system, a Speaker controls a local or national legislature, and a Senate Majority Leader rules his domain.

Women, however, face roadblocks across the most important avenues of upward political mobility. Although women are the backbone of most local organizations, they are seldom rewarded for their efforts. A typical case involved Ronnie Eldridge, who had served as Senator Robert F. Kennedy's liaison in New York City. She recalled that those who had used her clout with the Senator took her services for granted, never expecting her to have ambitions of her own, and never expecting her to cash in on the IOU's that constitute the backbone of American politics.

Several years later, after organizing women across the country for John Lindsay's abortive Presidential campaign, Ms. Eldridge found the same discriminatory treatment meted out by the Lindsay administration. "All I wanted was the job of First Deputy City Administrator," Ms. Eldridge recalled, "but I was given the job of Deputy City Administrator. The job paid four thousand dollars less. I said I was offended. I wanted the title and the money. Ed Hamilton [then Deputy Mayor] called and offered me part of the extra money, but not the title." The irony of this incident is that any man who had served in Ms. Eldridge's dual capacity as campaign organizer and top political aide would most likely have been rewarded for his efforts with a city cabinet post. Ms. Eldridge was unable to do better than third-in-command of a city department almost totally without power.

When politicians finally appoint women, they often try to kill two birds with one stone and appoint a woman who is also a member of a minority group. This forces women to do double duty. City Councilwoman Carol Greitzer has publicly attacked Mayor Lindsay for the injustice of this practice. "The real problem is making women stand for two minorities," she charged. "In the case of Amy Betanzos, the city's relocation commissioner, the post stood open for a year because Lindsay wanted a Puerto Rican woman."

But women in politics are also the first to admit that many of the obstacles come from women themselves. Some are convinced of their own inadequacy and decline to run. Others are jealous of the success of their sisters. Former Mayor Sam Massell of Atlanta says, "It is not at all popular, not only with the men but also with the women, to name a woman to anything. There's absolutely no political benefit whatever. Some women may be jealous. Some definitely feel that women should not play roles that compete with men. They feel a personal challenge in having to deal with another woman. I don't get any letters, any calls of support, other than from women's lib organizations. There's no good will in this at all."

Some women believe that a false sense of idealism prevents women from demanding a quid pro quo for their votes, money and services, in terms of appointive and elective office. Others do not see the necessity of electing women to replace good men. "The dilemma now is what do you do when there are good women running against good men?" asked Ronnie Eldridge. "What do you do with women who have worked for a long time for Al Blumenthal, Herman Badillo and Jerry Kretchmer?"

Donna Brunstadt, a Connecticut Democrat and member of the National Women's Political Caucus, answered this argument by recalling its parallels in the civil rights movement. "They did this to the blacks, too," she argued. "They said, 'Look, you don't need a black candidate. This man speaks out on civil rights, he has more power to speak out, he has the rest of the white community, so you just stay down there and let the rest of us do your job. You just sit there, black man or black woman, and you just let us do your job.' That's not the way it's going to be, though."

"We have friends who are legislators who vote right on all the issues," added her colleague Lee Novick, "and in their homes they are male chauvinist pigs. They do not have women on their campaign staffs; they fight the women's movement; and even though they vote properly, their consciousness is still at a different level."

Women in politics constantly confront reminders of this level of consciousness, represented in its most exaggerated form by an attitude expressed by their male colleagues that can only be described as a total denial of their presence. Representative Elaine Gordon, a member of the Florida legislature, recalled a typical story: "I was standing in an elevator in my office, and it was filled with people who knew that I was elected to office. And the county manager walks into the elevator and Vernon Holloway, who is another member of the House, walks into the elevator, and the county manager says, 'Hello, Elaine, how are you?' And Vernon says, 'Who's that pretty girl?' And I say, 'I am not a pretty girl. I am an elected official, Vernon.' And he says, 'Well, so am I.' And I say, 'Well, you're not a pretty girl, either.'"

Gwen Cherry, the first black woman elected to the Florida legislature, echoed her colleague's observations. "We are called he-women by other legislators," she said. "I get it every time we have a hearing. It is the sort of thing that you have to be exposed to constantly."

Liz Carpenter, whose career included a term as press secretary to Lady Bird Johnson, recalled that in the entire White House power elite "the only two people who didn't discriminate against women as far as the West Wing was concerned were Johnson and Jack Valenti. . . . It will be a cold day in hell before Larry O'Brien has a woman there, although I think he has learned a little because he has been roughed up.

"You still have the Irish Kennedy syndrome out of South Boston," she continued, "which is absolutely pigheaded about women. The worst male chauvinist pigs are intellectuals out of Harvard—right? They are terribly precious. They are so afraid they are going to lose whatever masculinity they have, which is too little anyway—and they all crook their finger over a cup of tea. Boston is ghastly. It is the old Irish Catholic attitude toward women."

The patterns, though, are changing. One hears less lamentation from politically involved women, and less rhetoric. No longer content to allow the rewards of the political system to go exclusively to men and to male-oriented policies, women are shedding the delicacy and aloofness that had precluded them from acting as decision makers, and accepting instead a gloves-off approach to the culture and the trade-offs of the political marketplace.

It was no coincidence that the women's movement acquired its life force during the upheavals of the 1960's, just as the civil rights movement and the peace movement began to wane. Indeed, many women defected from these movements after realizing, as women abolitionists had learned more than a century earlier, that women's rights were not included in the priorities of the men with whom they worked together for humanistic causes. Male chauvinism appeared as endemic to radical ideologues as it was to

Wall Street bankers, demonstrating that radical sensitivities were not transferable when it came to women's issues.

"Suddenly they were in a cause, but they were never equal," said Liz Carpenter, speaking of women's involvement in the movements of the 1960's. "They suffered the same discrimination that Susan B. Anthony got at the prohibition meeting, and Lucretia Mott got at the abolition meeting." Stokely Carmichael, the black civil rights leader, put women in their place with his well-publicized statement that they best served the movement "in a prone position." The early sparks of rage were fanned by statements like these, backed by the reality that women had failed to win leadership in movement politics for the same reasons blocking them in the world of practical politics. "Instead of cooking Betty Crocker casseroles in Scarsdale, she's stirring brown rice in Arizona or on the Lowest East Side, and instead of being the 'property' of one man, she's now the 'property' of all the men in the collective,"[6] wrote Robin Morgan of women who tried to liberate themselves through male-dominated movements.

Women discovered that the liberal patriarchy acted no more in their interests than male elites who professed no social conscience. They grew angrier still at carrying the coffee for men they considered their equals—and indeed, in many cases their inferiors—especially when the symbolism of subservience translated itself so clearly into political impotence for women and for women's issues.

Movement politics taught women yet another lesson about the limits of power: that confining their activities to interest groups not clearly identified with their interests produced uneven results when it came to realizing their goals; and that to achieve success more rapidly they needed representatives more sympathetic to their needs. Consequently, many women began to run for office as the logical next step following careers in other movements: Bella Abzug from the peace movement, Gwen Cherry from the civil rights movement, Pat Schroeder from Planned Parenthood, to name a few. Others appeared from such groups as NOW and the League of Women Voters, where they had taken an active part in issues involving women's rights. Still others had been active, though unappreciated, in the political parties.

The McGovern reforms brought women into the mainstream of American politics for the first time in the twentieth century. Experiencing real power all too briefly, they returned home with a taste for more, and a reluctance to rejoin the ladies' auxiliary of their local political party or the town branch of the League of Women Voters. The time has come to "take the bull by the tail and look the situation in the eye," exhorted Jill Ruckelshaus at the National Women's Political Caucus' first national convention in Houston.

Mounting evidence shows that women are doing just that: They returned from Miami Beach to circulate nominating petitions not for male candidates, but for themselves. In state legislatures, for example, women's representation has increased by an average of almost 50 percent—and in some legislatures by 100 percent. Similar trends can be shown on other elective levels throughout the country. In Anne Wexler's state committee district in Connecticut three of the district's five towns had women mayoral candidates in the 1973 elections. In one town, Darien, both political parties ran women candidates. "This was unthinkable a couple of years ago," said Ms. Wexler, a Democratic state committeewoman and nationally known political mastermind.

By 1974, the numbers of women seeking political office rose to unprecedented levels. Many leaders predicted that 2,000 women would be running before the year was out. According to current figures, 110 women have announced they are running for Congress, an increase of 24 percent over 1972 and 74 percent over 1970. On the state level, 13 women are running for governor—with Ella Grasso the front runner in Connecticut—13 for lieutenant governor, 45 for other state offices, and 1,007 for seats in the state legislatures.

The recent success of the women's political effort owes much to the National Women's Political Caucus (NWPC), a multipartisan group created in 1971 by Betty Friedan, Bella Abzug, Gloria Steinem, and Shirley Chisholm for the purpose of promoting women into more substantive roles in politics. The NWPC leaders seek, in the words of Betty Friedan, to get women "out of the purity that has . . . afflicted [them] in the League of Women Voters, and . . . out of the rhetoric and carrying on that have afflicted [them] in the women's movement." Since its creation the caucus has expanded to include many state and local branches throughout the country. The national office serves as a clearinghouse and policy center for its affiliates. Although the NWPC lacks the resources to supply women candidates with funds or workers, it has been able to help with publicity, speakers, moral support and, occasionally, political expertise.

Owing in part to the caucus' leadership, women across the country are beginning to realize that real political clout means the creation of their own political organizations that can supply money, votes, workers and overall support to women candidates and politicians sympathetic to women's issues. They are seeking and winning appointive and elective office, which will ultimately translate into reordered priorities, rechanneled government funds, and a new voice in decision making for half the population of the nation.

Washington began to get the message in the fall of 1974. President Ford, in the opening days of his administration, appointed Mary Louise Smith of Iowa the first woman to be national chairman of the Republican party. The President reiterated his support of the Equal Rights Amendment, abortion reform (but not day care centers), and met with the leaders of the National Organization for Women and the National Women's Political Caucus, among other women's groups, in a symbolic act based on their growing strength. Hardly a day went by without new evidence of women's increasing political power, even in the so-called Man's Country of Nevada where a woman won the Republican nomination for governor. The long march had finally begun, and the men were taking notice.

Chapter I

Growing Pains: Realpolitik in Miami

I don't think anyone sat out in that trailer and said, "How can we let the women down on those issues?" They figured, "They'll follow McGovern to hell and back." At that point most of us would have. I no longer would do that for any man.

—DONNA BRUNSTADT,
Connecticut Women's
Political Caucus

When the convention broke, Women Power 1972 *was real.*
—THEODORE WHITE, *The Making of the President 1972*

They rode the crest of each other's ambitions—the McGovern campaign and the women's political movement—and when it was over, despite the collisions, the bitterness and mutual sense of betrayal, they had altered, probably for all time, the role of women in American politics.

For George McGovern the inclusion of women, youths, blacks, chicanos and other minority-group members into the mainstream of the nation's political decision making was hardly altruistic. "We wanted to break the hold of the old, established oligarchy of politics," said the Senator in retrospect. "It had become rigid, encrusted, insensitive to new moods." The Democratic party structure was also singularly unreceptive to a Presidential bid by the mild-mannered Senator from South Dakota, one of the earliest opponents of the Vietnam War. McGovern was clearly at odds with the Democratic hierarchy, dominated by big-city bosses, organized labor, and the legislative leaders who had allowed blood to flow in the streets of Chicago in 1968 rather than permit an open convention.

For George McGovern, whose Presidential campaign had begun in quiet earnest immediately after President Nixon's 1968 election, the initial task was to change the party's structure, to make it more receptive to his candidacy. His vehicle, born of a frenzied floor fight at the 1968 Chicago Convention, was the Commission on Party Structure and Delegate Selection, commonly known as the Reform Commission. Its goal: to incorporate those excluded from the party's councils, and give them representation at every stage of the process of selecting a national ticket.

The McGovern reforms, which insisted that state delegations reflect the makeup of their populations—or at the very least, remove obstacles to minority participation—clearly influenced both major parties, increasing minority participation not only in the Democratic party, but also affecting the Republicans as well. As a result of the McGovern reforms, women made up 40 percent of the Democratic delegates at Miami Beach and 30 percent of the Republicans,[1] giving them their first real taste of in-the-trenches politics, along with the chance to solidify their new status.

At Miami Beach the relationship between George McGovern and the women delegates recalled the movie *Rashomon*, with as many interpretations as participants, each claiming ingratitude and betrayal. The conflict began as women constituted themselves an independent force at the convention—indeed, as it turned out, the largest independent force, even larger than the troops representing organized labor. They worked for their own objectives and at the same time supported George McGovern. When these two goals conflicted, as happened on a number of crucial issues, what began as a honeymoon turned to mutual disenchantment—but a disenchantment that ultimately propelled women toward a greater measure of political independence, as they experienced the hard crunch of practical politics.

For the women a sort of domino theory of betrayal seemed to have been operative, as they watched McGovern renege on a series of promises. Some women leaders claimed the McGovern forces initially betrayed them by backing down on a promise to support a cochairperson at the convention, agreeing instead to a male chairman and a female vice-chairwoman. Other breaches of promise soon followed. Women raised the South Carolina credentials issue, again with the Senator's promised support, and were again betrayed; then they raised the abortion issue and after failing once more, rallied to nominate a woman, Sissy Farenthold, for Vice President.

To McGovern, who had after all been the person most responsible for the presence of large numbers of women at the convention, fate seemed to have dealt an unkind blow, linking his fortunes to that of zealots, and amateur zealots at that. Rick Stearns, a top McGovern lieutenant, recalled, "There seemed to be an assumption on the part of some of the more active spokesmen for women's rights that the McGovern campaign should have collapsed its identity into the women's rights movement. That was absurd."

To professional politicians such as Representative Edith Green, veteran Oregon Democrat and a power on Capitol Hill, "The Democratic party was taken over by the kooks," a description she offered to justify her reasons for not attending the convention. "A ragtag mob of special interests and passions, put together in the course of the primaries," added Richard Dougherty, McGovern's press secretary, about the coalition. "Women, blacks, chicanos, gays, the peace groups—political in a sense, but fanatical about their positions." Both were right in the sense that a large percentage of top-level party regulars were noticeably absent from the proceedings. Mayor Lindsay was the only big-city mayor at Miami Beach. Absent were Daley of Chicago, Yorty of Los Angeles, White of Boston, Gribbs of Detroit, Rizzo of Philadelphia, and others, many of whom had cast their lot with Muskie. Of the 255 Congressional Democrats, only 30 were present.

The "ragtag mob" and the "kooks" felt different about their presence. "I would think that she would feel that way," said Yvonne Braithwaite Burke, the young, black woman selected as vice-chairwoman of the convention, of Edith Green's remark. "People are not used to seeing large numbers of minorities and not that many poor people. . . . They're accustomed to seeing one black in a crowd. When they see proportional representation, well, they can't get over it."

One of the convention's ironies was that the women did not know their strength. "If we had known in the beginning what we knew in the end, we could have had much more bargaining power, or we would have tried anyway," reflected Gloria Steinem, who worked behind the scenes sharpening strategies. "We had five hundred delegates there—we had a bigger bloc than the unions, than anyone else.

"We didn't know that before we got there, because our communications system is rotten," she continued. "There were even whole state caucuses or local caucuses that sprang up that we didn't know existed. And they would come and say, 'We are the caucus of Cayuga County.'" As for McGovern, "He was only interested in the question of delegates, how many could we actually deliver," she said, because "most of our delegates were McGovern delegates anyway."

Before the convention, at a meeting with women's leaders in his Washington home, the Senator had committed himself to appoint a woman to the Supreme Court, the National Security Council, and Cabinet posts. At the convention, however, the women pressed for further concessions while the McGovern forces saw no reason to capitulate. They had, after all, brought women into the party's decision-making process, given them status and power, and by all the normal standards of a political contract, expected women to sit back for the duration of the convention and at least not harm their benefactor. McGovern stood out easily as the male candidate most seriously committed to women's issues. And most of the women had accepted Gloria Steinem's judgment, published in *Ms.* magazine, that McGovern was the best of the *male* candidates.[2]

In spite of McGovern's promises the women pressed on at the convention, not only on issues, but also for jobs, and for more symbolic power. Years of anger, mostly self-directed, had welled up in them for allowing themselves to be used while others got the credit and the titles. The convention provided a constructive outlet for their rage: an opportunity with the potential for making a significant impact on party politics that they were not about to let pass.

Pragmatists in spite of their idealistic image, the McGovern forces refused to accept women's demands without clarifying just what women would do in return for them. "The National Women's Political Caucus was almost asking too much," Rick Stearns said. "They were asking, in a sense, to be taken into the upper echelons of the campaign without really providing very much help on the lower echelons. . . . As far as we were concerned, we had plenty of women in responsible positions who themselves resented any sort of outside pressure. They're the ones who felt that if anyone was going to be promoted, they ought to be promoted up through the organization, which in many cases they were. Why Gloria Steinem should be brought in as executive campaign manager or whatever—a lot of women in the campaign resented that.

"If they had people who wanted to work," he continued, "why didn't they send them to us? My God, we were desperate for people to go out and manage counties and cities."

In contrast to the Nixon campaign, the McGovern organization, to its credit, appointed women to top positions. (The Watergate revelations showed Nixon's apparatus distinguished by, among other things, the absence of women.) Of McGovern's ten regional directors, five were women. Women occupied other key posts: Liz Stevens worked with media; Marion Pearlman served as treasurer ("We owe her an immense debt," said Rick Stearns, "for always insisting that everything be done aboveboard"); Jean Westwood, a Utah mink rancher, who was to become Democratic National Chairwoman; and Anne Wexler, who ran the voter registration drive. Both Ms. Wexler and Ms. Westwood also served as the first women floor managers in a Presidential campaign. The press staff consisted of Dick Dougherty and three women: Carol Frieden-berg, Polly Hackett and Jackie Greenidge. The advance staff, according to Dougherty, was 50 percent women.

Significantly, the women who were recruited were not known as feminists. Their primary identity was as politicians, and in any showdown between women's issues and the McGovern candidacy they could be expected to come down hard on the side of the candidate—often to the surprise of the women's leaders, who felt especially betrayed by their sisters.[3]

The unusual degree of acceptance these women politicans experienced in the McGovern camp contrasted sharply with the resentment and bitterness expressed toward the more feminist-oriented women. It was especially hard for the men behind McGovern—and it appeared to be the men who made the hard decisions regarding women at the convention—to accede to their demands, while so many of the women leaders publicly supported Shirley Chisholm for the Presidential nomination. In view of their attitudes toward divided loyalty, Shirley Chisholm's decision not to withdraw her candidacy until nearly the end of the convention probably did significant harm to women's bargaining position with McGovern.

"I remember one scene that sticks out in my mind," recalled Richard Dougherty. "It was when the national committee met in special session. And I tiptoed out because I really couldn't stand it anymore. Gloria Steinem, with her rather long, elegant hands, was explaining in this jargon of the movement how McGovern seemed to be failing to sense the nuances. What they were doing, in effect, was insisting that there be big titles given to women, major executive posts, which indeed we did and which indeed we were going to do. That annoyed me. The schoolmistress explaining to the students. I am really fond of her. But early on she went off and supported Shirley Chisholm. And who the hell is Shirley Chisholm? She doesn't represent anything except her own radiant ego."

Dougherty continued to illustrate how he felt certain elements within the women's movement—what he termed "the purist factor"—acted against the interests of his candidate: "I was accosted in Springfield, Illinois, at the end of a long day, by three sort of granny-garlanded types, who were running as McGovern delegates. There had been, when we came into the reception, three or four or five pretty girls in hot pants, and 'McGovern Girl' banners on them—sex objects. And these three ripped into me, making the point that the issue, whatever it might have been, was really much more important to them than the candidate. One girl said to me: 'I don't give a damn about McGovern. I am for him because of the movement.'"

To the consternation of both the feminists and the politicians in the women's movement, McGovern appointed actress Shirley MacLaine to a key post as his liaison with women's groups. Many women charged that choosing a movie star instead of a serious woman politician downgraded the role of women. After all, they said, McGovern hadn't appointed a Hollywood actor to negotiate with Mayor Daley. "This was taken as a big insult," charged Gloria Steinem, a dilettantish move, especially in view of all the available women who had been active in politics for so many years. "Sissy [Farenthold] would have been ideal," said Ms. Steinem. "She'd been campaigning for him in Texas long before anybody else, and one of the reasons she lost was because she'd never hurt McGovern."

A further complaint against Ms. MacLaine was that she blocked access to the candidate. She had the power to sift through the numerous demands, requests, and offers of help from women and then channel those she considered most important back to the candidate. "It was the classic problem," said Gloria Steinem. "It must be true for blacks as well. There have been a few people working in the campaign, working very hard, with a fair amount of expertise. Then who comes in at the top and has the ear of the candidate? Some black athlete. That's what happened with Shirley. It wasn't her fault. But nonetheless if there was real respect for women as a political force, it would have been Sissy there, not just Shirley MacLaine. And it was a problem for women in the structure. She was the only one that was talking to him [McGovern] and she is just not a political person."

In her defense Rick Stearns argued that Shirley MacLaine had earned her job, having worked as one of McGovern's earliest campaigners, out touring New Hampshire and Illinois at a time when the polls gave McGovern less than a 5 percent chance of winning the nomination. "It's hard to think of people who worked as hard as she did, and as effectively," he remarked. "She's a very shrewd woman, a great campaigner. . . . I don't think she emerged in the campaign solely as a movie star." Shirley

MacLaine also reminded her critics that she had worked for McGovern as early as 1968, when she raised funds for him, and appeared as a McGovern delegate at the Chicago convention.

In the numerous showdowns between the McGovern forces and the women's movement, Ms. MacLaine invariably sided with the candidate. She acknowledged she had often been personally torn, agreeing as she did with the feminists on ideological grounds. But she was fearful of what this commitment would cost McGovern with the voters. An introspective and politically sophisticated woman, and an author as well as an actress, she reached her decision on what kind of role she would play after careful thought and consideration. In the end she justified her submission to practical politics on the basis of a higher priority, a more urgent priority—the defeat of Richard Nixon and the election of George McGovern.

"I understood what the feminist approach was, naturally, because I agree with them," Ms. MacLaine said, sipping a tall glass of orange juice in her duplex on the East Side of Manhattan. "However, my higher priority for the whole year—and I felt very strongly about that—was to get George McGovern elected. Something happens with strong, purist militant approaches to the necessary change in priorities. And for that reason a lot of the people were unsure, skeptical about the strong, militant approach where McGovern was concerned. I really don't think it had as much to do with issues, because none of the women out there could really be opposed to the Equal Rights Amendment or to abortion on demand, or to the need for day-care centers, or the fact that welfare is a female problem—all the things that Gloria and Bella and Betty and even Flo Kennedy were talking about are things that every woman feels either politically, philosophically, or psychologically in agreement with. So what we are talking about is what I learned is wrong with America, a kind of immaturity about the nation as a whole, and certainly about the McGovern campaign. And that is that we are not mature enough as individuals to rise above the question of image. . . . The McGovern men were threatened by the image of feminism—they thought.

"I tried to make it clear—and I still feel at that time it was the correct thing to do. I had made a decision, a very pronounced decision, to go for the higher priority of McGovern, and put my own feminist attitudes on the back burner for five months. And as he said to them [the women's representatives] at the meeting we had in his living room: 'Why are you forcing me to do something now which I am not capable of doing, when I can do so much more for you when I am President?'"

Her priorities were shared by Jean Westwood, who has attributed much of the women's discontent with McGovern to their impatience and political naïveté. "One of the things I found about women being new in politics was that I felt that they were back where blacks were in politics when the civil rights movement began," she said, relaxing on a grassy knoll outside the Capitol, the following spring. "The first convention they came to, they didn't feel that they had made very great victories. They did a lot of things that were quite amateurish, but that was because they were new at it. Maybe they're more refreshing when they're that way than when they get more professional."

Herself the victim of sexual bias—she was unceremoniously deposed after the November debacle[4]—she recognized tendencies along these lines in the campaign and acknowledged that women's complaints had some merit. "There was some resentment among the men in the campaign against women," she recalled. "I think Gary Hart [McGovern's campaign manager] did not like women in politics, even though he liked me. He once made a remark that there were no women involved. Somebody took him to task about it and he said, 'I didn't mean Jean; I never think of her as a woman.'" Her suntanned rancher's face broke into a sweet smile as she added that she wasn't sure whether to take that as a compliment.

Those who deposed her, she stressed, represented the conservative wing of the party, while her supporters fell into the liberal faction. But party conservatives also represented the male-dominated status quo prior to 1972; and when the suggestion was made that Ms. Westwood be replaced by another woman, they turned a deaf ear.

The men in the McGovern camp were quick to point out that while the appointment of Ms. Westwood showed their sincerity in promoting sexual equality in party politics, in choosing her, McGovern was paying off a very important political worker, one of his earliest supporters and closest advisers. McGovern felt deeply indebted to this woman, whose efforts, particularly throughout the West, made a considerable difference during those lonely months before his candidacy was taken seriously.

The Buzzsaw of Presidential Politics: Round One at Miami

To the McGovern camp the opening round at Miami Beach demonstrated the perils of dealing with the women and should have given them some indication of what lay ahead. At the same time women experienced their first taste of a new pattern displayed by McGovern and his aides: a willingness to submit to pragmatic considerations at women's expense.

At issue was the promised post of cochairperson. Representative Patsy Mink of Hawaii, the choice of the National Women's Political Caucus, was unacceptable to the black caucus, which urged the selection of one of its own members. To satisfy both the women and the blacks, a black woman, Yvonne Braithwaite Burke, was selected for the post of vice-chairman. She was elected to Congress that fall.

"It got all mixed up with black politics," Ms. Mink recalled, without a trace of resentment. This she reserved for the McGovern camp, for reneging on the commitment to appoint a coequal cochairperson. "The idea was to have an equal position, and not a second spot," she said. "We thought we had their commitment. We felt a sense of betrayal. They were so intent on playing consensus-type politics within the party." Too many women politicians had occupied vice-chairmanships in the past on a variety of levels in the party, and were well aware this was usually a figurehead post designed to give the appearance of equality. Women could not be blamed for trying to destroy the symbol as well as the practice of habitually being relegated to second place.

The McGovern forces, sensitive to the criticism that the party had been taken over by the "kooks," sought respectability in the form of Lawrence O'Brien, a party stalwart since the days of

President John F. Kennedy, when his group represented the insurgents. "We tried to get Larry O'Brien to agree to a cochairperson concept," Ms. Mink said. "O'Brien raised technicalities. He asked, 'How do you decide who presides?'" To Mr. O'Brien the objections were not technicalities but the very essence of the job, a symbol of his own influence and future in the party; indeed, his attitude proved an ironic example of how old-line pols were every bit as concerned with symbolism as were the women and the blacks.[5]

The women's resentment over this initial loss set the stage for a far more serious betrayal, involving the alleged failure of South Carolina to include a representative number of women in its delegation. Once again the McGovern forces expected the women to understand, to submerge their own cause into the common good, which freely translated meant feeding women's rights into the buzzsaw of Presidential politics.

The challenge to the seating of the delegation was raised by the National Women's Political Caucus on the grounds that the presence of only 8 women among the 32 South Carolina delegates indicated discriminatory practices running counter to the McGovern commission's guidelines. The credentials committee, noting that many women had run for delegate but lost and that 31 percent of the delegates were black, found no discrimination in the state's delegate-selection process. But the National Women's Political Caucus, believing it had Senator McGovern's support, pressed the case in Miami Beach.

"We wanted to get a reversal of the South Carolina challenge because we thought that was an evident case," said Representative Bella Abzug. "And we went to the McGovern people and we said, 'We are going to make the South Carolina challenge, and we expect your support. We have the figures and we can make it.' And they said, 'Okay. We'll fight it. You are right.'

"We started to produce the votes," Ms. Abzug continued. "And as we were producing the votes, there was suddenly an unclear picture on the part of the McGovern team, which was afraid that we might hit below the amount required, which would cause a point of order. They pulled back people—all kinds of people."

For the McGovern forces, the South Carolina challenge proved a nightmare that almost jeopardized their victory in Miami. The reason: The South Carolina challenge preceded the crucial California challenge, thereby introducing the possibility that any precedents set by South Carolina could be extended to California, where the stakes ran much higher. McGovern's strategists therefore sought to avoid a close vote that could raise a parliamentary issue. They wanted either to win big or to lose big. At issue were two questions: What constituted a majority of the delegates and who would be allowed to vote? The precedent at conventions has generally been that unchallenged delegates, even though members of delegations that otherwise were challenged, have been allowed to vote. The McGovern forces had 120 unchallenged delegates in California, whom they wanted to be able to vote. They feared that a parliamentary rule in South Carolina, which would prohibit the nine unchallenged delegates (along with the challenged members) from voting, would set a precedent for California, losing the McGovern forces 120 unchallenged votes and, therefore, the nomination. The California challenge involved the state's winner-take-all primary that gave the Senator all 271 delegates, without which he would have lost the nomination.

The second greatest problem with the South Carolina challenge was the general confusion surrounding the vote. Even McGovern himself was unaware of its dynamics until it was over. "The South Carolina challenge was handled by floor managers," said the Senator a year later. "I was not fully aware of what was happening until the challenge began to unfold. As it turned out, we might have won the South Carolina challenge with enough votes." He agreed with the overall strategy, however: "It wouldn't have done any good for the women to win the South Carolina challenge and have me blow the California challenge."

McGovern and some of his top lieutenants later conceded their strategy on South Carolina was a mistake, not for any moral considerations, and not for reneging on their promise to the women, but because in hindsight they realized they could have won, and avoided the antagonism generated by the loss. Their communications were faulty on two fronts: Their intelligence network failed to deliver an accurate projection of the South

Carolina vote; and then, having decided to throw the vote, they neglected to tell the women the real reasons for their decision. "We looked kind of silly trying to lie about that business," Richard Dougherty admitted. "We really did cut our count on that. Everybody knew we were doing it and, as far as I know, none of the ladies who were hurt most by it—namely, the South Carolina people—protested it."

For the women the South Carolina challenge was the climactic moment, recalled Rick Stearns. "I had made the argument that they had chosen the wrong place to make the issue. It was wrong not merely because the South Carolina challenge was debated before the California challenge, and therefore could set a parliamentary precedent, but because there were other, stronger challenges to be made. In Hawaii women were deliberately excluded. Not only was the case stronger, but it avoided a challenge that could jeopardize the California challenge. If we didn't win California, we weren't going to win the nomination." (Hawaii would be debated after California, under the rule by which challenges were considered on the floor in the order in which they were considered by the credentials committee.) "For the sheer politics I think it would be smarter to make it when it couldn't jeopardize the McGovern nomination. We wanted no opportunity for a test vote. The South Carolina challenge gave the opposition a chance to test parliamentary rulings that were largely in our favor.

"The women's caucus could have had our support for almost any other challenge," Stearns emphasized. "The political objective of the caucus, I assume, was to try to establish a precedent, and not punish or reward every delegation."

In view of McGovern's prior commitments on South Carolina few realized that the reversal on the vote meant a victory not a defeat for the McGovern camp. The confusion extended to the media, confounding CBS anchorman Walter Cronkite, who interpreted the loss as a serious blow for McGovern. The correct interpretation, reported by R. W. Apple of the New York *Times* and Robert Boyd of the Knight newspapers, revealed the South Carolina vote showed that McGovern controlled the convention in the sense that he could pull his troops back at will and change the direction of a major vote. The loss of the South Carolina challenge was, in fact, one of the great strategies of the Miami Beach convention, from a purely technical point of view. Once the vote appeared close, Stearns' command post in the trailer behind the convention hall sent out the instructions to 300 floor whips, one in each row. In addition, the delegation leaders were in direct communication with the McGovern floor leaders, who were telephoned from a communications center in the Doral Hotel. "Within five or six minutes, we had three hundred people on the floor who knew what the instructions were," said Rick Stearns.

Abortion Politics: The Convention's Civil War

For the women loss of the South Carolina challenge heightened their need for a victory—any victory—and marked their coming of age as mature politicians. They now realized that to male politicians ideological commitment meant little in the overall quest for power. It also demonstrated anew the undependability of a male politician—any male—and strengthened their resolve to go it alone in the future. Thus bloodied, the women resolved to bring to the floor an emotionally charged platform plank on abortion reform, a plank that could only bring fear to the heart of any national candidate with hopes of capturing the votes of the nation's Catholics.

"I felt that it was a mistake to press the traditional rank-and-file voters any further than we had," Senator McGovern explained. "It was an explosive issue. I thought it would all be decided by the courts anyway."

For the feminists, however, the abortion issue represented what Bella Abzug called "a transcending point of view." "We told the McGovern people that we had women there who were determined that issue had to be raised as a real political issue," she explained, "as a matter of platform. We believe it was their responsibility and even though some of us were supporting McGovern, we were going to press on the issues we are concerned with. I was on the drafting part of the platform, and I begged them to let me put something in. I said, 'If you don't, it's going to go to the convention. The issue that concerns everybody, which nobody wants to be concerned with, is going to come up. You are much better off to have it in the majority plank, and that's the end of it.'

"We said that even though some of us were supporters of McGovern, we have a responsibility sometimes when we go further than our candidates," she continued. "And that's the way it goes. That's part of life. We were told that nobody was going to support it because a lot of women who were for McGovern thought it would hurt them in their state campaigns. In the primaries they had bad experiences with it, and they thought we weren't going to get any support. The interesting thing, though, is that early in the vote [the abortion vote] there were some votes that registered for Humphrey, there were a couple of Alabama votes, some Wallace votes—and that scared the daylights out of the McGovern people. They thought what was going to happen was a big vote artificially produced to embarrass McGovern. They did not understand that abortion crossed many lines, including party lines."

The resulting floor fight was one of the most passionate battles of the convention, and one again characterized by betrayal and faulty communication. "It was a fight that divided sister against sister," reported Myra MacPherson in the Washington *Post,* "with Bella Abzug taking off on Shirley MacLaine, who spoke against the minority plank. It was a fight that had Gloria Steinem's usually controlled monotone quivering as she wept in rage, verbally attacked Gary Hart and called McGovern strategists 'bastards.'"[6] Feelings ran so high they divided husbands and wives. National Women's Political Caucus member Phyllis Segal and Massachusetts McGovern delegate Tony Chayes battled for the plank, while their husbands, Eli Segal and Abe Chayes, were campaigning against it.

Those who argued for the plank pleaded for the freedom to control their own fertility as an essential human right. As a practical concession the emotionally charged word "abortion" was never used; instead they spoke of "reproductive freedom." No one was fooled, though. Gloria Steinem emphasized the importance of phraseology, "a writer's conceit," she said, in formulating issues: "If you can just phrase it right, you can get support for it." Even the words "birth control"—anathema to many blacks who interpret this issue as a form of genocide directed at their race—were not incorporated into the platform.

Following Eleanor Holmes Norton's[7] plea to the delegates for "reciprocal respect for our rights," some women on the floor took out toy whistles, and started to blow them. They were soon joined by some of the men, including John Kenneth Galbraith, McGovern's economic adviser, who said, "This is one issue that simply has got to get discussion."

The women's feeling of betrayal was heightened by the appearance of a "right to life" speaker, Eugene Walsh of Missouri, who addressed the convention to argue against the reproductive-freedom plank. "The slaughter of the most innocent, whose right to live is not mentioned in the minority report . . ." he began. Gloria Steinem was livid, reported Myra MacPherson. "They put a right-to-lifer on, and they promised they wouldn't. She found Gary Hart and cried, 'You promised us you wouldn't take the low road, you bastards.'"[8]

Looking with disdain on the proceedings was Germaine Greer, the Australian feminist and author of *The Female Eunuch*, who covered the convention for *Harper's* magazine. "Womanlike, they did not want to get tough with their man, and so womanlike, they got screwed,"[9] wrote Ms. Greer, a theme *Harper's* regarded as significant enough to put on its cover against a backdrop of a naked female back. She was particularly disturbed by a McGovern meeting with the women at which a woman delegate pressed him on the abortion issue, while Gloria Steinem and Bella Abzug, who were chairing the session, feigned deafness. "I could hear her from where I was standing," commented Ms. Greer, "but Bella and Gloria stared glassily out into the room as if they were deaf or entranced." Gloria Steinem reflected later that the incident revealed Ms. Greer's lack of understanding of American politics, namely, the internal sabotage the Watergate hearings have revealed as common practice. "When the women stood up and yelled at McGovern about the abortion issue," she explained, "Germaine never thought to question why they were yelling only at him, and not at Humphrey and others, whose positions were worse. She never stopped to consider that they weren't feminists.

They were pro-Humphrey, pro-Jackson—but that is too complicated to understand." She added that when she met Germaine Greer in Miami, Ms. Greer dismissed the convention with the remark, "What a lovely imperialistic picnic you people are having." Some observers, however, concluded that Ms. Steinem and Ms. Abzug had protected McGovern at the meeting as a result of assurances they had given the candidate that he would not be embarrassed.

Still others misinterpreted the impressive victory attributed to Martha McKay of North Carolina, who convinced forty-eight members of her delegation to vote for the pro-abortion plank, with only nine voting no. While some members of the delegation might have voted for the plank to embarrass McGovern, it was apparent that the delegation was convinced by Ms. McKay on the merits of the case.[10] "Abortion is one issue you can't duck," concluded Ms. McKay in retrospect. "Once it's brought up, you can't duck it; it's so central to a woman's being. It's like the race issue. Politicians are fools to think they can duck these issues. Once it's there, you have to take a stand. We had no choice."

One of the more heartbreaking betrayals, as described by the women, was the split between the women in the McGovern camp and those on the floor. When Shirley MacLaine argued that the subject of abortion should be decided by each delegate as a matter of conscience, Ms. Abzug tried to shame her into changing her mind. "A sister never goes against a sister," Ms. Abzug admonished. Ms. MacLaine, who believed in reproductive freedom, later replied, "I'm not going against Bella. 'Sisters' have a right to have pragmatic politics as well as personal principles." Jean Westwood also reported being approached along the lines of "sisterhood" before the vote on the South Carolina challenge by Representative Abzug and several of her colleagues. "Jean," they told her, "we think it's just terrible you're going against the South Carolina challenge, and you're a woman." Apparently both Ms. MacLaine and Ms. Westwood were annoyed and uncomfortable at having been approached in this way—forced into reconciling their feminism to the exigencies of practical politics, then justifying a position they were not quite sure of themselves.

Reflecting on the battle, Ms. MacLaine explained a key fact, unknown to the general public, which influenced her own decision: George McGovern himself was ambivalent about abortion reform. In this light his unwillingness to commit his personal and political resources to the issue seems less cold-blooded. "The one thing that neither Dick, nor Gloria, nor Bella, nor any of the men in the campaign, or very few other people understood about George McGovern was that he personally was not certain about abortion," said Ms. MacLaine. "This was not a political act of his. He had seduced himself into believing that abortion in his terms was a constitutional issue.

"When you talked to George," she went on, "when you really got underneath it, he would always bring up the number of weeks. You saw that any man or woman who talks about the number of weeks involved is not really for it. He had a personal, very likely religious, traditional resistance to the notion of abortion. I was in touch with Paul Ehrlich back in January, before this ever came out to be the issue in Nebraska and Ohio. And Paul told me then that the field had shifted, that . . . four months later 65 to 75 percent [of the American public] were *for* abortion on demand. So, therefore, politically speaking, abortion on demand would have been a positive issue. But what nobody understood was that George McGovern wasn't for it. And the last thing in the world that I wanted to have happen was for him to come out really strong on something he didn't mean."

As his tactician on women's issues, Shirley MacLaine also understood that McGovern's ambivalence on abortion was better off hidden at least for the duration of the campaign; and for that reason she sought to protect him from the issue's adversaries as well as from its protagonists. Citing his awkwardness with the subject, she emphasized that even if the polls had reported 100 percent of the population favored abortion on demand, she would have protected McGovern from embarrassing himself. "McGovern would have trapped himself," she said. "He trapped himself every time he opened his mouth about abortion. First he would say it was up to a woman and her doctor. Then he would say it was a state's rights problem. . . . These are totally contradictory statements."

The vote finally came at 4:30 A.M. on the morning of July 12.

The plank was defeated by a vote of 1,572.8 to 1,101.37. Once again a combination of faulty communications and broken promises marred the proceedings and built up the residue of scar tissue. "I remember getting reports back, as the voting was going on, of women delegates in tears," recalled Rick Stearns. "They were women who disliked voting with the instructions, but felt they had an obligation to do that. This was one case where our intelligence on the floor utterly failed. I think the pro-abortion proponents were very vocal. We were very afraid, or we believed, that the plank would have passed if we hadn't taken a strong position against it. I was surprised when it was defeated so heavily. If we had just left things alone, it would still have been defeated, but it would have been defeated by a more respectable margin, and the women would have been less upset.

"Essentially we instructed the men and not the women on the abortion issue," Stearns continued. "We gave instructions that we wanted the plank defeated, although we did state that we were willing to make exceptions for people who felt that they had a conscientious or political commitment to the issue. We were much tougher with men on that."

The Dawning of Clout: Massing the Troops for Sissy Farenthold

Three successive defeats made the women's group hungry for at least a symbolic victory, one that was to prove costliest for McGovern in delaying his acceptance speech until 2:48 in the morning, well after even the people in California had gone to bed. "Only in Guam, where it was still a quarter of six in the evening, was George McGovern speaking in prime time under the American flag," Theodore White noted. "On the mainland, the audience for his speech had dropped from 17,400,000 homes to 3,600,000."[11]

"I thought it was a political catastrophe that we had to lose all that prime time," the Senator said, reflecting on the convention. "What I desperately wish now is that we had postponed the Vice Presidential selection until the next day, rather than lose this great network audience."

The main reason for the delay was the fairly spontaneous draft of Sissy Farenthold as a Vice Presidential candidate. (A secondary reason was a squabble in the New York delegation.) For once an issue arose *sui generis* for women, involving no unkept promises, no eleventh-hour betrayals, and no major disappointments. After the Farenthold vote, women returned home on an upbeat note, encouraged by the large turnout, enthusiasm, and solidarity among themselves.

Not even in contention for the Vice Presidential nomination, Sissy Farenthold had recently come to national attention with a surprisingly strong showing in the Texas gubernatorial primary. A tall, shy, elegant-looking woman with an ethereal quality about her, she edged out two well-funded political veterans—incumbent Governor Preston Smith (who received 9 percent) and the state's Golden Boy and heir apparent, Lieutenant Governor Ben Barnes (16 percent). Ms. Farenthold won 26 percent of the vote for herself. This made her runner-up to Dolph Briscoe, whose 49 percent tally landed him in a runoff primary with Ms. Farenthold. In the runoff Ms. Farenthold lost with a highly respectable 46 percent of the vote, and left many Texas politicians with the distinct impression that there would someday be another woman governor (remember Ma Watson?) in this bastion of male dominance.

In her two terms in the legislature Ms. Farenthold called herself "Den Mother of the Dirty Thirty"—thirty rebelliously liberal Texas legislators whose crusade for reforms, including financial statements from legislators, helped bring to light one of the state's worst scandals, involving the Sharpstown Bank. Before the scandal ended, the Speaker of the House, Gus Mutscher, was convicted of stock fraud, and the careers of two politicians, Governor Smith and Lieutenant Governor Barnes, were in tatters.

"I am a candidate in order to give the people of Texas a choice—a choice other than between two contaminated candidates [Smith and Barnes] and a legislator from the fifties [Briscoe]," she said in announcing for governor. "This past session, thirty or so of us in the legislature attempted to plant the seeds of reform in state government. We felt this was the overriding issue at hand. In this pursuit there was leadership neither from the governor nor the lieutenant governor, rather obstruction, nor was there any encouragement from the third major candidate in this race. Little more than a year ago the public became aware of the corruption that has prevailed in Austin. When this awareness could not be smothered, there appeared to be mass conversion to the reform movement by incumbents and candidates.

"Look at the other candidates for governor," she urged. "Who made $52,000 on a Sharpstown Bank stock deal? The present governor of Texas. Who has parlayed his $4,800-a-year salary into a fortune while supposedly serving the people of Texas? The present lieutenant governor of Texas." She traveled the state in a DC-3, and when it was over, Ms. Farenthold had a $60,000 debt and a national reputation.

How did this Vice Presidential campaign originate? From disarmingly simple origins, so casual the candidate herself failed to take it seriously until it snowballed into a full-fledged movement. "There were three students from Texas who worked with my campaign [for governor] and sold posters," reminisced Ms. Farenthold in Houston. "They had little designs, pencil sketches, very unpolitical posters. And they made a trip to Washington and they talked me up after I was defeated. They went up to see McGovern and they got sidetracked. So the first thing I saw was a little notice in the newspaper that an alternate named Chris Covino announced that she was going to circulate an open letter at the convention proposing me for Vice President. I was in a special session of the legislature. And a reporter came to me and said, 'Have you seen that story about the Vice Presidency?' And I said no. And he showed it to me and I smiled and said, 'I don't want to discourage the ardor of the young.'"

The three students then went to see Ms. Farenthold the Sunday before the convention. "You all go do what you want," she told them, and then promptly forgot about the whole thing. Only when economist John Galbraith came to see her on Tuesday morning did she begin to take her candidacy seriously. "He said it was the first time in twenty years there was anybody in the Texas delegation to speak to," she said with a laugh.

After Galbraith's visit the Women's Political Caucus entered the picture, drawing up petitions and conferring with B. Rappaport, Ms. Farenthold's Texas political adviser and patron. Working all through Wednesday night, the new Sissy-for-Vice-President group got the petitions out and pasted posters of their candidate over signs donated by Endicott Peabody of Massachusetts and Senator Mike Gravell of Alaska. The following day at noon Gloria Steinem called Ms. Farenthold to tell her that since Shirley Chisholm had decided not to run for Vice President, the caucus was now free to endorse her. "And that's the first time I took it with any seriousness," recalled Ms. Farenthold, described as "the reluctant dragon" by some caucus members; they find her an interesting paradox, a woman whose political successes are hard to reconcile with her cautious, self-effacing and introspective veneer.

Meanwhile Galbraith backed away from her candidacy, citing two reasons for his about-face. "First he said he had pushed Teddy Kennedy so hard that he could not nominate me because it wouldn't make sense to McGovern since he pushed Kennedy. Well, then Kennedy wasn't in the picture. Then he said . . . he couldn't nominate me because he had helped prevent a disaster, the disaster being keeping Kevin White [the mayor of Boston] out of the thing." Then she added with a twinkle in her eye, "I was so curious when he said, 'I think the man we have is going to be all right.' "

After the Eagleton choice was announced she had second thoughts about allowing her candidacy to continue, fearful that it be interpreted as an anti-McGovern move, and fearful—as any other politician would be in such an unpredictable situation—of not getting any votes. "You know," she admitted, with characteristic candor, "any time you run for office, you have that thought: Well, just suppose you don't get any votes."

In the end her fears proved unfounded, and she wound up with 420 votes, as opposed to 1,741 for Senator Eagleton. It was this vote that showed women the potential strength they'd had all along, if they had only been able to exploit it in their negotiations with McGovern. On this issue women seemed to unite more cohesively than they had on the abortion, South Carolina, and cochairperson issues. Shirley MacLaine surfaced on the side of the women and told the delegates to "vote any way they wanted to" on Ms. Farenthold's candidacy. "I thought it was just marvelous," she said. "I was delighted. It was one of those things . . . they [the McGovern people] tolerated with some amusement and then were stunned to find there was real strength there. It hadn't occurred to them to put a woman in the second spot."

In another act of feminist solidarity the Arkansas delegation cast seventeen of their votes (a whopping majority) for the Farenthold candidacy, a striking victory in view of that state's defeat of the Equal Rights Amendment. After the vote that night Sissy Farenthold told how she went up to Arkansas Governor Dale Bumpers, who profusely accepted her thanks for delivering his delegation. Only two days later, vacationing in Nassau, did she learn what really happened from a man whose wife was an Arkansas delegate and who was himself a personal friend of the governor's. "I'm ready to move to Arkansas and thank your governor," Ms. Farenthold told him. "Thank our governor? Well, it wasn't quite like that," he told her, relating the incident as it really happened. Bumpers had left instructions with his delegation, then had gone off to shake hands with the VIP's. While he was gone, in an act of political courage and feminist unity, the women delegates took over and switched the vote to Sissy Farenthold.

Although she'd campaigned for him vigorously in Texas, Sissy Farenthold left the convention somewhat disillusioned with McGovern. "You know," she remarked, "Eagleton called me and he couldn't have been more gracious. He said, 'You would have beaten me if I hadn't been anointed by McGovern.' I didn't expect that, of course, but what I would have appreciated would have been some courtesy from McGovern. You know, I was never on a list, never for consideration. It would have been a token thing, but it would have taken off the sting. Here I ran second, yet I was never on the list. But had I been a man, I would have been treated with more courtesy by McGovern."

Monday-Morning Quarterbacking

Although misjudgments abounded on both sides, the most costly were made by the McGovern forces, who miscalculated the depth of the bitterness they created—a feeling inevitably followed by a resultant loss of power and credibility. Sacrificing women's issues on the altar of pragmatism didn't work in the long run, as the altar became increasingly crowded with other issues, and other groups. The pols for the most part sat out the election anyway, unaffected by McGovern's efforts to conciliate them while many of the workers—especially women—responsible for McGovern's primary victories melted away as they watched the reasons for their commitment to politics evaporate. Although McGovern, to his ultimate credit, recruited idealists into politics, the convention taught him that idealists are fairly intransigent, especially when it comes to those ideals propelling them to enter politics in the first place. Despite his best efforts they could not be converted into a true political machine, reliable, chameleonlike, always ready to change at a signal from the leader.

Women regarded McGovern's actions as betrayals—indications they occupied low ranks in the political pecking order. But "betrayal" isn't really an operative word in politics, where promises are made only to the voters, who routinely expect them to be broken. Practicing politicians bargain with each other in the hard currency of their marketplace: Instead of promises, rewards are negotiated in return for votes, money and service. If the rewards fail to materialize, the quid pro quo is also pulled back, and the bargain invalidated. Women neglected to clarify promises into bargains; although each issue helped them to mobilize their own quid pro quo—in their case mostly votes and service—into a hard, clear strike force.

The bad blood spilled left the McGovern campaign devoid of the feminist political influence, a loss lamented by Shirley MacLaine: "I agree with them [feminist critics] that the McGovern campaign was void—practically completely void of the influence of women. And they suffered for that. Not just the women, but the McGovern campaign suffered. We definitely needed the women . . . to try and change the country." McGovern should have appointed a women's advisory council, she concluded, to take full advantage of women as a resource.

Some women who remained loyal to McGovern after Miami found the breakdown in communications precluded them from donating their best efforts to his cause. "We had absolutely zero priority as far as the McGovern group was concerned," recalled Gloria Steinem, "because we were captives. The state organizations didn't function in the election in the way they had in the primary. We would go there [to McGovern headquarters] and say, 'Just a mimeograph machine, mailing lists, that's all we need. We can mobilize the consumer groups, etc.'"

Their pleas fell on deaf ears, along with their requests to channel speakers to the McGovern cause. "It was like some group, some enormous thing plugging up the information," she continued. "Other state organizations were frustrated because they had requested speakers or certain strategic kinds of help and weren't even getting a reply." According to Ms. Steinem, they even neglected to coordinate her own speaking engagements, an inexplicable oversight in view of her well-known ability to attract crowds and press coverage: "It was as though I wasn't functioning. . . . the speaking requests would go to McGovern and never come out again, just due to inefficiency. So I began taking them separately. I finally was just functioning without reference, except I would call them up and say, 'Hello, there. I am going to speak at. . . .'"

Shirley MacLaine blamed this failure on a general breakdown in communications within the campaign organization. "It didn't matter whether you were a man or woman, a lamppost or a green monkey," she explained, stressing that women were not singled out for this treatment. "It was very hard to get anything through in the campaign because it was horizontally constructed. It wasn't a monolithic form so it didn't have a leader. George McGovern was the horse and the jockey. . . . In terms of the needs and desires of women there was absolutely nobody. But then there weren't very many people to contact in terms of the needs and desires of anybody."

Blocking their access to him also prevented women from helping McGovern sharpen his campaign oratory, in order to reinforce and win back a constituency that had helped him capture the nomination against overwhelming odds. "The major problem," concluded Gloria Steinem, "was that the issues weren't stated. The women's question was viewed narrowly instead of within a broader context. If he was talking about unemployment, say, why doesn't he also talk about unemployment among women, up 34 percent . . . this means six million or more women and kids on welfare. Nixon put these women and children on welfare. . . . Never in my hearing," she continued, "did he enunciate a full range of issues in those terms."

Faulty communications also plagued the women's movement, which itself contained diverse factions within its ranks. There was no clear-cut strategy, charged Martha McKay, among women at the convention. Policy was formulated by Gloria Steinem and Bella Abzug, with little or no consultation with other caucus representatives. "There was supposed to be a committee of four or five people which should have included representatives of all candidates. It never materialized." It was a mistake, Ms. McKay argued, for women to have followed Gloria Steinem's argument that supporting McGovern was a woman's issue. "That was not a woman's issue," she said emphatically. "Our issue was to get a position in his campaign and get some commitments from him about appointments. We didn't have a whole lot of bargaining power but we had some. We had some troops."

Herself a supporter of Terry Sanford, the governor of North Carolina and their favorite-son candidate, Ms. McKay stressed the importance of emphasizing women's issues to the candidates so they understand that if their ambitions and women's interests collide, women's interests would come first. There must never again develop the kind of situation that occurred in Miami, forcing women to sacrifice their own interests. Things will change for women, said Ms. McKay, "only when we form coalitions and have the guts to withhold our support. This is what we did not do in Miami. What Gloria did not do, what Bella did not do. In the plane with Terry I said, 'You understand, Terry, if it comes to a case of your interests or women's interests, which one it's going to be, don't you?' And he said, 'Yes, I understand.' "[12]

Within the context of American pressure politics Martha McKay's approach is well taken. To be effective a group must be willing to mix its ideology with solid, pragmatic tactics, such as withholding or delivering its support in a massive bloc. One can't imagine George Meany, for example, continuing to support a candidate who had explained that for the duration of his campaign he would have to speak out against the minimum wage but after he was elected would continue to be a friend of the working person.

Martha McKay also believed from a strategic point of view that if women had won a solid victory from the start, they might have developed enough of a power base to carry them through the rest of the issues. The issue she settled on as ripe for victory was the seating of the Chicago delegation, and she attempted to get the women's caucus to dramatize that issue. "I tried to get the caucus to take the seating of the new Chicago delegation as their number-one priority," she recalled. "They had taken on the Daley machine. They had eight women, the lives of whose children had been threatened over the telephone. Two had been assaulted, one in a church by Daley's thugs.

"Doesn't that story have appeal?" she asked. "It was the right cause. We needed a victory, and I had a gut feeling that the convention was not going to seat Daley's delegation." With all this in mind she tried to get the caucus to back the issue. "The women from Chicago were there," she recalled, as she described the first meeting of the caucus. "They spoke to us and said, 'We need your help.' I moved that we take that as our number-one priority. Then Bella said, 'We're not doing this that way.' " She said it wouldn't be fair because there was going to be another caucus the next day. She got it put off, and it lost by a few votes. The fact of the matter was at that time McGovern was playing footsy with Daley.

The timing killed the issue for the caucus, she continued, since the press conference called for the following morning was called off. The press was forced to leave without identifying the full-fledged commitment of the women's caucus for their sisters in

Illinois. The challenge prevailed anyway and the Daley delegation was never seated.

Women Power, 1972

And so the women left Miami, many to pursue careers in public office back in their home states. In Sissy Farenthold's Texas, where she had been the only woman member of the legislature, 6 women were elected the following fall. This represented progress, but only minimal progress, in the 150-member body. More important, it reflected a national trend, given impetus by the McGovern commission and the McGovern campaign, which stood out as the first campaign in history that systematically recruited women into positions of responsibility.

Despite some setbacks, women left the convention with substantial victories for the women's political movement under their belts. "When the convention broke up," wrote Theodore White, "Women power 1972 was real."[13] On the convention floor, a thousand women delegates acted with substantial solidarity considering the fact that 88 percent of them had never been to a convention before. On the third floor of the sea-sprayed Betsy Ross Hotel, where the National Women's Political Caucus encamped, functioned a "power center," White observed. "Mimeograph and Xerox machines spewed out leaflets in thousands of pink, yellow, green, blue sheets; the switchboard at the Betsy Ross Hotel jammed; fuses blew; and each night, after dark, couriers boarded the buses to travel north on Collins Avenue and persuade the night clerks of the 40 or more major hotels to stuff mailboxes or let them slip leaflets under delegates' doors. 'WOMEN POWER 1972' remained stained on the Betsy Ross's third-floor carpet, in faded red paint. . . ."[14]

Women proudly watched other women in high, visible positions; Patricia Harris, for example, who managed the credentials-committee challenges with "toughness and skill,"[15] and Yvonne Braithwaite Burke, who presided over the platform debates. They saw the Democratic National Committee unanimously elect Jean Westwood its chairperson. A sweeping fifteen-point women's rights plank was written into the platform, including pledges supporting "the Equal Rights Amendment; the elimination of discrimination against women in public accommodations and jobs; equal access to educational opportunities, tenure, promotion and higher salaries; the availability of maternity benefits to working women and the appointment of women to positions of top responsibility in all branches of the Federal Government."[16]

In contrast to Martha McKay's interpretation, other members of the women's caucus attributed the credentials committee's decision to oust Mayor Daley and fifty-eight others in favor of more women and more blacks as their own victory, won by intensive lobbying efforts. Women could be proud, too, that their efforts within the Democratic party forced the Republican party to open its convention doors to women.

The women had made progress, but the progress merely whetted their appetite and heightened their critical evaluation of men and of the political system. They left Miami Beach with a sense of accomplishment coupled with a sense of betrayal, a feeling that sharpened their cutting edge and made them more determined to use their resources for women and for women's issues. "I don't think anyone sat out in that trailer and said, 'How can we let the women down on those issues?'" said Donna Brunstadt, a Connecticut delegate. "They figured, 'They'll follow McGovern to hell and back.' At that point most of us would have. I no longer would do that for any man."

Chapter II

Stag Party: Patterns of Exclusion in Party Politics

I still say that both political parties discriminate more than government itself—far more.

—REPRESENTATIVE
MARGARET HECKLER

Women are just mad. Mad at themselves more than anything else, that they let themselves be used all these years. They were the ones who did the work and somebody else not only got the credit, but got the title. Women are no longer going to be vice-chairmen.

—ANNE WEXLER

In the autumn of the 1972 Presidential campaign Anne Martindell, vice-chairman of the New Jersey state Democratic party, failed to receive an invitation to a meeting called by her fellow leaders to discuss election strategy. The meeting, held at the home of Salvatore Bontempo, the state chairman, was for top party strategists, including former Governors Richard Hughes and Robert Meyner, Senator Harrison Williams, and key party aides. Ms. Martindell made an uninvited appearance and lashed out at her fellow Democrats for excluding her. She refused to be shut out, she said, because she "represented all the vice-chairmen, as well as all the women in the party." One leader tried to calm her, explaining she hadn't been invited because all the other leaders were afraid she would be offended by their language. Not so, retorted the feisty Ms. Martindell, "I don't give a —— what kind of language you use. You had no right to exclude me."[1]

Ms. Martindell's experience was typical of American party politics, where a "males only" sign hangs on the clubhouse door. A good example is the practice of relegating women to the post of vice-chairman, a figurehead position viewed as meaningless by most practicing politicians. Nominally second in command, these women are in fact outranked by lower-ranking male functionaries. Although most vice-chairmen accept their roles as more symbolic than substantive and virtually lacking in power, some, Ms. Martindell for instance, rankle when slighted.

For women, winning elections has proved less difficult than getting nominated, a process that forces women to choose between breaking down the locker-room door, as Ms. Martindell did, or finding a route that allows them to circumvent the room altogether. In either case the choice usually boils down to whether or not the political hopeful can obtain the resources to create a separate organization to run her own primary race, keep that organization intact until the general election, and then face the possible liability incurred by functioning in a legislature without party support.

Like other professional male elites, party leaders are conditioned to regard women in supportive rather than leadership roles, and often neglect to reciprocate their support when women achieve some leadership of their own. In fact they seem all too ready to sacrifice women politicians at the drop of a district—as the Brooklyn Democrats did when they ditched Representative Edna Kelly, then second-ranking Democrat on the House Foreign Affairs Committee and a nine-term member of the House, when it became necessary to create a black district. Ms. Kelly had no illusions about her exclusion from the inner circle of Brooklyn politics, despite her power in the House. Arriving late at county headquarters for a meeting called to oust Stanley Steingut, then county leader, Ms. Kelly (who was his coleader) entered a large room of district leaders who pointed to a small office, where Mr. Steingut and the six most powerful leaders were locked in private combat. Representative Kelly knocked on the office door, which was opened wide enough for the men to see who was seeking to enter, then slammed shut in her face.

Other women expendable to the party have been more controversial than Representative Kelly, who quietly faded from view after the party had made its decision. In 1972, when the Democrats had to relinquish a Congressional seat in Manhattan, it was Bella Abzug, one of two Congresswomen at that time in the thirty-nine-member state delegation, who was redistricted out of her seat. Her entire district, the 19th Congressional District (C.D.), was eliminated from the drawing boards.

In Massachusetts in that same election year, Representative Louise Day Hicks, best known for her campaigns against school busing, failed to win reelection as predicted after her 9th C.D. in Boston was expanded to include several suburban communities.[2]

In Bella Abzug's case the reason for her expulsion was more complicated than expendability. As Bella explains it, she is "A woman *who* . . ."; a woman who had constantly put herself in opposition to the party in her outspokenness on the peace issue and on women's rights. Totally in character, she also fought her party's attempt to eliminate her politically, announcing she would oppose incumbent William Fitts Ryan in the 20th C.D. primary election. "I suspect," she said, "that the attempt by male politicians to dismember a district represented by a woman, a woman who happens to be an activist and a leader of the women's rights movement, will provide us with an initial test of the strength of organized womanpower."[3]

Earlier in her term, Ms. Abzug had locked rhetoric with the late Representative Emanuel Celler, the dean of the House and chairman of the Judiciary Committee, who said that he opposed the Equal Rights Amendment because he felt that women were basically inferior to men. After all, he pointed out, there were no women at the Last Supper. Ms. Abzug rejoined, "There may have been no women at the Last Supper, but there damned well will be women at the next one." As a twist of fate Mr. Celler was unseated in the next election by Elizabeth Holtzman, a thirty-two-year-old lawyer.

When women come close to achieving some real power in the party organization, they often find the party resorting to outright sabotage. To stop Ronnie Eldridge from becoming county leader in 1967 the New York Democrats simply changed the rules in the middle of the balloting. After seeing that Ms. Eldridge had won a majority of the votes among the district leaders—traditionally all that was required to elect a county leader—the party suddenly changed the rules to require a two-thirds vote. With a tinge of bitterness in her voice Ms. Eldridge recalled the incident: "I was a very serious candidate. I remember one of the leaders standing up and saying—and this was a reform leader—'How could a woman be a county leader? She couldn't sit and talk with the other county leaders. We couldn't get any business done.' " The strategy worked, though few objected at the time, and Ms. Eldridge, then Senator Robert Kennedy's liaison with the New York Democrats, lost the election.

Women are often selected by the party for ceremonial roles, party posts in which their actual power is minimal although their visibility is great. Women activists complain that both parties tend to select women they can control, women who will not challenge the status quo. "In my own home state, Indiana," recounted Jill Ruckelshaus, a Republican activist who worked for Anne Armstrong in the Women's Unit in the White House, "there was an at-large race for House of Representatives in the Merion County district. And the selecting committee picked out who the candidates would be, and they all ran at-large. They tried for some kind of balance, geographically and racially, but they didn't ever try to balance it sexually. They always had one woman or two out of every fifteen or sixteen candidates. But they never chose anyone who was active; they always chose someone they could control, someone who would listen to the male leaders in the group."

Ms. Ruckelshaus added that her party is still not promoting women who come from the ranks of the feminists, or from the women's political movement, but that she and Ms. Armstrong travel around the country making speeches encouraging women in general to become more active in politics. She admitted she never tried to convince individual women to run for office, although she implied that Ms. Armstrong did: "She knows Republicans all over the country, including the chairmen, so she will very often encourage women to think of themselves as possible candidates, or as a campaign manager, instead of thinking of themselves as a forty-eight-hour-a-week volunteer."

The small number of women in public office reflects the pattern of discrimination that begins at the precinct level. Of a total of 310 state offices, only 24 are held by women, 19 of whom are Democrats and 5 Republicans. Women, therefore, account for only 8 percent of the total.[4] In the state legislatures the percentage is even lower: Of 7,603 state legislators, 450 are women—189 Democrats and 261 Republicans—constituting 6 percent of the total.[5] In Congress the percentage is lowest of all, the 16 women members representing less than 4 percent of the total population on the House side. The Senate has had no women since the defeat, in 1972, of Maine Republican Margaret Chase Smith.

As salaries for public officials increase (Congressional representatives, for example, earn $42,500 a year, which they're trying to increase to $52,000), party officials seem even less inclined to relinquish nominations to women candidates, a fact many fear will further hurt women's chances. In fact, statistics seem to indicate a pattern, showing that the lower the salary, the greater the number of women. Only in the state of New Hampshire, where legislators earn $100 a year, have women made a numerical impact: 68 women have been elected to the House, of 400 representatives, the highest number of any state legislature in the country. Connecticut, with its 22 women legislators of a total 151, comes in a close second. Other states with a high percentage of women legislators also conform to the pattern of paying lower salaries: Vermont, a state with 21 women legislators, pays $1.50 a day, plus expenses, the total stipend not to exceed a biennial ceiling of $4,500. Connecticut pays $5,500 a year. Maine, a state with 16 women legislators, pays $3,500 over a two-year period. Conversely states whose legislators receive salaries high by the standards of the other states show lower percentages of women, a formula illustrating that as salaries escalate, the jobs become more desirable, and women have a harder time obtaining them. California, which pays $19,200 a year, has elected only 3 women to the state Assembly, and none to the Senate; Illinois, paying $17,000 a year, elected only 4 women representatives; Michigan, paying $17,000 a year, only 7; New York, paying $15,000 a year, 3; and Pennsylvania, paying $15,000 annually, 7.[6]

The Primary Battle

After working for many years in reform Democratic politics, organizing peace groups citywide to work for candidates in the party, Bella Abzug decided to run for office herself. To her surprise the party closed ranks against her when she first announced her intention to unseat incumbent Congressman Leonard Farbstein. "You're the one that *helps* sides," her friends in the reform movement admonished. "Why do you want to run yourself?" "Well," she informed them, "over the years people always asked me to run, and I said I didn't want to. Finally, when it came to 1970 and we still had no peace and no change in priorities, I decided that we needed a different kind of Representative: an activist. I then said, okay, I'm running."

At that point the reform clubs told her that they had a number of candidates of their own, that she wasn't a member of the reform club in the district in which she wanted to run, and that they would select a candidate from among their own ranks. Angered, Ms. Abzug determined to run in spite of their resistance. In spelling out her decision to them, she informed the club their procedures were too limited, excluding from nomination representatives from the community. "They all knew me," she recounted. "I had worked very hard. I had organized five boroughs to work for Ted Weiss, in addition to other reform candidates like Ed Koch. Whenever a candidate took a strong position on the war, I then helped mobilize forces throughout the city. I said you can't just select a candidate and say this is who we have to work for. We want to have the chance to work on a broader kind of thing." Bella Abzug won the primary and the election, unseating Representative Farbstein, a feat the reform clubs' candidate Ted Weiss had been unable to accomplish in the past.

If the party doesn't laugh at them outright, say many women who have tried to seek office, it attempts to stall them, in hope of discouraging them more permanently. Bonnie Andrikopoulos, a Colorado Republican who campaigned for Representative Patricia Schroeder, observed, "If you go to the party and want the party's support . . . and this was one of Pat's greatest obstacles . . . they told her, 'Don't do that this year; you haven't had the experience.' We had a lot of qualified women who should have been running a long time ago, but they've gone to the leadership and the leadership has always said, 'Oh, it isn't time yet; don't ruffle the waters. We'll run a man.' I think that from the success that we had in Colorado, that hopefully women won't believe that anymore. You can do it without the backing of the party leadership. Pat didn't ever have strong support from the party."

When a woman manages to win a primary fight, the party often tries other strategies to block her success, apparently willing to lose an election rather than win with a woman. In Pat Schroeder's case, according to Doris Meissner, former executive director of the National Women's Political Caucus, the Democratic party of Denver deprived her of funds usually given the candidate who has won the primary. This was followed by a cutoff of AFL-CIO funds normally given a Democratic candidate. As a result of the efforts of the caucus, continued Ms. Meissner, "We were able to get a good chunk of money to her because we pushed the Democratic Study Group [an informal group of liberal Congressmen] as well as some of those groups involved with the whole discrimination issue."

More disappointing to Pat Schroeder personally were the women in the Colorado Democratic party to whom she also turned for support. "It's too early for a woman to run," they gently explained. Her candidacy, they felt, would "set back the woman's movement"! Failing to endorse Ms. Schroeder, the Democratic Women's Caucus considered supporting her opponent—a man—but eventually remained neutral, chastened by Ms. Schroeder's warning that "the press would never stop laughing at them if they did."

"I was so dismayed at their reaction," said Representative Schroeder, as a quorum call buzzed in her office, "and yet it was typical of that part of our conditioning . . . you know, 'You can't be too pushy, and we'll support you if you run for the State House. Start a little lower.'"

To their surprise Pat Schroeder turned out to be an excellent candidate—young, attractive, articulate—who had the capacity to draw large crowds to her speeches, and ultimately to the polls. With little money and party support, she beat her primary opponent Clarence "Arch" Decker with the vote of 24,792 to 20,497, and in the general election, won her seat from Congressman James McKevitt with a final tally of 100,858 to 92,178. Ms. Schroeder pointed out that after the primary, even though the party leadership failed to help, many precinct committee people turned out to help her win the general election.

The Colorado Democratic women reacted predictably and as the party would have wanted them to, relegating women's goals well behind the party's interests. Rarely acting as a catalyst within the party, women's auxiliaries generally serve as support pillars, to reinforce the service and fund-raising functions in the general interest of maintaining the male status quo. In Essex County, New Jersey, for example, the Peter Rodino Ladies Auxiliary holds annual parties for the purpose of raising money and generating support for their Congressman. All the county committeewomen in the district are invited. Recognizing the real purpose of segregating these groups from the mainstream of party life, Betty Friedan advised a group of Democratic women in New York City, before whom she had been invited to speak, that their first order of business ought to be to disband.[7]

Recently women's chances for nomination have increased in what are known as "throwaway districts," districts in which the candidate is expected to lose, either because of a strong incumbent, a strong machine, or a combination of both in the opposition. In 1972 New York Republican County Chairman Vincent Albano chose Jane Pickens Langley, a wealthy former actress, to run against Representative Edward Koch in the 18th Congressional District in Manhattan, and Joyce Ahrens to run for the Assembly in the same area against Peter Berle. As Albano expected, both men won handily, although Ms. Ahrens ran a strong race with support from members of the Women's Political Caucus. No one could determine, however, whether Chairman Albano gained any mileage with women voters as a result of his nominations.

Party leaders also look to widows of officeholders at nomination time, in the hope of capitalizing on the voters' goodwill and sympathy, as well as on some of the power held by the late politician. Most recently, two widows of Congressmen killed in plane accidents were nominated and elected to fill their husbands' seats: Lindy Boggs of Louisiana and Carliss Collins of Chicago.[8] Women who enter politics this way often turn out to be fine candidates and politicians and may well, as Martin Gruberg has noted, become more prominent than their husbands. Edith Nourse Rogers of Massachusetts polled a larger proportion of the total vote in the special election held after her husband's death than her husband had polled the previous fall, and went on to defeat a former governor and serve for eighteen terms in Congress, chairing the Veterans Committee in the 80th and 83d Congresses. Frances Bolton, who served for fourteen consecutive terms, became ranking minority member on the Foreign Affairs Committee. Margaret Chase Smith became the only woman to serve in both the House and the Senate. Widows also benefit from being permitted to assume their husband's committee assignments, Gruberg also noted, while other freshmen are assigned to less powerful committees.[9]

Competent or not, the practice of nominating a widow "over her husband's dead body" has aroused the ire of members of the women's political movement, who accuse the parties of perpetuating "dynasties" within a democratic political system. The dispute came to a head in the fall of 1972, when the widow of Representative William Fitts Ryan, of Manhattan's Upper West Side, tried to wrest the Democratic nomination from Bella Abzug; failing that, Ms. Ryan later opposed Representative Abzug in the general election as the Liberal party's nominee. Despite Priscilla Ryan's experience and ability, the contest was portrayed as one between a legatee candidate and a candidate who had achieved political success on her own. Ms. Ryan lost badly.

Statistics on the number of widows who have succeeded to their husband's offices are deceiving, because they fail to show the extent to which sexist discrimination has affected the careers of these women. Scarcely different from other women in the eyes of the party, many political widows have faced hostile party leaders before deciding to run their own races, independent of the party hierarchy's support. Although Margaret Chase Smith "succeeded" to her late husband's Congressional seat, she went on in 1947 to face a recalcitrant state GOP and three primary opponents, one of whom was the governor and the candidate with the "monetary backing of the regular Republican organization."[10] After her victory she stayed in the Senate for four terms, a total of twenty-four years, before being defeated in 1972 by a young Democratic Congressman, William Hathaway.

The career of Leonor Sullivan, a Democrat from St. Louis, Missouri, also challenges false impressions of succession, for she, too, conducted her own fight to seek the Democratic party nomination. According to Representative Sullivan, the Democratic party organization refused to support her in the special election called after her husband's death. "We don't have anything against you, but we want to win," the party leaders explained, according to Ms. Sullivan, after nominating a relatively unknown man from the state legislature. With relish Ms. Sullivan recounted how the Democrats lost, while she returned to Washington, working for a full year to save enough money to run her own primary fight before the general election. Without the party's support she succeeded in winning the primary, shrewdly spurning advice to forget the party and run for Congress as an independent. "When you run as an independent, you come in as a zombie," she explained to them, because Congress is organized along party lines. In the primary, where she faced six men, she found it a distinct advantage to be a woman, and more readily identifiable to the public. Her high rate of recognition with the voters was enhanced by the fact that she had been born and reared in St. Louis, and was remembered as being one of the first women to accompany her husband on the campaign trail.

A soft-spoken woman with a ready smile and crinkly blue eyes, Ms. Sullivan tends to wear bright clothes and lots of large jewelry, to the consternation of some of her more fashion-conservative colleagues in the House. As the only woman in Congress to vote against the Equal Rights Amendment, she has also caused dismay among women political activists, who say that despite her nonfeminist stance she is the most powerful woman member of Congress. She now is the only woman in Congress to chair a committee (Merchant Marine and Fisheries); in addition, she holds a seat as the third-ranking Democrat on the powerful Banking and Currency Committee—positions of power she has built up on her own, not via the legacy system. Despite her stand on the Equal Rights Amendment, however, Ms. Sullivan hasn't forgotten her early difficulties before her first victory in 1953, pointing to the party as the most difficult obstacle facing women who seek to enter politics in a meaningful way: "The hardest thing for a woman is to get nominated," she concluded. "It's difficult for a woman to get in. You don't just bluster in. It's the same twenty years ago as now."

Party Challenging: A David and Goliath Fable for Women

A woman can't bluster in, as Representative Sullivan advises, but neither hard work nor talent guarantees a woman political success no matter how superior she may be to whomever the party is offering the public. "I still say that both political parties discriminate more than government itself does . . . far more," said Representative Margaret Heckler of Massachusetts, recalling her early fight for political recognition. "The party did not encourage me. In fact they discouraged me. At first they ignored me, and then they discouraged me. When I was finally elected, they had to accept the fact."

Before deciding to run for office, Ms. Heckler—then a young lawyer with three small children—recalled contributing considerable amounts of her time and energy campaigning for the Republican party and its candidates. She soon realized her candidates were not investing as much of themselves in their campaigns as she was. "I'd have a whole team of women taking all the abuse that one receives . . . at a railway station with commuters, about three days before the election, when all the worst things come out, right at the end, and report back to my candidate, and he would have been at home with his feet up by the fire sipping a cocktail. And that really annoyed me, and it happened repeatedly. So I decided that I would run."

Once again service counted for little when Ms. Heckler sought the party's blessing before stepping into the fray. In her case, though, the party would have been wise to support her, for after winning a seat on the Governor's Council (a statewide office), she went on to challenge Joe Martin, former Speaker of the House and in 1966 its Minority Leader. Ms. Heckler beat him in a primary election, which led her to her first term in the House in 1966. Republicans thereby lost one of their most powerful men in the House, a leader whose power had taken years to build and to develop.

Reflecting on her victory, Ms. Heckler stressed the chasm between the party leadership and those like herself who "toiled in the vineyards." Finding the leadership wouldn't support her, she turned to the grass roots, Republican precinct committeepeople, where Martin's support had eroded and where her best and most effective campaign workers were recruited. Many independents, she continued, also entered that primary to help her get nominated. In a strange twist of fate Ms. Heckler benefited from the party's contempt. Poor intelligence allowed for a certain laxity, and party leaders never recognized their opponent as a real threat. "Martin's supporters didn't believe any woman could ever unseat him," she said with a laugh. "And they drew a parallel between my race and that of another woman, a brilliant woman who apparently spoke many languages and was extremely competent. But the time was not ready for her. She ran against Joe Martin maybe twenty years before I did. And so, they thought, 'Here's another woman,' and they expected me to be defeated."

Most important, she stressed, she was able to capture the support of lower levels of the party organization, people not ordinarily consulted on nominations and who, in populist fury, occasionally turn their backs on the leadership. "It was really a populist kind of thing," she recalled, "where people expressed their point of view. It was not a bloody campaign by any means because I respected Joe Martin, but I felt my support really had come from the people—and though that is a moldy cliché in politics, that is really what politics is about." In her ability to compartmentalize in politics, to separate, as she puts it, "the chiefs from the Indians," Margaret Heckler has been able to supplement and to bypass the top layers of the party machinery, creating in essence her own organization, an organization she credits with giving her more independence as a legislator than that enjoyed by men who have come out of the top levels of the party structure.

In many cases the party machinery will go along with a young, attractive, insurgent candidate like Margaret Heckler—if he is a man and if the candidate demonstrates his abilities among the electorate. There are cases, in fact, where the party has actually promoted an insurgent as a fresh new face to present to the electorate. More commonly, though, the system operates within a protégé context; the party father trains his protégé for his seat in Congress, or his seat in the state legislature, or his office in the party hierarchy. In this framework the politically ambitious woman is almost always forced to go the primary route (as indeed, to a lesser extent, are many men who are regarded as insurgents) for offices from dogcatcher to governor. First they must openly challenge the leadership, then hope to raise the votes and the funds necessary to win. Such a feat requires considerable financial and emotional resources—resources many women are beginning to muster, encouraged by the successes of women like Margaret Heckler and Pat Schroeder.

The Penalties of Political Independence: Coping with Ostracism

The parties eventually accepted Representatives Sullivan and Heckler, although many Republican leaders never quite forgave Margaret Heckler for beating Joe Martin. But other women, audacious enough to challenge the machinery, must face what amounts to eternal excommunication in their future relationships with the party hierarchy, an experience best illustrated by the career of Michigan's Martha Griffiths.

Representative Griffiths has managed to stay in Congress for nineteen years despite her isolation from Michigan's Democratic party, whose present organization she and her husband, Hicks Griffiths, helped build. Compounding the liability of her separation from the party, Ms. Griffiths also lacks support from organized labor[11]—a strong party ally and a powerful force in the state. "I don't have anything to do with them, and I never have," says Ms. Griffiths of the state party organization and their labor allies. "I always help in my district around election time. I give the district money, and I supply workers on election day. I don't do anything for anybody else."

What is striking about Martha Griffiths' experience is the absence of loyalties politicians normally exhibit. The quid pro quos traditionally extracted for party service just didn't seem to operate in Ms. Griffiths' case; perhaps they would have if her husband had been the candidate. "I had a very peculiar situation," recounted Ms. Griffiths in her strong, raspy voice. "My husband reformed the Democratic party in Michigan to elect Mennen Williams. He was Williams' first campaign manager and was state chairman after that." In spite of this, when she decided to run for Congress, she found not one ounce of support forthcoming from either the labor unions, whom she had supported as a state legislator, or from the party. "I worked harder than anybody else. They did nothing to assist. Nobody in labor and nobody in the Democratic party. The woman who was the vice-chairman of the Democratic party lived in my district. My husband had made her the vice-chairman. I ran a campaign from a trailer. She never even saw the trailer. So I never got any help from any of them. They really didn't want me to win."

Like Bella Abzug, Representative Griffiths attributed part of her problem with the party to the fact that she was an independent woman who couldn't be counted on as a predictable political force. This was especially disturbing to the labor people, she said, who resented her inclinations toward leadership in the legislature. "The labor guys came in and they wanted to take over the whole thing," she recounted. "And their biggest problem was that I was sitting there in the Michigan legislature. I had been the law partner of the governor. And I was the best educated. So when I said, 'Do this or that,' the rest of them did it. And they didn't like that. So they invited me to run for Congress." Hoping to defuse Ms. Griffiths, the party-labor leadership offered her what amounted to a "throwaway district," an area considered a Republican stronghold. They had no idea that Ms. Griffiths would even come close to winning, one of the many reasons they didn't bother to work for her, and they banked on a solid defeat that would discourage her from future political forays. She surprised the leadership, however, by coming within two and a half percentage points of winning in the extraordinarily tough election year of 1952, with Eisenhower carrying the district by an overwhelming margin.

On a more personal level political alliances also failed Ms. Griffiths, who expressed her disappointment at Governor Williams' refusal to promote her political career. Encouraged by her husband to run for the Senate, she approached Governor Williams less than two years after her first Congressional race in order to clear the idea with him and, she hoped, win his support. "I had always assumed that you would run," she began. No, he told her, he wasn't going to run, but Blair Moody, who had received an interim appointment as Senator on the death of Arthur Vandenberg, would run for a full term. By this time, she recalled, it was February of an election year, and Moody had showed no signs of declaring. "Well," she told the governor, "if he's not going to run, and you're not going to run, I will run. . . . Hicks will send the plane to pick me up and I will hit every town in Michigan." No, the governor assured her, Moody was going to run. And Moody in fact ran, while Martha Griffiths acceded to the governor's wish, and kept out of the race. Moody lost the election and died shortly afterward. In hindsight Ms. Griffiths seemed genuinely sorry she hadn't run for the Senate, as well as deeply resentful at Governor Williams' refusal to let her try. "My husband and I made Mennen Williams governor," she said indignantly.

The next time she decided to run, she kept her own counsel and ran again for Congress, this time succeeding both in the primary and in the general election.[12] By this time the hostility toward her was so entrenched the Democrats endorsed her opponent in the primary, settling on a candidate who was an absolute stranger to them—to their ultimate regret. "They nearly died," recounted Representative Griffiths gleefully, "when he turned out to be the head of the White Citizens Council. But I beat him, and I beat him two-to-one. And everybody they endorsed down to precinct delegate won, except the man they ran against me."

Why such hostility to her? "Well, they really resented this ability, an ability to lead. They didn't want an individual voice speaking up. You were supposed to take orders. This was particularly true as long as Walter Reuther [then head of the United Auto Workers] was there." It is also true that male elites, products of the culture, find it more difficult to accept leadership from a woman, a shrewd, feisty woman, than they would from a man whom they could accept in politically active roles.

National party leaders also took their cue from the Michigan Democrats' excommunication of Ms. Griffiths, as she found when presidential candidates failed to include her in their campaign plans. "In 1960," she said, "when Kennedy was running, we had an all-day event in Michigan. A women's affair. And they had women coming into the city of Detroit from all over the state, and Mrs. Rose Kennedy was there. They had a man from the University of Michigan discussing one of the issues before Congress. And after they were finished one of the women from the back of the room got up and said, 'In the name of God, if we've got a Democratic Congresswoman, what are we doing listening to college professors?'"

To Representative Griffiths few factors explain the hostility and isolation she has experienced in her political career as much as her independence. In the state Assembly where she had helped labor get an unemployment compensation bill passed, she nonetheless failed to win their support. "You would have assumed that any fool would have supported me, after that performance," she said. "The manufacturers' representative was sitting up in the gallery, you know, putting his thumb up to vote yes, and down to vote no, to the Republicans." After she got through explaining the bill to the legislators, many Republican legislators voted with her, along with a sufficient number of Democrats, to pass the bill. "Those guys should have been so grateful to me and so pleased with what I had done that nothing I could ever have done again should have stopped them. The truth was, the minute I did it they wanted rid of me. I had a brain and I could speak, and I could get something done. I was a dangerous person; and I've been dangerous to them as far as they're concerned ever since."

Does this isolation from the power blocs in her state leave her too isolated to be effective? Perhaps on the state level it would, but Representative Griffiths feels the effect has been salutary: She's come to Congress a free agent. "I was in an absolutely glorious position. Because they couldn't ask me anything, or offer any advice, they couldn't say we want this, we want that, and I never heard from any of them again. I just love the whole thing," she exclaimed. "I've had a great life, and you know, it's been sheer accident."

Ms. Griffiths' independence, particularly from the unions, has freed her to become one of the most effective feminists in Congress. Her campaign for the ratification of the Equal Rights Amendment (ERA), which she initiated and shepherded through its final passage in the House in 1971, succeeded despite the strong opposition to ERA by most unions, including, at that time, the AFL-CIO. The UAW, however, the major union in Michigan, supported ERA, but many Congressmen enjoying the support of other unions were inhibited from fighting for this issue. Ms. Griffiths, however, by virtue of her independence, could proceed unobstructed by political obligations.

Unexpectedly political isolation also accrued added benefits to her account with the voters, affording her a credibility not given her colleagues. On the issue of school busing, which Representative Griffiths opposes, she illustrated this point: "I have a district that would hate busing more than any other district in Michigan. I didn't have any trouble, but two of the Congressmen were darn near beaten because they were so close to the UAW, which espoused busing. Everyone knew they would vote the way the UAW wanted them to—and everyone knew I wouldn't. So when I said, 'I'm not going to vote for busing, I'm against busing,' they believed it. But they didn't believe those guys. It was a real plus."

Ms. Griffiths' case is unusual. Most women forced to run outside the party organization eventually return to the fold—if not embraced by the leadership, at least tolerated. Confronted by the strong alliance between labor and the party, Representative Griffiths faced an unusually powerful negative force, which probably precluded her reentry into the party orbit. Her early experiences, however, no doubt affected her deeply, for throughout her Congressional career Ms. Griffiths has championed all manner of proposals, causes, amendments and bills involving sex discrimination.

Women as Vote Getters

Perhaps the most difficult problem to sort out is just why American political parties—pragmatic to the core—neglect women who have proved themselves as vote getters. Sissy Farenthold claims the party organization in Texas made no overtures to her after her near victory in the 1972 gubernatorial primary. In a field of seven candidates Ms. Farenthold ran second, with 26 percent of the vote, surpassing the incumbent governor and lieutenant governor. As a further indignity, she recalled, she had to conduct a bitter struggle to become a delegate to the 1972 Democratic convention (a fairly low-level political prize). "Down here," she said, "it is pretty much winner take all. I know that, and really one of the most difficult things I ever did, personally, was to go to the state Democratic convention after my defeat. And I had to fight to be a delegate to Miami. I had to fight within the McGovern ranks." Citing the low numbers of women in American politics, Ms. Farenthold advises, "For any woman who wants to go into politics, I advise that she run first. If she waits to be drafted, she won't ever make it to the legislature."[13]

The notion of women's potential as vote getters is beginning to strike some segments of the national party leadership, where active efforts to promote women candidates can be seen. Harriet Cipriani, head of the women's division of the National Democratic Committee, now travels around the country trying to encourage women to move out of the supportive roles in the party into more active ones.[14] "We realize," she said, "that women have more credibility now with the voters, and can therefore attract voters from the other party more readily than a man can. A voter tends to look more at the person than at the party when a woman is running." The Democratic Women's Caucus in Illinois, she said, approached Mayor Daley with the idea of getting him to slate more women on the Democratic ticket. After warning representatives of the women's group that he would give them only five minutes, he ended up talking to them for fifty minutes, after which he agreed to slate a woman, Joanne Alter, for a spot on Chicago's Sanitary Commission. Ms. Alter ended up by leading the other commissioners by more than a million votes, according to Ms. Cipriani.

Despite their willingness to slate Ms. Alter, the Democratic party in Illinois remains the only state party organization without a woman elected to its state committee. To change this situation, says Ms. Cipriani, would involve a long and complicated process to change the state's election law; but until this happens, women's chances of being slated on a regular basis remain limited.

In Chicago, the patronage capital of the world, the record on women being included as a meaningful part of the Daley organization remains grim, according to the authors of an excellent study of political women in the Cook County machine. The study concludes (and the conclusions could be applied to strong party organizations in urban areas across the country): "While women have a role in the Daley organization, they have no status, never had status, and will not attain status."[15] Daley's appointment of Ms. Alter, the authors say, was made to "get the IDWC [Illinois Democratic Women's Caucus] off its [the organization's] back," and should not be regarded as the beginning of a new trend toward increasing the number of women as candidates on a regular basis. Keeping women on a "short lead" is as much a function of limited attitudes as anything else, explain the authors; they cite Mayor Daley's praise for a committeeman who increased female involvement in his precinct by holding a card party and a fashion show at his ward's headquarters—the organization's idea of women's activities. Only if the ethnic picture of Chicago politics is changed, the study concludes, will women's political future brighten: "The only way this . . . can change, is, we think, if ethnic Catholics, particularly the Irish, lose control of the organization to blacks and/or to the Spanish-speaking. Women from these groups . . . are becoming aggressive politically, while other ethnic women remain passive. Furthermore, it is the black and Spanish-speaking women who represent the groups most in need of patronage jobs."

The Task of Changing Attitudes: The Party as Culture-Bound

Rejecting the widespread notion that women just do not belong in the inner councils of the major parties involves a massive change in attitudes. Women activists tell an apocryphal story about a young boy whose mother practiced law. One day he was asked if he, too, wanted to be a lawyer when he grew up. "Oh, no," he said, shocked, "that's woman's work." Young and old, male elites—whether in the party or in high-status professions—fear the direct correlation between including women in their ranks and suffering a subsequent loss in professional prestige.

"The presence of a woman in a male group devalues the group," said Gloria Steinem, explaining this syndrome. "I remember interviewing the astronauts right after the Soviets sent a woman up, and they were furious. It has always stuck in my mind as a kind of example. . . . It is masculine affirming, if I can use that term, to have an all-male group. The addition of a black male is okay, as long as there aren't too many. It is even kind of good because it is the masculine image. But as soon as a woman can do it, too, it literally devalues the whole function, whatever it is."

Exclusionary practices toward women originate in the nuclear-family unit, which structures women's lives in such a way as to preclude their normal and natural entry into the life and subculture of the clubhouse. In the normal political family, for example, an evening scenario might find the woman putting the children to bed, while her husband ambles over to the clubhouse, hoping to cultivate the friendships and relationships that will provide him with the foundations of his political career. If he doesn't choose the clubhouse, he might attend the Rotary Club or the local bar association or a wide variety of all-male organizations that tie in with politics. The network of clubs patronized by women, on the other hand, is far less likely to be connected to party politics or to political success.

Geri Pleshaw, an aide to Mayor Kevin White of Boston, succinctly described this system in Massachusetts: "Traditionally the men who have gotten into Massachusetts politics are men who have been with the Knights of Columbus or Chamber of Commerce. And they get attached to some guy who is either in office or running, and they work for them. And then that guy moves on, and then someone says, 'Hey, Bill, why don't you run?' And he is out four nights a week—K of C one night, Chamber another night, etc., etc. He gets elected and he is essentially a man who likes the company of other men. So essentially he becomes a member of a men's club, which is the legislature or the city council. . . . I don't think there is an overt 'no women' policy, but the women who have run in Massachusetts have been strong issue women. They've had to be, because the only existing forms of sociopolitical organizations available are closed to them."

Women's chances in the party system depend, to a large extent, on the enlightenment of the leaders themselves, some of whom have consciously, with varying degrees of vigor, opened their organizations to women. Among the most outstanding in this regard has been Kevin White, who has appointed Massachusetts women to high political and policy roles in his organization. (A talented young woman named Joie Prevost acts as personnel director, overseeing all job patronage; an older woman, Barbara Cameron, a former law partner of the mayor, reviews city contracts.) New York's former Governor, Nelson Rockefeller opened up the executive branch of state government to women. And John Bailey, the Democratic state party chairman of Connecticut, has promoted women within the party to high-ranking roles and candidacies. But the evidence is meager of other attempts by individual party leaders to accept women as political leaders. Esther Newberg, executive director of New York State's Democratic Committee, points to the sociological background of New York's organization leaders as the major impediment to women. "New York didn't produce the kind of woman in politics that Connecticut did," she explained. "Connecticut produced [Congresswoman] Ella Grasso, Katherine Quinn [vice-chairwoman of the party] and Gloria Schaffer [Secretary of State]. Part of the reason is the kind of party leader. Bailey went to Harvard; he wasn't a Buckley [Charles Buckley, former Bronx Democratic county leader] immigrant type of leader. The wives of the organization leaders in New York, except for Pat Cunningham's [Bronx Democratic leader] wife, stay home and cook."

Party leaders will always be reluctant to promote women, when they can use them so readily as volunteers. In 1965 the Department of Labor reported that 22 million women served as unpaid volunteers in all kinds of jobs, mostly in the social-welfare field. (In New York 77 percent of all volunteers were women.) The Department of Labor also estimated that volunteers did $14.2 billion worth of work annually.[16] Although political voluntarism has never been calculated, the same patterns prevail—women volunteers keep the system going, earn nothing for their services, and find their influence proportionate to their earnings.

While male volunteers do not get paid for their efforts, there is considerably more evidence to indicate their payment comes eventually, if not in the form of nominations for political office, then in a myriad of other ways. The young lawyer who donates his services to the party, for example, finds business channeled to him in the form of new clients or lucrative legal work from the courthouse, such as refereeships, guardianships or receiverships. The man who runs a copying service may add the party's mailings to his business, the advertising executive may bring the party's advertising work to his firm, etc.[17] All of which shows that political voluntarism also follows the double standard.

Relegated to voluntarism in the party, women with political interests often seek a more serious role for themselves in such groups as the League of Women Voters, where they can at least achieve some status to compensate for their distance from any real power and influence. Many fine women politicians are drained off by the league, which despite its value as an issues lobby has not changed its post-suffrage stance against noninvolvement in electoral politics, thus excluding itself and its members from gaining any real influence in the political world. The league itself has spawned some excellent candidates, but once these women run for office they must sever their formal ties with the league, a handicap not suffered by men who can benefit from their fraternal ties.[18] The league's position became glaringly apparent (some might say ludicrous) in the spring of 1972 at a Seton Hall

University panel discussion featuring Ann Klein, past president of the league and then a gubernatorial candidate in the state's Democratic primary, and Nina McCall, president of the league's New Jersey chapter. Calling the chairperson of the panel aside for a private word, Ann Klein asked if she could publicly ask Ms. McCall to endorse her candidacy personally. Despite years of league ties between them, protocol precluded her from asking the league's president herself.

"I Should Have Said, 'Never Mind, We'll Go'"

Many good women who surmount the party obstacles succeed and go on to distinguished careers in public service. For unlike other professions more elitist in nature, in politics the voter ultimately decides, rendering that profession at least theoretically open to women, should they seize the opportunity. "I've said many times, time and time again, that I'd rather take my chances with the electorate, with whatever prejudices or diverse attitudes . . . than with the legal profession," said Sissy Farenthold, now national chairwoman of the National Women's Political Caucus. "I've been through too many battles to fight that one."

But many women, talented and qualified women, find that at this point in time they cannot circumvent the party organization or compete with its vast resources. A case history in the frustration of a woman who tried to run is provided by Ross Graham, the widely respected and knowledgeable administrative assistant of State Senator Manfred Ohrenstein. She decided to run for office on Manhattan's West Side, an area abundantly stocked with young, liberal, politically ambitious men. After serving as a legislative aide, taking an especially active role in the fight for abortion reform, Ms. Graham decided it was time to branch out on her own political career. "There came a time when I wanted to cast my own vote," she said. "I resented the fact that there were so few women in the legislature, especially during the battles over abortion. I was the one who persuaded Al Blumenthal to sponsor the bill. Even Fred [Ohrenstein] complained that a woman ought to be saying those things. I became aware that I had to move out."

Finally Ms. Graham decided to run for the West Side seat of

Assemblyman Richard Gottfried, a member of an opposing faction of the reform Democrats. In choosing his district, she calculated on the basis of two factors: Who would be the easiest state legislator to beat? And who had served his district, in her estimation, without distinction? Aware that anywhere in Manhattan she would be running against a man, she settled on Gottfried as a likely choice. "I watched Richard for the first year and a half in Albany and it seemed as if he did nothing," she explained, aware that on the West Side she would be called to task for running against a useful legislator.

At the beginning her campaign generated tremendous momentum. A respectable number of district leaders in Gottfried's district encouraged her and promised they would run on the ticket with her; rich Democratic contributors promised to hold fund-raisers for her; and individual members of the Manhattan Women's Political Caucus threw their moral support behind her. "I sent a fund-raising letter to old friends," she said, "to people on an abortion list, a woman's list. I raised fifteen hundred dollars. A hundred dollars was the largest contribution from a woman friend. There were several fifty-dollar contributions. The rest were five-dollar and ten-dollar and some twenty-five-dollar contributions."

Suddenly, without warning, her campaign went into reverse, as it became apparent that top political leaders were using the threat of her candidacy to negotiate with Assemblyman Gottfried. As Gottfried began to cooperate, the leaders in turn quietly began to pressure the district leaders loyal to Ms. Graham (as well as some of her other supporters) to renege on their commitments. As the heat intensified, many dropped away, fearful of losing housing projects, day-care centers, and all the things political leaders use as leverage in the struggle to maintain power. One very good friend, Ross Graham recalled, a state committeewoman from the lower half of the district, had promised to run on the ticket with her; but, threatened by her district leader with some difficulties in a housing project she had been involved in, she decided not to run at all, rather than face this retribution.

With the loss of the district leaders went all their resources—the use of the clubhouses, their telephones, mailing lists and moral support. This alone, estimated Ms. Graham, doubled the cost of her campaign, putting it in the neighborhood of $15,000 at that point, instead of the original $7,500 on which she had figured.

After the departure of the district leaders went the financiers, sealing their pocketbooks and their connections. Especially disappointing were close friends, big-name politicians in the reform Democratic movement whose endorsement would have made a difference, who also reneged on their promises and told candidate Graham they could no longer publicly support her. If she had pressured them, she says, some of her political allies would have endorsed her: "Ted Weiss and Al Blumenthal would have endorsed me eventually, kicking and screaming. They owed it to me." But Mr. Blumenthal, who had long been arrayed against Mr. Gottfried in a series of fratricidal primary campaigns, had finally made his peace with the Gottfried forces, and says he was disinclined to return to open political warfare.

One rich reform Democratic woman who had promised to hold a fund-raising party for her, also withdrew her endorsement, and with it the planned party. "That was a real blow," says Ms. Graham, who added that the women melted away as quickly as the men. "Even Bella Abzug, who is a great feminist, wouldn't support me, because Gottfried had supported her in a primary fight against Bill Ryan." Representative Abzug says Ross Graham never *formally* asked for her support, the semantics of which escape Ross Graham, who claims she did ask Bella for her support.

She then approached women from outside the party, women from the Manhattan Women's Political Caucus, to see if she could tap another source for some badly needed funds. Not getting any significant financial help from the women's group, she concluded, "Women were clearly not prepared to spend as much as they would on a dress or a pair of shoes; and until women realize this, we're not putting our money where our beliefs are." Much later, with this in mind, she also concluded that one of her biggest mistakes was trying to raise money through women; "women don't give money," even in Manhattan, one of the few areas of the country where there are women who earn large salaries.

Realizing she couldn't run a campaign for state assembly on a budget of $1,500 and without a party organization to back her up, Ross Graham eventually withdrew. "I couldn't see where I was going to get the next hunk of money," she recalled in despair. "When things begin to slide, they really slide. I called my two wealthy relatives . . . who think I'm a pinko. They gave me nothing. I felt I had to ask everyone. I didn't want to shake everyone down again. I sent back all the money I'd raised. This isn't often done. Many of my supporters wrote back to me to say they'd support me if I ran again." In hindsight Ross Graham believes it was a mistake to back down, since Gottfried won by only 2,500 votes. "No one's to blame but me," she said. "I should have said, 'Never mind, we'll go.'"

Chapter III

Biology Was Destiny: Overcoming Role Obstacles to Political Success

> *Have your babies in August.*
> —M. CAREY THOMAS

"Yes, I have a uterus and a brain, and they both work," Representative Patricia Schroeder, a Colorado Democrat and mother of two small children, told an elderly Congressman who had expressed astonishment at her dual roles. When Ms. Schroeder arrived on Capitol Hill, in 1973, she was the only one of the sixteen Congresswomen with small children—the rest were unmarried, married but childless or with grown children. Since then Representative Yvonne Brathwaite Burke, a freshman California Democrat, has had a baby girl; she was the first Congresswoman in history to become pregnant during her term of office.

Ms. Schroeder, whose dual roles evoked criticism from the start of her campaign, tackled the problem directly. Instead of being apologetic about how much she loved her children, she would begin her speeches by announcing, "Hi there, I'm that radical you've all heard about, who doesn't shave under her armpits and leaps over barricades screaming obscenities. I keep both children in the freezer, and my husband is short, has feathers, and goes 'cluck, cluck.'" The tactic worked in reducing questions about her domestic life, although one woman came up after a meeting to ask her what was wrong with short people anyway and to inform her that she'd lost both her vote and her husband's.

Still, at least one "household question" was raised wherever she appeared. "I'm not saying it was a plant," she said, "but the same person would be in the audience at all functions asking the same question. So I finally got tough and said, 'You'll notice that my husband isn't here, because he and I feel very strongly about contact with the children, and so we rotate, so that when I'm out, he stays home in the evenings, so that one of us can put the children to bed.'" Then she would smile at her male opponent, sitting across the stage next to his wife, subtly indicating that both of them were out campaigning while their children went unattended.

Since Pat Schroeder's life-style in politics differed so widely from the norm, many psychologists and journalists asked to interview her children to see what peculiarities they would exhibit. She finally relented and allowed one reporter to talk to them, although she warned her they were only six and two-and-a-half and probably wouldn't have much to say. The reporter came, interviewed the children, but couldn't write a story. To her surprise they were no different from other children.

"She came over and interviewed them for over an hour, and it was really hysterical because she'd say things like, 'Well, don't you find this life kind of different?' And they'd say, 'What do you mean?' They'd see all these people come and go, and they'd say, 'That's my friend Dan, and that's my friend. . . .' And she finally left saying, 'They don't notice anything's different.' And why should they? They're used to a very exciting life and they're very much involved." Ms. Schroeder felt that since she ran her campaigns from her home, with her husband as her campaign manager, her children really benefited from an extended family, with exposure to many people and many new situations.

Greeting the public as the politician in her family forced Pat Schroeder into repeated encounters with the double standard. "My husband ran for the State House two years ago, and they would tell me how nice it was to see a young wife out supporting her husband," she said. "I come back as a candidate and knock on the door, and they told me to go home and be with my kids. What an inconsistency. Both ways, I'm out of the house."

The question "Why isn't your husband the candidate?" dogged

her footsteps and strained her patience. Even after she won her Congressional seat and arrived in Washington, the same question cropped up, with a different cast of characters. "I think there have been only two or three Congressmen in all of Washington who, when they met my husband, had not immediately said to him, 'Why the hell didn't you run?'—translation being, 'Where is your ego? What's wrong? How did you let her?'" she told the Women's Political Caucus at their first convention in Houston. "They absolutely can't understand that we could have a marriage that can survive that way." She later added that her colleagues were "very shocked to meet him [her husband] in that he appeared to be quite masculine, able to take care of himself. I don't know what they expected," she said reflectively.

The public experienced a kind of culture shock in coping with the roles Pat Schroeder presented to them. Campaigning for her husband was acceptable: She remained within the cultural norms functioning without responsibility in an essentially supportive role. If the children got sick, she could run home and remain there without taking time away from the affairs of state. As a candidate, on the other hand, she communicated the full meaning of her new role, acknowledging that she would be out of the house for long periods of time and that her family would be adapting to an erratic life-style—including a trip from Washington to Denver every other weekend. She asked the voters not only for their votes, but indirectly for their acceptance of a way of life still alien to most middle-class Americans.

"I'm in this because of the next generation," she would tell potential constituents, "and the planet they're going to inherit. The water's full of bubbles, they can't breathe the air, and the educational system is lousy. We must realize there's more to a person's life than how many times they're home and have fresh-baked cookies."

Although her example may encourage other women, Pat Schroeder remains an exception; most women in politics rose to power unfettered by family life. Of the women in our book sample—and this included women in a wide range of political roles from the clubhouse to the White House[1]—only 0.8 percent had young children (under ten); 38 percent were unmarried; 29

percent had no children; and 40 percent had older children. Smaller samples selected at random invariably produce similar results. Of the fifteen women administrative assistants in the New York, New Jersey and Connecticut Congressional delegations, the following statistics emerge: Eleven are unmarried; of those who are married, only two have children; and of those who are unmarried, one is a widow, and one is divorced (both have children).

The dearth of young women with children in politics not only narrows the talent base, but guarantees shortened careers in which the women are unable to amass requisite political power. For if women wait until their children are grown before seriously entering politics, their careers will be limited to lower-level offices. Representative Ella Grasso, Connecticut Democrat, knows she will never acquire any real power in the House, where the decades are tolled before a member enters the inner circle. "I can be a gadfly here," Ms. Grasso said. "But you don't make a long-term career out of Congress at the age of fifty." Unhappy with the slow mobility of the House of Representatives, Ella Grasso soon set her sights on the State House and filed for the Governor's race.

Endowed with great resilience and wit, Ella Grasso and Pat Schroeder have somehow overcome the cultural pressures and emotional stresses affecting other women seeking to enter the political arena. Fred Greenstein, a political scientist known for his studies on political socialization, notes that politics is regarded as a male preserve, "more resonant with the natural enthusiasms of boys. Women who find it especially threatening not to be 'feminine,' and who see politics as a male function, will be drawn into the political arena only at the cost of great psychic discomfort."[2] Indeed, men are equally discomfited by women in power: After reaching a position of power in the male world, Joan of Arc was burned at the stake for being a "witch."

Politics is a stunning example of how cultural imperatives work to maintain the status quo of one of the so-called male professions.[3] Politicians do not require brute strength or the ability to sustain physical onslaughts—although women have plenty of both—and, indeed, there is no justification for its phallocentric bias. In politics there is no heavy lifting, although, as

Bella Abzug has pointed out, women during pregnancy carry excess poundage around for months at a time. It is true that politicians exhibit great stamina and can survive on three to four hours' sleep during campaigns, but women exhibit this kind of stamina—and more—during labor and while giving birth. There is, then, no biological reason why women should be excluded from politics, yet this exclusion persists as one of the principal realities afflicting women in politics.

Cultural Relics: The Origins of Second-Class Citizenship

Ambitious women often find themselves in limbo, constantly fighting society's strictures. Seeking political office means engaging in an active, male-type activity, with all the trappings, language and symbolism common to other preserves also considered male, such as wars and spectator sports. Politicians "run races," "fight battles," "make deals," "wage wars," "win," and "bring home prizes." Women who seek these prizes must ignore the passive roles into which they've been boxed and branch out into more active roles to achieve success. When they cross these role boundaries, they risk being branded aggressive, tough, and ruthless, qualities that bring respect to male politicians but carry the full thrust of social disapproval to women who exhibit them for the same goals. Bella Abzug, to take one example, is frequently criticized for being hard-driving and aggressive, ruffling the public's sensibilities with those very attributes required for upward mobility in New York City politics and, indeed, much admired when they appear in men.

The interpretations of women's roles funneling in from the disparate social sciences all blend into a distinctive pattern—women as "passive," the "other," entering politics at great "psychic risk and peril"—have all served to fossilize women into secondary roles in society. Freud's writings, widely popularized on this subject, had considerable impact in reinforcing the passive-active belief system. Equating women's psychological health with passivity, Freud considered women who aspired to active roles (i.e., male professions) as suffering from "penis envy," their ambition a neurotic state requiring psychiatric help.[4]

Study after study gives rise to the danger that women will begin to believe the stereotypes of themselves and develop what amounts to a ghetto mentality toward developing their own political leaders and participating on a more active level. They start to believe they *can't* lead, that women become too emotional, or that they don't have the talent or the training for politics. In a study for UNESCO a French political scientist, Maurice Duverger, concluded: "Women . . . have the mentality of minors in many fields and particularly in politics, they will accept paternalism on the part of men. The man—husband, fiancé, lover, or myth—is the mediator between them and the political world."[5] Additional voting and public-opinion studies have supported this view: "At all levels of political action, from discussing politics to voting to political letter writing to holding party or public office, women participate less than men. They appear to be less interested in politics, to belong to fewer organizations, to be less informed politically, and to display a lower sense of political involvement and political efficacy. . . . To one degree or another, women have tended to defer to the political judgment of men . . . sex roles have been so defined that politics is primarily the business of men."[6]

Feelings about women's lack of competence in the political arena run so high that even as recently as 1970 Dr. Edgar Berman, Hubert Humphrey's personal physician and a member of the Democratic party's Committee on National Priorities, argued against promoting women into higher policy-making positions in the party on the grounds their physiology hampered their judgment. "Raging hormonal influences," he argued, "subject [women] to curious mental aberrations," which might prove dangerous in the delicate balance of national politics. "Suppose that we had a menopausal woman President who had to make the decision on the Bay of Pigs?" he asked.[7]

Representative Patsy Mink, who was also on the committee, demanded Dr. Berman's ouster, charging him with the "basest sort of prejudice against women." Her demand, coupled with the publicity generated by his ill-advised remarks, forced Dr. Berman to resign from the committee under a cloud of notoriety. Representative Mink's attack, along with the reinforcement she received from members of NOW and other prominent feminist organizations, indicated that women were finally beginning to challenge their own political stereotypes and finding the resultant publicity an extraordinary vehicle for change.

Mounting evidence also shows women dismantling another popular myth: the inherent superiority of male lawmakers. Fighting for abortion reform, ratification of the Equal Rights Amendment, and for other issues in the state legislatures has given women a ringside seat from which to observe political reality—an experience bringing them renewed confidence in their own abilities. As they discern the human failings of political men, they are shaking off the ghetto mentality. Donna Meyer, who has lobbied the Oklahoma state legislature for the ERA, has concluded, "There is a wealth of mediocrity running rampant in the entire legislative body. Those men do not study the issues. They do not find answers. They just turn around and look to each other and say, 'Well, how are you going to vote, Tom?' "

Women across the country lobbying the state legislatures have found the same situation: Legislators are not as uniformly expert as they have portrayed themselves and the field is wide open for women willing to move in. Donna Meyer, recalling the myth and its hold on women, repeated her determination to overcome it: "I told a woman not so long ago—we were both in the Senate gallery—that I was going to be down there one of these days. And she looked at me and said, 'Well, do you have the qualifications?' And I looked at her and said, 'Well, of course I have the qualifications. What do you mean?' And she said, 'I thought you had to be a lawyer.' And I said, 'That's what the lawyers would like us to believe, but that's not true.' "

Spokeswomen for the women's political movement have not only challenged the concept that men are better equipped for public office, they have, indeed, argued the reverse—that women's presence in government would lead to vast improvements in society. Bella Abzug has advocated this point. "Women look at a nation run by a male executive branch, a male Congress, a male Pentagon, and male corporations and banks, and they rightly ask, 'Would we, if we shared equally with men the authority of government . . . condone the spending of more than a trillion dollars in the past twenty-five years for killing and useless missiles when our cities are dying of neglect—when families go homeless and hungry? . . .' I think not."[8] In Aristophanes' play *Lysistrata* the women stopped sleeping with their men until the men stopped waging wars, a drastic measure to be sure, but an early suggestion of the feminine perspective on war.

Women have also been kept away from the political arena to protect them from what men consider the necessary sordidness of political life. Politics is no place for women, they say, revealing their fear that if women become too involved in the political process, its corrupting influences will reach into their homes and touch their personal lives. This attitude is curiously similar to the way mobsters protect their families.[9]

Political Consciousness-Raising: Coping with Biology Through Image, Style and Ideas

It is not entirely coincidental that the feminist movement, dormant since the passage of the Nineteenth Amendment, took root again in the 1960's, a period in which birth-control pills were introduced and used on a widespread basis, and abortion became more readily available than it had been in the past. The use of the pill, along with other perfected birth-control devices, gave women more control over their biological destiny, a feeling of security not enjoyed by their mothers or grandmothers. Women now exercise certain rights traditionally reserved by society for men: the right to enjoy sexual relationships without marriage; the "right to orgasm"; and in general the right to grow, to experiment, and to develop professionally, without facing the restrictions imposed by early marriage.[10] Biology could never have exerted as tight a grip over women's lives were it not for the laws that intruded into an otherwise personal area of life. Asserting their right to control their own anatomical destinies, women's groups in the 1960's took up a new cause, abortion reform, an issue that served to solidify the women's movement into a political force to reckon with. It was largely through the efforts of women's groups[11] that the first liberalized abortion law was passed by the New York State legislature in 1970. The movement for abortion reform brought into public view the rage women felt on realizing that men wielded almost total political control over women's physical destinies. Women began to point out recurring disparities along these lines, such as the the all-male New York State legislative committee's choice of witnesses to testify at the hearings on the state's abortion laws: eleven men and one woman, a nun.

Women are fighting battles on many fronts to win for themselves a greater degree of control over their own bodies. NOW, for example, is leading attempts on a state-by-state basis to reform rape and prostitution laws, which have discriminated against women for so long. On a more frivolous level younger women have also begun asserting their right to wear less restrictive clothing, a by-product of their generation's new political and sexual freedom. Spike-heeled shoes, girdles and brassieres are no longer *de rigueur* for women, who want to be free to move about in comfort, as men do, unimpeded by the confinements of dress and culture. Pregnancy itself has become less of an impediment; many women won the right to continue working throughout gestation.[12] In an earlier era when a more delicate word was needed, pregnancy was known as "confinement"—an accurate description of a custom forcing women to disappear from public view.

Recognizing how solidly she is linked in the public eye with bottles, babies and breeding, the new political woman has developed a set of coping mechanisms designed—consciously or unconsciously—to meet cultural prejudice head on. Many women in politics find they can deal most successfully by asserting themselves repeatedly as independent entities, not defined by husband or family. "Most people in Austin wouldn't know whether I had a husband for sure," said Sarah Weddington, the twenty-six-year-old state legislator who tried the case involving the Texas abortion laws before the U.S. Supreme Court. Ms. Weddington, who does have a husband but wears no wedding ring, stressed that she "tried, as far as my public image was concerned, not to associate myself with my husband. . . . I have very definite feelings about the fact that I was running as a person and not as his wife . . . and if at some future time we were no longer together, I would still be able to serve as well." Like many other women in politics, Sarah Weddington wears neutral, tailored clothing, very little makeup, and a simple hairstyle, with her dark blond hair swept back in a bun; although with her fine features and porcelainlike skin, she suffers little from the lack of feminine artifice. Quiet, genteel, and very soft-spoken despite her strong feminist feelings, she has developed a reputation for political skill, gaining great respect for her ability to harmonize disparate groups, iron out their disagreements, and get them to work in concert.

An equally effective technique for neutralizing the public's response to a woman candidate was developed by politically astute Margaret Heckler, an attractive strawberry blonde, who conducted her first primary campaign wearing a gray flannel suit at every appearance on her schedule. It was a costume, she says, designed to allow her to blend into the gray Massachusetts sky and into the equally gray male political arena, so that the voters would be forced unconsciously to identify her with the issues, and forget about the fact that she was a woman. The strategy worked, for after her victory, her opponent said he had belatedly discovered some devastating material concerning her background, which he would have used against her during the campaign. "You're a mother," he said accusingly. "You have children."

Also representative of this new style is Congresswoman Elizabeth Holtzman. Tall and spare, with long hair and dark-rimmed glasses framing wary, remote eyes, Representative Holtzman has succeeded in drawing a cool, neutral image of herself. She confronts the political world with no husband or children in tow to disturb her colleagues or the voters. Interested only in being effective, Ms. Holtzman soft-pedals feminist issues, preferring instead to portray herself strictly within the confines of what she has delineated as her personal political identity: effective, competent, unemotional, to be judged on her mind and her actions alone.

Representative Julia Hansen of Washington, who is married with one grown son, recalled that throughout her long career in politics she never allowed herself to be photographed—as do many male politicians—in campaign literature or in press releases with her family flanking her; for the same reasons, she said, she would not allow herself to be photographed walking out of a church. Both her religion and her family are private, not to be confused with her public life. In this way she avoids the flak Representative Schroeder has chosen to confront in such a highly visible fashion. Ms. Schroeder has brought her young daughter with her to the floor of the House of Representatives and to demonstrations over cuts in day-care funds. The presence of her daughter added considerably to the drama and urgency of the day-care issue.

Political women have not chosen to negate their sexuality, nor do they care to conform to society's stereotype of the career woman: drab-suited, sensibly shod and unmodishly coiffed. But in their struggle to be taken seriously as candidates they find it easier to avoid the more overt symbols of femininity, which in the past have served to keep them in subservient roles in society as well as in the home. To neutralize their image many women politicians have developed a style designed not to ruffle the public's sensibilities about career women. The style is low key, emphasizing qualities of integrity, levelheadedness and rationality, in hope of countering the popular (e.g., Dr. Berman's) image of women as hysterical and flighty.

Women have adopted political styles deemphasizing their biological roles for the single purpose of increasing their ability to compete with men on a more equal basis. Their public posture does not mean they do not love their children. Nor does it mean they do not possess sexual feelings, nor that deep down they want to be men. They merely want to compete with men on an equal footing, and to do that means making the public more interested in what they offer as public officials than in what they offer as homemakers.

Biology and Equality: Family Life and Political Success

Comedians—both male and female—have had a field day with the women's liberation movement, with variations of jokes about bra burning and role reversal—who does the dishes and who drives the trucks. But political women who find themselves lampooned have often revealed a deep sensitivity to this kind of humor. At one Inner Circle show, for example, New York City's political reporters portrayed Bella Abzug's husband as a tiny man wearing an apron, while an actor who portrayed an ungainly woman pranced about the stage. Ms. Abzug, who was in the audience, dissolved in tears. Sissy Farenthold's husband is called "Mr. Sissy." Too often it is assumed that any man married to a woman active in politics is bound to be emasculated, unhappy and relegated exclusively to scullery-maid roles. One such husband, overcome by the pressure, ruined his wife's Congressional career right before she was to announce that she would seek a third term. Publishing the now-famous "Coya Come Home" letter in the newspapers, the husband of Representative Coya Knutson of Minnesota wrote that as a result of wifely neglect, his "home life has deteriorated to the extent that it is nonexistent." The voters firmly rejected Ms. Knutson at the polls, leaving her the only Democratic incumbent in the country to be unseated by a Republican in 1958.[13]

To its enduring credit, the women's liberation movement has developed the idea of shared child care and household functions in order to free more women to enter the working world. No biological determinants have ordained women better equipped than men for domestic functions; and realizing this, many couples who cannot afford child care and domestic help have structured their marriages along more egalitarian lines, so that neither party is forced to interrupt his or her career development.[14]

The ideas promoting equal partnership in marriage are highly relevant in women's struggle for upward political mobility. Successful political women who have married have followed a similar pattern, choosing husbands who have encouraged them in their political ambitions and, in some cases, have shared domestic functions well before the women's movement popularized the importance of this issue. Whether he does the dishes or not, a political husband needs an extra dose of masculinity and compassion to take in his stride the strains political life puts on his marriage: the teasing, the eighteen-hour days, the traveling, the cold dinners, and the fact that his wife may have to be away from home—at the state capital or in Washington—to fulfill her political roles. Representative Martha Griffiths, for example, returns home every weekend to be with her husband, who practices law in Michigan and runs her campaigns. "I go home every weekend," she said firmly, "and have for nineteen years." She added she felt the main problem with getting women to run for national office is the dislocation that distance puts between their roots and their public responsibilities. "Where is home?" she asked hypothetically. "It puts a tremendous strain on a marriage for a woman to be in politics, unless the husband really is supportive." Political wives also suffer the same pressures and inconveniences, but given the dynamics of the double standard, their sacrifices are rarely called into question.

Other Congresswomen have worked out their family lives in different ways. Benefiting from an extended family situation, Representative Ella Grasso has left her husband and two children back in Connecticut. "My husband [a school principal] was always very helpful," she said. "And we shared many of the tasks I might have had to assume alone. I was very lucky because I had parents who lived right across the street. And I had uncles and aunts all around. My children were living in a familiar neighborhood . . . where their mother had been born. So it was almost like a little enclave, and I had no qualms." A generation older than Pat Schroeder, Ella Grasso wouldn't have considered going to Congress if her children were home and needed her "to comfort them and to cook for them and to clean their house . . . and do all the traditional things that I had done, which I felt I had to do. And when I didn't have to do it anymore, then I was free to come here." But it didn't keep her from political activity on the state level; she served in the state legislature in Hartford when her children were younger and she felt compelled to remain nearer home. She recalled a unique way of combining family life with political activity, showing the protean character of successful political women: "I remember once having to work on a budget message when I was in the state legislature, and Suzanne [her daughter] had this awful case of the measles. I was so scared. So at least while I was sitting up all night, I could work. I measure all these events in my life by what my family was doing at the time."

Some women actively involve their families in their political lives. Elaine Gordon, a bright young legislator from North Miami, Florida, described how her decision to run for public office turned out to be a collective decision, one that involved her three teen-aged children. Ms. Gordon, who is divorced, said, "Before I decided to run, I sat down with them and had a long talk and told them what would happen, that I was going to have to spend a lot of time away from them, that they would miss being with me personally but that there would be a lot to gain in other ways. . . . And all three of them [two boys and a girl] said, 'Absolutely, Mother. No question. Go. We'll help you, we'll work with you.' And they were all thrilled." Her son, she recalled, became so caught up in her feminism, that he came home from junior high school one day, incensed that only boys were allowed to take the creative cookery course. The school's rationale, he told his mother, was that men became chefs, not women. Between the two of them they persuaded the school to change its policy.

Gwen Cherry, one of Elaine Gordon's colleagues in the legislature, also says her family is tremendously supportive and helpful to her, especially her husband, whom she regards as ballast in her hectic political life. "I guess if it wasn't for my family, I wouldn't make it," she mused. "Because I always come home to them. My husband takes it in stride. He explains to me when I get impatient and when I say, 'Why does this have to happen like this?' . . . He has no doubt at all about his masculinity. He has no qualms at all about where he is going." Her children, though, have not adjusted as easily to her political career; they vacillate between support, resentment and humor. She says her son will wake her in the morning with the humorous rebuke, "Get up. Don't you know I pay your salary. See, we pay our taxes and she is laying around here. Where are your constituents? Go out and see your constituents. Do something."

Some husbands are supportive to the extent that they run the household, take over basic household administration and allow their wives to submit full time to the demands of political life. Still others will share domestic tasks, if additional household help is needed, and a rare few change career plans to help their wives advance politically. Pat Schroeder's husband left his job in Colorado to move to Washington when she won her Congressional seat. He found himself another job with a Washington law firm after the family relocated. For a month and a half, when they arrived in Washington, he served without pay as his wife's administrative assistant, to the consternation of some of Representative Schroeder's colleagues. "I saw your husband in your office, and thought you ought to know that you can't employ your spouse," an older Congressman scolded Ms. Schroeder on the floor of the House. "I don't give him any money," she retorted. "I just let him sleep with me."

Representative Margaret Heckler's husband and children have also been supportive. In fact, her husband encouraged her to enter politics initially. Part of the reason she entered politics was that her husband, a busy stockbroker, was occupied with a highly demanding career that kept him away long hours. This left her with the time, and the gap that time created, to devote herself to politics. "He never had regular hours and was never really home," she explained. "And the last thing he needed was a wife who would be a drag and who would say, 'When are you coming home for dinner, dear?' And even though I was practicing law, I was saying it. So he said, 'Isn't there something more you can do?' And one thing led to another. He encouraged me to run. He was my campaign manager and has always been. . . . He truly feels strongly about giving women an opportunity in every field." Representative Heckler added that her husband lived in Boston during the week and commuted to Washington on the weekends. Her children, too, are supportive. "They are the best assets I have," she says, because people are so amazed that they are "normal, happy, loving children. I don't know what they expected, but it's incredible." One of her teen-agers, she chuckled, has offered to supply his musical group to perform on their electric guitars and drums during her next campaign. "Mother," he told her, "people are tired of speeches. You simply announce for reelection and when called upon to address any group, our group will perform. Let us carry on."

Warm, supportive families give women the wherewithal to enter politics, for a secure background cushions some of the burdens they must shoulder during the course of their political careers. Liz Carpenter, a prominent activist in the women's political movement, is fond of pointing out all the stable family lives of women politicians in the hope of counteracting what people think is stereotypical about women in politics. "I always love to tell people that Bella Abzug's been married for twenty-six years and has two children, and Shirley Chisholm's married. They all think we're unhappy. And most of them are pretty fulfilled women or they woundn't have the courage to enter politics."

Ms. Carpenter also pointed out that family lives can often constrict a woman's personal success, because so many women cannot leave their families or move their families to take advantage of better career opportunities. This has kept many women, particularly women who live far from the northeast corridor, from running for national office; the commute seems prohibitive. During her stint as press secretary to Lady Bird Johnson, Ms. Carpenter recalled many efforts on the part of the Johnsons to recruit and name women to top-level jobs: "Johnson was doing his best to try to name women. And I helped. And you would get somebody who you thought was just great, and when you hit somebody who was the right age of, say, forty to fifty-five, which is right to bring into the government, they are still on the nest. And they can't leave it. Well, can you disrupt a husband with a job in General Motors to come down here? It's hard. Julia Montgomery Walsh was one. Mr. Johnson wanted to name her to the SEC [Securities Exchange Commission]. And she was well qualified."

Time is a major obstacle to women; most of them are not married to husbands who would sacrifice for their wives' political careers, and many have children who are still young enough to require constant care. These women don't have the time necessary to participate in the political process, especially at higher levels. How can they get involved in campaigns from ten in the morning until eleven at night? Women still can't say "I can't come home to dinner" with the ease that men can. Many women politicians point out that if they want to be involved in policy-making decisions, they must remain at the clubhouse (or any comparable forum) until ten o'clock when the crisis occurs and everyone is huddled around saying, "What are we going to do about it?" And they must be willing to be there, not with one eye on the clock, but with their full faculties focused on the important decisions to be made.

But time is now becoming more readily available, thanks to an accommodating technology. Jet travel enables a politician to travel across a state in hours, not days as in train travel, and thus attend a rally or conference and still spend some time at home. The long-distance telephone sometimes makes it possible for the politician to avoid making the trip altogether.

Combining political life and family life reaches its most treacherous course when a politician's activities become controversial enough to affect her children. This is especially true on the local level, where the immediacy of issues and actions carry this potential and cause many women untold anguish. "Nothing ever hurts you as badly as to see your family hurt, because of your activity," said Julia Hansen, recalling a painful incident involving her son. "When I was on the City Council, I insisted on a man paying his water bill, which he owed while I was chairman of the water committee. Immediately afterward, his son tried to kill mine, by pushing his head into a brick wall. He was nine years old, and he and two of his friends were looking at the moving-picture billboard, which was right beside our home. They were admiring it and talking about going to see it when this boy came along and said, 'You're never going to another show because I'm going to kill you.' And he pushed his head into the wall. The doctor was out of town, so I had to paste his forehead together as best I could with Band-Aids, and the scar is still there. These are the things that make you hurt." Representative Hansen—whose son was born between sessions of the legislature while she served as a state representative—ran one of her primary campaigns from her hospital bed right after delivering her baby.

Marriages become strained not when women branch out into politics—or similarly demanding careers—but when excessive demands are made on them, preventing them from professional fulfillment. As long as societal pressures force women into perceiving themselves primarily in roles of child care and home maintenance, then biology *will* control destiny and women should prepare to accept continued paternalism. Karen De Crow of Syracuse argues that unless marital attitudes are changed, women will not only have difficulty entering politics, they will have difficulty going to pottery class. Many of her friends, she reported, became radicalized in their late twenties, thirties or forties, when they decided to go back and finish college or get a graduate degree. "When they saw the hostility they were encountering at home, they got kind of scared. Families where all the kids are off at college, with trips to Europe, their own cars, thousand-dollar skis and everything. And the wife wants a couple of hundred dollars for college tuition, and well, all of a sudden everyone asks, 'Well, can the budget stand it?'"

Men as well as women need considerable reorientation in terms of their expectations of women, and once this occurs, there will be no limits to the progress women will make in politics. Public acceptance of the politician as mother is one step forward in this direction and the pace is quickening, thanks to women like Pat Schroeder who have forced the issue out of the woodwork. Political mothers will have a very positive effect not only on the political arena, but on their children as well, despite the fact that their presence in the home will be decreased. "I personally think," speculated Karen De Crow, "that the best thing that could happen to a child . . . particularly a girl child . . . would be to have a mother in the Congress of the United States. Maybe she would have a bad day when the sitter got sick, and Daddy wasn't around and she had to go into the drugstore and sit for two hours. But what that girl has going for her is that she knows she could do anything in the world, and that would be just fine."

Chapter IV

The Equal Rights Amendment: Ending Paternalism Through Politics

You understand that we're playing a power game here, we're not playing a game where you run and cry if somebody knifes you in the back. You just wait in a dark alley with a baseball bat.

—MARTHA McKAY,
North Carolina

The Equal Rights Amendment finally got to the Rules Committee, and I looked at the Rules Committee and I said, "Oh, my God, once again it's a man's decision."

—REPRESENTATIVE
GWEN CHERRY, Florida

Harnessing Clout: How Connecticut Ratified the ERA

The state capitol at Hartford, an imposing Gothic structure capped by a gold dome, rises majestically above the city. It is perched on the bank of a swirling, muddy river, while inside, like most state capitols, it has marble floors, cavernous hallways, and displays of richly polished woods. Upstairs there is a small public cafeteria, resembling a corner luncheonette, where visitors and lobbyists dine at Formica-top tables wedged against each other. The legislators drift off to one side, toward their own special dining room, the Hawaiian Room, restricted until very recently to male legislators and their guests. Women legislators could enter the spacious dining area, decorated with large bamboo poles and red, white and blue streamers, only if accompanied by a man. "I would just stand at the door and look hungry," said former State Representative Ella Grasso, "and someone would always invite me to sit down." But Connecticut's twenty-two women legislators (nineteen in the House and three in the Senate) were not all as sanguine as Ms. Grasso. Some were deeply resentful of what they viewed as a daily reminder of their second-class status.

The Hawaiian Room's males-only policy was permanently relaxed after March 16, 1973, one of the first casualties resulting from the Assembly's ratification of the Equal Rights Amendment —soon to be followed by the Senate. The preceding year the House had defeated the amendment by six votes and the bill had never reached the Senate.

The victory for equal rights in a heavily Roman Catholic state offered by its example a master plan for the twenty-one states that had not yet ratified the proposed Twenty-seventh Amendment. The setting was a cold, sunny day in Hartford, warmed slightly by the first breezes of an early spring struggling to break through the New England chill. Starting early that morning, the friends and foes of ERA descended on the State House, girded for what they knew would be a close fight. Until they packed the galleries for the final debate and vote, they spent the day closeted with legislators, plotting strategies, grouped in hallways, passing out literature, and eager to talk to anyone who would listen.

The ERA supporters, stung by their defeat the previous year, seemed less in evidence than their opponents, and more deliberately low key. Their opponents, mostly young to middle-aged housewives, carried signs and wore large, homemade buttons with the inscription: STOP ERA. Others wore American flags and sought to identify their cause with patriotism. "God created us different," exclaimed Amy Rogers, one of the leaders of the STOP ERA group. "ERA will open up a hornet's nest. We'll have unisex. We'll have open restrooms."

The STOP ERA women declined to say who had alerted them to the vote in Hartford on that fine brisk day, or who had organized their visit. They admitted no group affiliation. "A friend just called me up this morning, as I was drinking my coffee," one woman said, "so I thought I'd come on out." When asked if they were members of the John Birch Society, many waffled, neither admitting nor denying membership, but generally uncomfortable at being asked.

Their secrecy extended to the leader of the group, Sandra Gormley, who declined to be interviewed on the grounds that she was writing a book herself on ERA, and didn't want to share her material. A tall young woman with elaborately coiffed, teased blond hair, Ms. Gormley stood out above the crowd as she moved about the House gallery in a long white wool hostess skirt and a ruffled purple blouse. Throughout the day, two long, thin men with slicked-back hair, trimmed in the ducktail cut of the fifties, remained at her side; whether they were bodyguards or advisers was unclear.

Another opponent, Doris Sherrow, said she was upset by the ERA because, "It is so general, it will uproot too much. The pressures are going against the family structure, and that offends me personally." A three-year-old girl in a bright pink dress tugged at her hem, as she joked that she'd left her one-year-old at home because "she didn't have the stomach for politics." As she warmed to the subject, some of her personal fears emerged. "I don't want ERA because I have a college degree and my husband doesn't," she admitted. "By all rights I should go out to work because I can make more money." Ms. Sherrow, who said her husband was employed as a drapery hanger, saw the male working world as especially unattractive. "I don't want to work sixty hours a week like men do," she said. "Sure there are times I'd want to go out to work, to dress up, not have oatmeal on my dress, but I feel I should be home with my children." She came down to Hartford, she said, because a few friends called her up.

In the press room reporters identified the STOP ERA group as an affiliate of Phyllis Schlafly's national organization, STOP ERA, a group that has been connected with the conservative wings of both the Republican party and the Catholic church. It has also been linked with the John Birch Society, although Ms. Schlafly has denied this affiliation. None of the women in Ms. Gormley's group mentioned Phyllis Schlafly's name, however, and each insisted she was sitting in her kitchen drinking a second cup of coffee when the word came through on the ERA vote. Some pro-ERA lobbyists recognized several STOP ERA participants as "the same Birchers into book burning in Ridgefield [Connecticut]." Others charged that many of these women were going around the hallways asking pro-ERA people if they were Jewish.

A strange bedfellow for the STOP ERA group was the AFL-CIO's Hartford lobbyist, Madeline Matchko, who stood outside the chamber chatting with legislators. "The Communist Party is also against the ERA," she answered, when asked about the curious coalition between the John Birch Society and the AFL-CIO. "The ERA will take away a helluva lot more from women than it will give them," she explained, as she ticked off her reasons for opposing ERA. "Take pensions, for example. Women state employees are allowed to retire earlier [at age fifty] than men [at age fifty-five]. Women also pay less for life insurance. In the area of protective labor laws—the major reason the AFL-CIO opposes the ERA—where we fought for thirty years, everything will be lost. A woman who spends her day at a drill press now has a seat. She has always been provided with a seat. Now she won't be."

A large, tanned jovial woman with twinkling eyes and short white hair, Ms. Matchko dressed proletarian-style in blue pants and a blue and white pinstriped overblouse. Pointing with disdain to the pro-ERA lobbyists, mostly young, white middle-class women, she said, "These women have never worked in a factory. How do they know?" An otherwise cheerful woman with an open, friendly manner, she seemed angered by the fact that the women supporting ERA were not working women. The evidence contradicts her on two counts. At the time, an increasing number of union women nationwide supported ERA, such as Cele Carrigan and Dorothy Haener of the UAW. Second, many of the lobbyists from NOW, the NWPC and the other groups gathered in Hartford to support ERA were working women. The fact that their jobs didn't take them into the factories—as indeed was true of most of the other lobbyists, legislators and political participants in Hartford—should not detract from their overall status in the working world.

The pro-ERA lobbyists, a coalition of women from NOW, the American Association of University Women (AAUW), the League of Women Voters (LWV), and the Connecticut Women's Political

Caucus, provided a dramatic contrast to the STOP ERA women. Hurt by the defeat of the amendment the year before, they acknowledged previous mistakes in approach and remapped their strategy accordingly. Their first rational decision, to lobby in a low key, was immediately apparent; for unlike the STOP ERA group, none of their members wore buttons, passed out pamphlets, or otherwise blitzed legislators with their material. "Critics last year said we were too abrasive," said Lee Novick, one of the group's key strategists, who is president of the Connecticut Women's Political Caucus and a lecturer in political science at the University of New Haven. "This year our approach is more personal."

In keeping with their new approach, pro-ERA forces fashioned an educational strategy, based on supplying legislators with information on ERA in the hope that they could be quietly convinced to vote for the amendment on its merits. "I've chatted with every legislator on the phone, and over half personally," said Judy Pickering from NOW, who organized the ERA coalition. "We're in a position to answer all sides of the question." Like many activists new to the political arena, she realized the usefulness of becoming a data bank for legislators, many of whom lack the information necessary to render and explain their decisions. Indeed, a major role played by skilled lobbyists consists merely of supplying information to undecided legislators.

Ms. Pickering's group had the advantage of working with a new legislature, with one-third of its representatives seated for the first time, and anxious to win new supporters. Paradoxically it was also the new conservative Republican majority that held out hope for ERA's passage, since so many of the Democratic votes were controlled by the AFL-CIO. Madeline Matchko was far less sanguine about her prospects for defeating the amendment than she had been the preceding year. "We had better rapport with the Democrats," she said. "We were better organized last time."

The milling in the hallways finally began to thin out, as the representatives took their seats, while upstairs the supporters and antagonists packed the gallery so densely that many were forced to find seats on the steps. Blue-haired matrons from the Greenwich suburbs were wedged between young dungareed couples with small children on their knees. Groups of women still passed out STOP ERA buttons and throwaways. To counter the patriotism claimed by the STOP ERA group, several young men sported buttons with pictures of the American flag, bearing the motto: "Ratify ERA, it's the American way." "Why should the Birchers have a monopoly on the flag?" one of them said.

The excitement generated in the gallery by those who felt they had a stake in the outcome contrasted with the levity on the floor below, many legislators joking about whether they could disqualify themselves from the vote. Before the debate, in a display of gallantry, they all stood up to applaud the women in the gallery, followed by individual representatives who arose to introduce visiting constituents from their districts, seizing the opportunity to dispense recognition and win some votes. Harold Harlow, a dark, handsome young legislator from Litchfield, evoked laughter when he introduced two women from his district, and neglected to introduce his wife, also sent from central casting, who, throughout the session, sat behind him daintily embroidering a sampler.

Representative Dorothy Osler, a Republican from Greenwich, then stood up and introduced House Resolution 1, the ratification of the ERA. Carefully selected by the pro-ERA coalition to endow the ERA with respectability, Representative Osler stood out as a testament to the middle-class woman: white-haired, slightly plump, conservatively dressed in navy and white, with a sweet smile and gentle demeanor. Recently elected by the town of Greenwich, Ms. Osler had risen from the ranks of the League of Women Voters to enter party politics.

In a slightly nervous but clear voice she began her speech, immediately disassociating herself from what she considered the wilder elements of feminism—a pattern that was to prevail throughout the afternoon, as legislator after legislator prefaced his speech with a reassertion of his sexual identity. "As a woman happily married to the same man for twenty-six years," she began, "who has raised two sons, I am not exactly what you would call a feminist, or a women's libber. I have not changed my life-style, or burned my bra."

Representative Osler continued with her main theme, to heap legitimacy on the Equal Rights Amendment by listing the amendment's supporters, including groups such as the League of Women Voters, the General Federation of Women's Clubs, and the Republican and Democratic National Committees. (The Republican National Committee actually sent out palm cards to the legislators listing the reasons for voting for the ERA.) She also added the names of prominent individuals—Sissy Farenthold, Jill Ruckelshaus and Lenore Romney—who supported the ERA. Lenore Romney sent a telegram to the legislators, which Representative Osler distributed. In listing the groups and influentials supporting ERA Ms. Osler displayed the political heft behind the amendment to her colleagues, hoping to convince them they were in good, solid political company with ERA.

Despite her emotional reaction against women's liberation, Representative Osler found herself recently radicalized, the result of a glaring incident in her own hometown. With anger slipping into her normally mild voice she told the audience what happened when she tried to borrow money from her local bank for an auto loan so that she could buy a car to drive to the state capitol in Hartford. Even though she had just been elected to the state legislature, where she drew a salary of $5,000 a year, the local bank refused her a loan without the cosignature of her husband. This despite her personal friendship with the bank president and the fact that she had banked there for the last twenty-five years.

Whether she regarded it that way or not, Representative Osler had experienced what women in the feminist movement call "the click," the sudden realization, usually the result of a personal experience, that women—all women—are really second-class citizens. Representative Osler had experienced the pain and indignity women universally feel when they attempt to get anything without the protection of their husbands and fathers—whether it is a bank loan or a job or a credit card. In any case the realization is dawning, in all classes and races of women, that the continuation of paternalism urged by the ERA's antagonists means an uncertain future for women who either lack or reject male protectors.

With a sigh of relief Representative Osler finally sat down, and the battle lines were drawn, as one legislator after another got up to make a short speech for or against the amendment. Following

Representative Osler, Representative Joseph Pugliese, a Republican from Plainville, rose to argue strongly against the ERA, citing excerpts from the 1,800 cards he claimed he'd received in opposition to ERA. "Please vote no ERA. My boyfriend likes me the way I am," read one. "Let's keep our women ladies," read another. Charging that a secret ballot would result in a defeat for the bill, Representative Pugliese continued with a few choice arguments of his own: "We have no right to subject women to the animal facts of front-line existence," he intoned, referring to the possibility that ERA would subject women to the draft. "Some men would be able to cop out on their responsibilities and not pay alimony," he added, although he was later contradicted by a woman legislator, an attorney, who reminded him many men already neglect to pay child support or alimony without benefit of an equal rights amendment. He concluded his argument with the affirmation, "It may be male chauvinism to put a pretty receptionist in the office, but this is also good business," and sat down, content that he had justified his position on the grounds of "protecting women against themselves."

Further arguments against ERA were offered, surprisingly, by two women legislators. Representative Ruth Clark, a Republican, opposed the ERA for the following reasons: that ERA was unnecessary, that adequate legislation already existed on discrimination, and that women would do better to launch massive legal suits appealing lower-court decisions on discrimination than to fight for the ERA. Another Republican woman legislator, Marilyn Pearson, declined to support the amendment, preferring instead to have the voters decide the issue through a referendum in 1974.

Still others, like Bernard Avcollie, a Democrat from Naugatuck, rejected the bill because it would mean changing 400 statutes in Connecticut alone, a fearfully difficult prospect to a legislature in session only part time.[1] Representative Avcollie repeated almost verbatim lobbyist Madeline Matchko's argument, that it was "of little consolation to the woman on the drill press when they take her stool away. What will the psychological lift do for her then?"

Those who stood up in support of ERA ran the gamut from the deadly serious to the jocular. Many male legislators seemed compelled, if they were supporting the bill, to assure everyone that they were not sexual deviates. "I have a wife and three daughters," proclaimed Representative Gerald F. Stevens, a Republican, in a typical remark. Others tried to link their masculinity to the bill's defeat. "I vote no for women to be like men, look like men, and act like men," thundered Representative Rosario T. Vella, a Republican from the town of Enfield, to much applause.

Other legislators indicated they felt threatened by the women lobbyists, even though lobbyist Lee Novick admitted they did not yet have the clout to follow through with primary fights against legislators who opposed the ERA. In other states, however, there were indications that members of the Women's Political Caucus were planning races against male legislators who have been particularly antagonistic on women's rights. In fact, before he emerged as such a folk hero in the Watergate hearings, one such target was Senator Sam Ervin, Democrat of North Carolina, who led the fight against the passage of ERA in the Senate. One particularly threatened legislator stood up and expressed his colleague's fears, announcing, "If they have the power to vote us out in two years, let 'em." This showed, if nothing else, that at least the women's groups were able to supply the illusion of a threat power, which is always partly illusory anyway. Another legislator cornered in the corridor between the speeches, admitted he, too, felt the groups supporting ERA had more influence and ultimately more power than the groups opposing the amendment. "Let's face it," he said. "The STOP ERA people are going to go home and forget it; the women's movement people are not."

The tension heightened as the speeches grew shorter and the time neared for a vote. Representative William Ratchford pointed around him as he expressed his convictions: "Look around you if you don't think there's discrimination . . . nineteen women out of one hundred and fifty one Representatives." Two black male legislators then followed in support of the ERA to say that they identified the women's rights movement with their own struggle for equality and a just society.

By late afternoon, after a two-and-a-half-hour debate, a motion was made for a roll-call vote. All eyes turned to the giant electronic tabulating board, off to the side of the House floor, as the votes were speedily tallied. A quick glance across the gallery, packed with predominantly pro-ERA supporters revealed hands clutching each other. Suddenly loud cheers broke forth as the final tally showed an overwhelming victory for the ERA: 99 votes for, 47 against. Women in dashikis hugged women in McMullen flowered blouses, and children danced on the seats. The women whose lobbying efforts were responsible for the amendment's ratification cried openly, released from the tension that had built up over the bill. The STOP ERA followers silently picked up their pocketbooks and their pamphlets and walked out of the gallery, without a word from their leader, Sandra Gormley, who gathered up her long skirt and strode from the chamber.

The House action paved the way for the Senate, which ratified the bill the following week by a vote of 27–9. Like the House, the Senate had also changed its makeup. Nearly half the state senators were new, compared with more than a third in the House. Both houses had changed to Republican leadership as a result of the Republican landslide in November, 1972.

Later that evening, at a celebration dinner at a roadside steak house, the leaders of the ERA effort analyzed their victory. Judy Pickering attributed their success to several factors, most notably the fact that they had been quietly working on passage since the defeat the year before; the STOP ERA people, on the other hand, had been working—at least in Hartford—for only a few days before the vote. Aided by a computer, Judy Pickering had analyzed the legislators in great detail and predicted the vote within ten votes, winning for herself the press-room pool. Most estimates predicted the vote would be very close; hence the sense of drama in the chamber. "Everyone was afraid of our computer," said Ms. Pickering. "Everyone else was saying it would be very close, either way. The legislators were frightened of our computer."

There was ample cause to be afraid. While the STOP ERA people were standing in the hallways indiscriminately handing out literature, Judy Pickering and her colleagues worked with carefully annotated print-out sheets, noting those legislators who supported the bill, those against, those who were undecided, and those who had been contacted personally. Also at their fingertips on the sheets were such pertinent data as every legislator's sex, party affiliation, address, home and business phones, and prior vote on the ERA. This data enabled lobbyists to maximize their time and concentrate their efforts on the undecideds.

Lee Novick, a formidable tactician in her own right and veteran of many political wars, explained that the legislators knew them all as a result of past fights. "They had developed personal relationships with us," she said, "and even though we were often adversaries it meant more to them to know us personally."

Another factor in their success was the new emergence of women in leadership positions in the legislature, some of whom helped the women in their fight to pass the ERA. The most influential, Audrey Beck, had just won her position after organizing the younger and newer members of the House to demand the right to choose their own leadership instead of allowing the old guard to retain the power to choose exclusively from within their own ranks.

Is there much sexual bias in the legislature? "See that group that just walked through the door?" asked Ms. Beck, pointing to a group of men who had just left the lobby of the capitol and passed through the revolving doors. "That's the leadership of the House. I'm now in the leadership, and they haven't asked me to join them."

A woman, of quiet strength and character, Ms. Beck was prevented from joining her friends for their victory dinner; she had just met a young girl from her district who had come down for the ERA vote and, fearful that the girl would hitchhike home in the dark, Ms. Beck drove her home.

Congresswoman Ella Grasso advised the women lobbyists on matters of tactics and strategy, intimating that she'd also used some influence of her own regarding the issue. She convinced ERA's advocates, she said, to lower the pitch of their message, in the hope of reducing some of the hostility they'd built up the year before.

Taking their cue from classic interest-group tactics, the pro-ERA coalition made its greatest impact in developing a capacity to supply information and in learning how to effectively apply their individual powers of persuasion behind the scenes.

Larger and wealthier pressure groups exercise their research functions routinely, funneling data in support of their interests to Congressmen, bureaucrats and public officials.

The ERA victory was advised on a budget of only $400 donated by NOW. Other lobbyists have lost campaigns that cost thousands of dollars. The victory showed women's potential impact on politics, once they pooled their resources and joined the fight.

The Battle Lines

Connecticut's success stands against a background of fifty state-by-state conflicts, some already waged while others prepare for future skirmishes. To date, thirty-three of the necessary thirty-eight states have ratified the bill, including some, such as Vermont and Connecticut, that initially voted against ratification. But it looks as if getting five more states to ratify will prove troublesome, particularly since many of the remaining states are located in the deep South and in the conservative Bible Belt. Some states have reversed their initial decision to ratify, possibly canceling out Connecticut's change of heart.

The counteroffensive to the ERA, as well as the difficulties in garnering support for the amendment in the Southern and rural states, have punctured the initial enthusiasm and hopes for the amendment raised by the overwhelming majorities the bill won in the House and the Senate, and by the encouraging response of the twenty-two states that immediately ratified the amendment. The fight over ERA caps a struggle that began nearly forty years ago, when the amendment was first introduced.[2] It originally read: "Men and women shall have equal rights throughout the United States and every place subject to its jurisdiction." The amendment was rewritten in the Senate Judiciary Committee in 1943, and since that time has been introduced with the following language: "Equality of rights under the law shall not be denied or abridged by the United States or by any state, on account of sex."

On October 11, 1972, the House passed the ERA by a vote of 354–23. Representative Martha Griffiths of Michigan, who led the ERA forces, succeeded in a rarely tried parliamentary maneuver to bring the amendment to the House floor without the approval of the Judiciary Committee, which had refused for decades even to hold hearings on the measure.

The Senate followed suit and on March 22, 1973, passed ERA by a vote of 84–8, against the vigorous objections of that chamber's leading constitutional authority, Senator Sam Ervin. Thirty-two minutes later Hawaii became the first state to ratify the amendment, at 12:10 P.M. Hawaiian Standard Time (5:10 P.M. Eastern Standard Time), and the ratification fight was on.

Representative Martha Griffiths notes that the amendment has until 1979 before it can be counted out by the states, and calmly proclaims, "We're going to win. It will become an amendment to the Constitution. We've got six [now five] more years. We had hoped it would be ratified by May, but we had setbacks in Florida, Ohio and Illinois. I am concerned now, especially with states that came so close. But we're still going to win."[3]

Countering Ms. Griffiths' efforts and her optimism is her opponent, Phyllis Schlafly, who has diagnosed the ERA as a "terminal case." The only question, she continued, "is whether its sponsors will let it die peacefully and with dignity, or whether they will engage in massive bloodletting in a vain attempt to save their offspring."[4] Sharp-tongued, attractive, intelligent, and herself rather liberated, Ms. Schlafly appeared rather suddenly as a leader on the ERA scene—to all observers, self-appointed—to launch what is now regarded as the major counteroffensive. Before her crusade she had achieved national recognition as a political conservative who has held high posts in the Republican party, and for her support of Senator Barry Goldwater for President.[5] After the overwhelming defeat of Senator Goldwater in 1964 Ms. Schlafly vanished, along with others who were strongly identified with the right wing of the Republican party and blamed for its failure at the polls. Fighting the ERA has brought Ms. Schlafly renewed recognition, as well as her own morning show on CBS television. Her STOP ERA group now claims several thousand members, particularly active in Arizona, Florida, Illinois, Louisiana, Missouri, Ohio, Oklahoma and Virginia. Most share Ms. Schlafly's philosophy, best described as a form of nineteenth-century grass-roots populism.

In popularizing the opposition to the ERA, Ms. Schlafly has

made hundreds of speeches and television appearances throughout the country. Thus far, the women's movement has not produced anyone with her force and charisma to present the other side—anyone who can be identified, as Ms. Schlafly has, with the ERA as her primary issue. "If we got an adequate public debate whereby the issues were presented, I think it would be defeated," Ms. Schlafly explained. "Getting that debate will require a lot of work and effort on the part of a lot of people, because the women's libbers are people who like to agitate and the women I deal with are not the kind who normally like to make themselves obnoxious." She continued in a vein that recalled some of that anti-Eastern, Bible Belt, Goldwater campaign rhetoric: "The business and professional women who are for the amendment can get time off to go and lobby, whereas the women who are taking care of their husbands and families can't."[6]

Ms. Schlafly repeatedly disavows any affiliation with the Birch Society. Her group is financed, she claims, by small contributions, none of which exceeds one hundred dollars. Most striking about Ms. Schlafly is the inconsistency by which her life-style clashes with her rhetoric. A topflight career woman, she spends much time flying around the country spreading the gospel of homebodiness.

The ERA has attracted a roster of powerful enemies in addition to the AFL-CIO, which reversed itself and now supports ERA, ranging from conservative groups within the Roman Catholic church, who believe ERA will erode family life, to the more extreme fringes, where the opposition includes the Ku Klux Klan, the Birch Society, and the Communist party, all of whom oppose the ERA.

Arrayed against this curious coalition is an impressive list of individuals and groups, armed with more "legitimacy" than most of the opposition's constituent groups, but lacking their emotional intensity and passion.[7] The League of Women Voters, the General Federation of Women's Clubs, and the Citizens Advisory Council on the Status of Women—an arm of the executive branch of government—are among the groups that have undertaken the bulk of the work under an umbrella coalition called the National Equal Rights Amendment Ratification Council, which includes

Common Cause, the National Education Association, the National Woman's Party, the National Women's Political Caucus, the American Association of University Women, the National Organization for Women, the Democratic National Committee, the United Auto Workers, the Federation of Professional Women, and the National Association of Women Deans, Administrators and Counselors.[8] All told, the coalition consists of twenty-five national organizations, not all of them women's groups, now working on a master plan designed to achieve ratification by 1975. They had received some help from the White House women's bureau: Anne Armstrong, counselor to the President, and her former special assistant for women's programs, Jill Ruckelshaus.

Clearly political in outlook, the council's master plan centers on applying pressure on the legislatures reluctant to ratify ERA. Rather than risk precious time and resources in duplication, its leaders have coordinated basic tasks suited to the specialties of its member groups: "The National Women's Political Caucus will attempt to identify . . . the legislators opposed to the amendment who look defeatable and to find candidates to run against them; NOW plans to analyze the records and the political and economic alliances of every anti-amendment legislator to determine what individuals or groups might bring pressure on these opponents to change their minds . . . ; Common Cause plans to analyze the arguments that had been raised against the amendment and to prepare answers. It also plans to assist in training grass-roots lobbyists for the amendment."[9]

At a meeting in July, 1973, Common Cause undertook a basic coordinating role committing its telephone and research staff to the ERA effort. Pat Keefer of the ERA told the council her group's WATS line (Wide Area Telephone Service—unlimited calls to certain areas) would be at their disposal and that Common Cause was preparing a research packet to aid pro-ERA speakers and activists across the country. The establishment of Common Cause as a data bank filled a crying need expressed by representatives of affiliated groups at the meeting, some of whom reported getting SOS-type requests for more than a thousand pamphlets at a time from their state organizations. To augment the research capability of Common Cause, NOW offered the use of its computer, so that council operatives in other states could analyze their legislatures as Judy Pickering had done so successfully in Connecticut.

Working the partisan political end—in addition to women on the White House staff—is Harriet Cipriani of the Democratic National Committee. A spirited woman with a deep sense of commitment to increasing women's power in politics, Ms. Cipriani has circulated memos on the ERA to Democrats in states that have not yet ratified the amendment. She has also circulated and publicized letters indicating support for the ERA from governors of the following states: Arkansas, Florida, Georgia, Illinois, Maine, Montana, North Dakota, Ohio, Oklahoma and South Carolina, none of which had yet ratified ERA.

Members of the council gleaned their lists and established a nucleus of two or three people to serve as field coordinators in targeted states.[10] Of these states they decided (at their July, 1973, meeting) to focus on those states whose legislatures were scheduled to meet in 1974. They hoped to set up workshops to focus the ERA lobbying effort, and to utilize the centralized functions of the council, namely, its speakers' bureau, media experts, legislative data bank, and personal political connections.

Another workshop was held several months later in St. Louis for members of the NWPC. Run by Anne Wexler, a high-ranking official in the McGovern campaign, the workshop succeeded in developing a systematic three-year program for initiating an all-out ERA effort in those states where the women's caucus was strongest (defined by Anne Wexler as having at least 200 members). "I would like to see the caucus take a systematic approach toward the '74 elections," wrote Anne Wexler in a memo to herself in preparation for the workshop.[11] She then mapped out a game plan involving a detailed analysis of state legislatures, with an eye to replacing mediocre legislators (as well as legislators opposed to ERA) with women supported and helped by the caucus. Should they succeed, Ms. Wexler concluded, they will be doing the country a service by eliminating some of those "Amvet-Jaycee lawyers responsible for the deplorable state of state governments."

As it progresses, the fight for the ratification of the amendment clearly demonstrates women's newfound political clout, shown by the wariness and respect with which they are now treated by politicians. The Texas legislature, for example, surprised the National Women's Political Caucus meeting at Houston with a resolution of greeting, and expressed hopes for the conference's success. In Texas, where the legislature ratified ERA two weeks after its adoption by Congress, the Texas voters passed an amendment to the state constitution that would guarantee equal rights for women. In states less cooperative than Texas, ERA supporters threatened to wage campaigns to defeat recalcitrant legislators. In Vermont, ERA supporters had helped to defeat the legislator who had led the opposition to the amendment in 1972, and succeeded in gaining ratification the following year.

Matching Ms. Schlafly in fervor and determination, ERA supporters in Florida began a drive to get women to sell their blood to raise money, an idea that appeared likely to be copied elsewhere.[12] "You understand that we're playing a power game here; we're not playing a game where you run and cry if somebody knifes you in the back," speculated Martha McKay, whose caucus was unable to win ratification in North Carolina. "You just wait in a dark alley with a baseball bat." In North Carolina the day after the Senate voted against ERA, the House sent the Senators a large bunch of roses for letting them off the hook; they enclosed a note that said, "With thanks from a grateful House." Although ERA cannot come up again in North Carolina until 1975, the caucus there is mobilizing with baseball bats, to help them meet the next legislative challenge.

The Wheat from the Chaff: Why ERA?

If equality kept pace with its rhetoric, America wouldn't need a Twenty-seventh Amendment, guaranteeing that "equality of rights shall not be abridged on account of sex."[13] Bearing an uncomfortable resemblance to race prejudice, sexual bias in American culture runs deep—firmly embodied in its mores, attitudes and laws. Women in the front ranks of the ERA fight experience the full thrust of sex prejudice; they are forced to counter it in its most extreme forms, expressed, for example, by the Arkansas legislator who railed against "all these college-educated women in Little Rock, running around sticking their nose into politics when they ought to be home." In Perry County, he continued, "we keep 'em barefoot and pregnant so they can't run around, and give 'em a cow to milk so they don't have time for these things."

Although laws reflect the customs of a culture, they also have the capability of modifying traditions, particularly when these traditions are undesirable or change too slowly. The civil rights movement effectively used the tactic of changing the laws to combat race prejudice, beginning with the Brown decision in 1954, which slowly turned the tide against segregated schools by making them illegal. A similar approach has been suggested to leaders of the women's movement, emphasizing legal reforms rather than such political measures as a constitutional amendment; but the movement has rejected this as a total approach. When Ann Scott, NOW's vice-president for legislation, was asked why the discriminatory laws were not attacked individually instead of under a blanket amendment, she replied, "If we waited to change the laws, law by law, we would wait something like two hundred years before we would have complete equality under the law."[14] The gradual approach to making inroads into deep-seated, culturally rooted problems is reflected by the Civil Rights Act of 1964, which enabled blacks to make significant strides, while Harlem, Watts, and Hough stood ten years later as grim reminders that America had not yet absorbed blacks as an integral part of its culture. Similar legislation and executive decisions have helped women,[15] but failed to integrate them into American political life. Women have been raised, as Gloria Steinem says, only to token levels in our culture. The Equal Pay Act, affirmative-action programs and the creation of an Equal Employment Opportunity Commission often put women and blacks on a collision course, as both groups competed for the limited tools available to fight discrimination. The Equal Employment Opportunity Commission, for example, soon found itself in the midst of a dispute over whether to commit the bulk of its resources to fighting race prejudice or sex prejudice, a choice that must be mind-boggling to those involved. Some token-conscious politicians and administrators found they could solve such dilemmas by appointing and promoting black women, thereby defusing accusations of sex prejudice and race prejudice in one fell swoop. This fails, however, to solve the problems of white women and black men.

As feminism resurged again in the mid-sixties, women began to realize how pervasive were the patterns of sex prejudice in both the culture and the law. "While there has been some progress toward . . equal rights . . . there is overwhelming evidence that persistent patterns of sex discrimination permeate our social, cultural and economic life," concluded the Senate report on the ERA amendment.[16]

"The legal status of women has changed very little since the adoption of the Nineteenth Amendment . . . there is no denying the fact that women are still . . . subject to discrimination in many phases of everyday life. This is particularly true in the areas of legal rights, education and employment," added Senator Edward Gurney, Florida Republican, in the 1972 Senate debate on ERA. President Nixon also lent his support to the ERA, arguing that the piecemeal case-by-case approach waged in the legislatures and in the courts for the last fifty years had not succeeded in eradicating sex discrimination. "Throughout twenty-one years I have not altered my belief that equal rights for women warrant a constitutional guarantee," he said on March 18, 1972.[17]

Discriminatory laws affect all women regardless of class, race or social status, and make the middle-class woman who can't get her own credit card as incensed as the prostitute who finds herself subject to criminal sanctions while her male customers go free. Both receive unequal treatment under the laws. If the ERA achieves final ratification, it would nullify all those laws that create a distinction on the basis of sex—and there are hundreds in each state—and signal a new era in the history of women's rights. Since many of these laws discriminate in favor of women (divorce and alimony law, to name one example), the passage of ERA offers relief to men who suffer from legal inequities as well as to women.

In the larger categories of statutory and case law most laws that differentiate between men and women affect women more adversely than men, either by imposing harsher penalties on women for the same crime or by preventing women from exercising the same opportunities as men and thereby precluding them from achieving the same measure of economic and social independence men have enjoyed. In the area of criminal law, for example, opponents of the ERA fear the courts will invalidate sodomy or adultery laws that contain sex discriminatory provisions, seduction laws, statutory rape laws, laws prohibiting obscene language in the presence of women, and prostitution laws. In the case of prostitution law, the proponents of ERA argue, the fact that women are penalized more heavily than men displays a "contradictory social stereotype" of women, which considers "women more evil than and depraved than men who engage in the same conduct."[18] The elimination of these laws through an equal rights amendment would help correct the imbalance in a society operating on a sexual double standard.

Many who fear legal chaos from the passage of the ERA envision state legislators working round-the-clock for a long period of time to change all the laws affected. Others argue that the creation of societal upheaval does not justify the introduction of equality between the sexes. Since much of the intelligent opposition is based on misinterpretation and on inaccurate data, an attempt will be made to analyze several areas causing the greatest concern and political flak.

ERA opponents argue that women will lose their privileged status, a price they consider too high for the dubious commodity of equality. What they and the general public fail to realize—unless they've had a brush with the legal system—is that the pedestal is a myth, best debunked by looking at the legal status of women. In the area of domestic-relations law, to take a prime example of legal inequality, women find themselves little more than chattel property, subject to the dictates of paternalism, with virtually no independence of their own. Under the common law the legal rights of a married woman are defined by her relationship to her husband. State laws define a wife's domicile as that of her husband and require her to follow her husband, otherwise she risks facing charges of desertion. In many states women are required to assume their husband's name and may marry without parental consent at eighteen, whereas the legal age for men is twenty-one. In effect the state encourages men to complete their career preparation before marriage, not women. Discriminatory domestic-relations legislation provides that the father is the natural guardian of minor children, and requires married women, not married men, to go through a formal procedure and obtain court approval before they may engage in an independent business.

In the area of alimony and child support, opponents of the Equal Rights Amendment argue that it would weaken men's obligation to support the family, thereby attenuating the family unit. Justifiably fearful is the woman who has been indoctrinated with the belief that men should support women, and who neglects in the fulfillment of her role as homemaker her own occupational development. The percentage of American women in this category is large enough to present a serious problem, especially as no-fault divorce becomes increasingly imminent. If alimony is eliminated, where does this leave the woman, untrained and unprepared, who cannot support herself? In reality no better off than she was before, according to a report issued by the Citizens' Advisory Council on the Status of Women, which dispels these fears as myths, based on misconceptions about how divorce and alimony work.

"The rights to support of women and children are much more limited than is generally known and enforcement is very inadequate," concludes the report. "A married woman living with her husband can in practice get only what he chooses to give her. The legal obligation to support can generally be enforced only through an action for separation or divorce, and the data . . . indicates that in practically all cases the wife's ability to support herself is a factor in determining the amount of alimony; that alimony is granted in only a very small percentage of cases; that fathers, by and large, are contributing less than half the support of the children in divided families; and that alimony and child support are very difficult to collect."[19]

In the famous case of *McGuire* v. *McGuire* [20] the emptiness of the support obligation was dramatized, when the Supreme Court of Nebraska overturned a district court decision requiring a husband to provide his wife with the "necessaries of life." The plaintiff in the case, Mrs. McGuire, testified that her husband, a well-to-do farmer, had not given her any money or provided her with any clothing except for a coat in the last three to four years. Their house had no bathroom, bathing facilities or inside toilet, and no kitchen sink. The furnace had not been in good working order for five or six years, and she was driving a 1929 Ford equipped with a broken heater. In overturning the lower court, which had ordered Mr. McGuire to provide his wife with the necessities of life, the Supreme Court of Nebraska ruled that if husband and wife were still living together, their living standards were not a matter of concern for the courts to decide.

A woman's status as her husband's chattel becomes increasingly apparent when viewed through the eyes of family law, which offers little protection to "intact" marriages. Within the marriage contract the woman clearly suffers in terms of a fair quid pro quo; when she marries, a woman's legal and domestic burdens increase, without concurrent assurances of support into the bargain. Mrs. McGuire was a "dutiful and obedient wife," the court decided, who had "worked in the fields, did outside chores . . . raised . . . 300 chickens, sold poultry and eggs . . ." for fully thirty-four years of her marriage, yet there was no way to compel her husband to provide her with even the barest necessities.

Given the reluctance of the courts to interfere with intact marriages, the concept of guaranteed support emerges as a highly promoted cultural myth, likely to be unaffected by the passage of an equal rights amendment. "Any legal changes required by the Equal Rights Amendment," conclude the authors of an article in the *Yale Law Journal*, "are unlikely to have a direct impact on day-to-day relationships within a marriage, because the law does not currently operate as an enforcer of a particular code of relationships between husband and wife."[21] With no legal sanctions to be taken against a niggardly husband, women are left with social pressure as their only tool of enforcement. A blunted tool today, local mores and pressures can still be effective in small towns or villages, or in tribal cultures or ethnic strongholds; but the high rate of transience and growing absence of community renders them largely ineffective in modern society.

The council's report also revealed astonishing evidence on the ineffectiveness of alimony laws, showing the low percentage of cases in which alimony was actually awarded. In California, where divorce is now relatively easy to obtain, one judge reported that in his county alimony was awarded in less than 2 percent of all cases, and only where highly unusual factors existed. In 98 percent of all cases cited by a nationwide sample of judges, the wife's capacity to earn was taken into account, showing that as a national practice, alimony is not awarded *carte blanche,* but only after all considerations are factored out.[22] Indeed, as early as 1926 a California court upheld the earning capacity of one woman, even though she had phlebitis and could not be on her feet, to justify its decision not to award her alimony. Another California court denied alimony to a woman married thirty-six years who had reared eight children. Alimony was denied on the grounds that her husband, a day laborer who earned from $40 to $57 per week, lacked the "ability to earn more than sufficient for his own support and maintenance . . . and . . . no ability to pay further for the support and maintenance of plaintiff or for her attorney's fees or court costs. . . ."[23]

Equally surprising data relate to child support. This indicates Americans' delusions about divorce. Newspaper headlines regularly report the astronomical divorce settlements of movie stars, jet setters, tycoons and other celebrities, but payments for child support, the report shows, generally are "less than enough to furnish half of the support of the children, . . . and even these small payments are frequently not adhered to." Since most judgments for child support are so small to begin with, the report continues, "the mother is forced to fulfill the role of nurturant and supporter at the same time if she, as is usually the case, keeps the children."

"Since most judgments for child support allow such minimal sums of fifteen dollars a week, twenty-five dollars a week, thirty dollars a week, . . . we know that the mother is giving at least half of or close to half of the support; the mother is actually fulfilling a coextensive duty of support to the child," testified

Adele Weaver, president of the National Association of Women Lawyers, before the House Judiciary Subcommittee studying the ERA.[24]

Just as surprising in the realm of family law is the rate of noncompliance in the collection of support and alimony funds. In the only study the authors could find,[25] the results showed that in a metropolitan county in the state of Wisconsin, only 38 percent of the fathers were in full compliance with support orders within one year after a set of divorce decrees had been adjudicated. After that year the percentage had shrunk considerably, even from that low percentage. By the tenth year "only 13 percent of the fathers were fully complying, while 79 percent were in total noncompliance. Legal sanctions taken against the fathers by welfare authorities appeared to be almost nonexistent. In the first year only 19 percent of the noncomplying fathers was subjected to legal steps; while in the tenth year, action was taken in only 1 percent of the cases."[26]

Most distressing about the widespread acceptance of a husband's responsibility to support his wife and children is the equally widespread ignorance regarding the extent of noncompliance in child support and alimony decrees. The net effect cripples young women who enter marriage in the belief it represents financial security, failing beforehand to prepare themselves for careers outside the home. Should they then become divorced or widowed, they find their capacity to earn is sharply limited (60 percent of that men), while their burdens are multiplied. In addition to erasing the gross inequalities in family law, an Equal Rights Amendment would also open up career opportunities to women that would expand their earning capacity. In essence, their only *real* protection is the knowledge that they have the capacity to keep their families financially secure.

Facing the Brotherhood: Labor's Case Against the ERA

"Dear Sir or Brother," wrote AFL-CIO lobbyist Andrew Biemiller to the heads of all the state AFL-CIO councils.[27] "As you know, the AFL-CIO has opposed passage of the ERA by the Congress and since its passage, has opposed its ratification by the states." The letter continued in this vein, urging the "brothers" to take all appropriate action to prevent their state legislatures from ratifying ERA, and in those states that have already ratified, to exert an effort to rescind their ratification actions.

Eight months later, in the fall of 1973, the AFL-CIO formally changed its position and withdrew its opposition to the ERA. Their action signaled a response to pressures exerted on them by union women, who were just beginning to close ranks on the ERA issue. The Coalition of Labor Union Women (CLUW), meeting the following spring, officially endorsed the ERA. The AFL-CIO's shift made a considerable difference in getting Ohio to ratify ERA. According to Irene Murphy, who coordinated strategy for the ERA task force, AFL-CIO lobbyists in Ohio worked as hard for the amendment as they had worked against it in the past.

Nevertheless, there remains stiff resistance from some elements in the labor movement, from a few state affiliates of the AFL-CIO, and paradoxically from such women's unions (with male leadership) as the ILGWU. In terms of clout labor movement opponents far outweigh Ms. Schlafly's devotees; their advocates are still firmly convinced the ERA will eliminate the body of protective labor laws they worked so hard to enact.

These laws limit the hours that women work, the conditions under which they work, and the kind of jobs women are permitted to take. Many states have laws that prohibit women from being employed in jobs involving the lifting of heavy weights, working long hours, or accepting employment in an atmosphere society might consider unsavory. Although some labor unions have supported the ERA,[28] many have dismissed the amendment as a middle-class phenomenon that ignores the working woman.[29] The general phrasing of the amendment, they argue, would not accomplish more clear-cut specific goals, such as ensuring equal pay for equal work, or promotions free from sex discrimination.

Explaining her initial opposition to ERA, Esther Peterson, former Undersecretary of Labor in the Kennedy administration,[30] analyzed the problem in class terms. "I've been in Congress [as a lobbyist] and have seen all these guys who are against the minimum wage and for the Equal Rights Amendment, and it was so clear to me. The NAM [National Association of Manufacturers] was, of course, for the amendment and I didn't trust any of those people. I didn't trust the Chamber of Commerce; I didn't trust the National Association of Manufacturers, the Retail Federation and all those groups." Those groups, recalled Ms. Peterson, fought against her in 1938, when she and her colleagues in the labor movement were trying to get twenty-five cents an hour enacted as the minimum wage. They also opposed her efforts on behalf of the Equal Pay Act.

To Esther Peterson, who now supports ERA, the amendment originally assumed the shape of a tool wielded by mercantile interests designed to cut wages, not increase them—a move that would affect women more than men. "Equal rights," she accused the manufacturers, "would mean that they did not have to pay a minimum wage." Pointing to the groups that initially supported ERA during her years in the Kennedy administration and as a lobbyist on Capitol Hill, she recounted the evidence proving how deeply the labor movement's interests clashed with those of ERA's proponents, setting up a portrait of the ERA as a class struggle, labor pitted against the upper and middle classes. "They're just not on our side," she explained. "What would make me mad is that they would go out and make these great speeches for the Equal Rights Amendment, then they'd go in and argue against covering domestic workers." They argued against her in the 1950's and 1960's, "against covering hotel, restaurant, laundry workers, every area where women had the bottom of the barrel" within the Equal Pay Act. "I just got turned off on Equal Righters during that period."

Labor leaders share Ms. Peterson's fear that their hard-fought protections will be pulled back instead of being extended to men as well; and quite correctly mistrust big business to safeguard their past victories. "My theory in those days was that we should not have an equal rights amendment where there's a danger of wiping out state legislation, until we have been covered by the Fair Labor Standards Act . . . to get laundry, food processors, beauticians, hotel, and all these big women's occupations covered by the Fair Labor Standards Act," said Ms. Peterson, who added that she received no help on these women's labor issues from women's liberation groups until recent sessions of Congress, when these groups started to help extend the minimum-wage bill to domestic workers. Until then, she added, there was no evidence the women's movement had worked to pull up the lower-class groups of women: "They have not joined hands with the working woman," she concluded.

Echoing her objections, Andrew Biemiller, Director of Legislation for the AFL-CIO, testified before the House Judiciary Subcommittee examining the ERA. "We are not opposed to equal rights for women," emphasized Mr. Biemiller, but to the amendment, which will "destroy more rights than it creates by attempting to create equality through sameness."[31] The ERA, he continued, was essentially negative, containing no positive laws within its framework to combat discrimination against women. In place of the amendment, he suggested, discrimination could be remedied more effectively through specific legislation—such as the Equal Pay Act—and through strengthening existing enforcement agencies, namely the Equal Employment Opportunities Commission [EEOC], by giving it the same cease-and-desist powers granted to the National Labor Relations Board and other regulatory agencies.

What disturbs Biemiller and other labor leaders are the absence of guarantees written into the amendment to ensure that labor protections now applicable to women would be extended to men. Given the strength of labor's opposition, one wonders why the ERA's advocates failed to write these guarantees into the amendment at the outset. Legislatures could just as easily eliminate laws as extend them, argued Biemiller: "Nothing in the amendment prohibits the reduction of present benefits and privileges as a means of complying with the equality standard set out by the amendment."

A rider to this effect, the Hayden rider, was incorporated into the ERA passed by the Senate in 1950 and 1953, guaranteeing that the amendment would not be construed to "impair any rights, benefits or exemptions now or hereafter conferred by law upon persons of the female sex." If such a rider had been attached to the present ERA, perhaps labor might have united behind the bill earlier instead of mounting such heavy opposition.

In Pennsylvania, argued Biemiller, the attorney general abrogated the Pennsylvania Women's Labor Law because of sex-discrimination provisions covering working conditions and hours, rest periods and washroom facilities, rather than extend what they termed preferential treatment to men.

Like Esther Peterson, Andrew Biemiller perceived the ERA alignment in terms of a schism between business and labor, accusing the Citizens' Advisory Council, appointed by President Nixon in 1969, of being "notably unrepresentative of any group except business and professional women." A careful look at the list of women on the Advisory Council bears out Biemiller's accusation. The question arises of why not one woman from the labor movement was included in the twenty women selected for the panel. In addition to the council's chairwoman, Lieutenant Colonel Jacqueline Gutwillig (U.S. Army, retired), the panel includes six women executives and businesswomen; three attorneys; one editor and publisher; assorted interest-group leaders, including representatives from business and professional women's organizations, the U.S. Citizens Committee for Free Cuba, and the National Council of Jewish Women; four teachers and scholars; and Patricia Saiki, a member of the Hawaii state legislature. The work the group has accomplished, however, has been notably outstanding and scholarly in tone, although Biemiller was correct in scoring the President's failure to include labor representation, and the council's omission of labor's objections in its literature.

There is no doubt the AFL-CIO always found itself uncomfortable with its position on the ERA. Its arguments were cogent but difficult to communicate; its lobbyists were all too often faced with defending the untenable position of opposing equality for women. They were equally discomfited in finding themselves in the company of the large body of extremist elements crowding the anti-ERA coalition.

Also chalked up on the debit side is labor's own sad history regarding women. The "Dear Sir or Brother" letter is a typical example of how women have been excluded from leadership positions in the union movement. It was not entirely coincidental that the UAW, which has promoted women into leadership positions, supported the ERA. "Women are not in leadership positions within the unions," acknowledged Ken Meiklejohn, a lobbyist with the AFL-CIO specializing in the ERA. "This is true of staff positions as well."

Those within the labor movement who objected to the AFL-CIO's former opposition to the ERA argued that the loss of protective labor legislation would be no loss to women at all, since many "protective" labor laws have been used to prevent women from taking high-paying jobs, from being promoted, and from being paid on an equal basis with men. Limiting a woman's work hours, for example, limits her ability to work overtime, to earn as much pay as a man, and to advance, since supervisory positions often require longer hours. Not allowing a woman to work at night may prevent her from working when her husband could be home caring for their children, thereby precluding her from contributing to the upward social and economic mobility of her family.

Weight-lifting laws also limit a woman's ability to advance; such regulations should be based on the physical capacity of the individual, and not on sex. Some women in low-paying jobs, such as waitresses, lift more than men in many categories of high-paying jobs. Indeed, in the last few months of pregnancy, women may carry well over twenty pounds of extra weight without relief.

Restricting a woman's occupation also lowers her earning capacity. It is atavistic to prevent women from being hired as bartenders, while they serve as waitresses in bars. They are working under the same conditions but earning a lower salary. "So-called protective legislation," argued Martha Griffiths, "that said that women could not work at a certain job—for instance, she could never be on the desk of a hotel at night—ignored the fact that right beside the male clerk there was a charwoman working, and that down in the entertainment rooms there was a woman singing or playing the piano."

Looking Forward

The future of the ERA remains uncertain, but some recent breakthroughs—most notably the reversal of the AFL-CIO—have given its supporters renewed hope. Catalyzed by the women's movement, many groups have mobilized, cohering into working alliances of considerable potential for meeting the amendment's five-year deadline. (Connecticut's pro-ERA coalition was one of the most outstanding examples of this kind of coalition.)

Whatever the outcome, the amendment's success to date has been a barometer of women's newfound political power. After forty years on the shelf, the amendment finally won decisive victories in the House and the Senate and managed to obtain twenty-two ratifications within one year of passage. The ERA demonstrates that women want to take their full place in society, even at the expense of losing some protective legislation and special privileges. The pro-ERA women clearly feel that the paternalism reflected in the protective legislation is too closely allied with exploitation and second-class citizenship, similar to the patterns of paternalism that "justified" slavery.

Finally the ERA battle is politicizing tens of thousands of women, and involving them directly in party and legislative politics, dispelling their self-consciousness and their inhibitions, their feelings of political inadequacy, and their belief in the innate superiority of male politicians. These women now have a solid, firsthand knowledge of the legislative process, and a healthy, hard-won respect for their own ability to change the course of history.

Chapter V

Getting It All Together: The Women's Movement Coalesces

As a black and as a woman, I am especially concerned about the extension of coverage to domestic workers. My own mother was a domestic, so I speak from personal experience.

—REPRESENTATIVE SHIRLEY
CHISHOLM

Hormones, birth control and wedding rings are not matters of credit.

—BETTY FURNESS, former
NYC Commissioner of
Consumer Affairs

Coalescing I: An End to Slave Labor

The women's movement had suffered the criticism of being too middle-class, too dominated by well-heeled, well-dressed, well-educated women who were too involved with the advancement of business and professional women, and less concerned with the plight of blue-collar and minority women. Although this criticism was leveled mainly by the male-dominated leadership of organized labor—and came to a boil during the battle over the Equal Rights Amendment—many women accepted the criticism and became wary of the women's political revolution.

At last the women's movement came together under the leadership of Shirley Chisholm to deliver a blow to its elitist image, and in the spring of 1973 won its first legislative victory since Congress passed the ERA: enactment of legislation to include domestic workers under the protection of the $2.20 minimum wage law. Welded together by Ms. Chisholm, an alliance of women's groups successfully combined with organized labor to win a fifteen-month campaign, following a defeat on the same issue the year before. Their combined clout produced heady results for working women and for leaders of the women's movement, proud not only that their muscles were flexed, but that their power was used to upgrade the most exploited group of women in America.

"As a black and as a woman, I am especially concerned about the extension of coverage to domestic workers," said Ms. Chisholm in a speech before the House of Representatives. "My own mother was a domestic, so I speak from personal experience."[1] Earning a median income of $1,800 a year, domestic workers in America suffer such rank exploitation one wonders why Congress—and the women's movement—came so late to this issue—and why domestic workers weren't covered originally along with the 47 million Americans benefiting from the protection of the minimum wage? One explanation lies in the fact that although more than one and a half million people (97 percent of them women) fall into the category of domestic worker, no single group with any real influence represents them on Capitol Hill, where their interests might best be served. Another factor is that domestic workers suffer from three of society's most serious prejudices: sexism, racism, and a generally low regard for household technology.

Shirley Chisholm adopted this orphaned constituency, striving to bring new dignity to their lives and to their professions. As their new field marshal, she strode to the well of the House, where in a calm, but high-pitched voice, she told her colleagues, "Mr. Chairman, on the days when this house has debated the welfare bills and poverty bills, this chamber rings with fervent speeches about the work ethic. Yesterday and today it has echoed with warnings about inflation. What I would like to know is, when are the members of this House going to apply the same standards to the working poor as they do to themselves. If we are going to talk about the work ethic, we ought to be talking about fair compensations for work performed. If we are going to talk about inflation caused by wage increases, we ought to look not at the workers at the bottom, but at ourselves and at the other high-priced workers whose 5 percent cost-of-living increases exceed the actual income of the workers who are seeking coverage by the Fair Labor Standards Act today."[2]

Behind the scenes Representative Chisholm's Congressional suite served as the command post for the legislative battle, a check-in point for those who came to Washington to lobby on the bill's behalf. It housed a telephone-calling center, a mimeograph center, organization meetings, and meetings involved with garnering support in key committees and on the floor. "It was an eight-hour-a-day seminar on how to lobby," said Shirley Downs, Ms. Chisholm's key lieutenant, who oversaw the effort. "It looked like a battleground." The initial strategy of the Chisholm forces involved tapping the resources of many diverse groups. They involved as many pressure groups as they could to provide the strike force necessary to overcome the twenty-six-vote defeat suffered the year before. Civil rights coalitions, social action groups, church groups, labor unions, women's groups, consumer groups—indeed, a wide variety of groups coming under the umbrella of "the public interest"—all joined their legions, an exciting new conglomerate in the ongoing history of Congressional alliances.[3] Especially encouraging to Shirley Downs was that this year women's groups had begun to treat such issues as the minimum wage and welfare reform as *women's issues*; in fact, at their first national convention in Houston the previous February, the National Women's Political Caucus had held two workshops on these issues for their members.

The major drive began a few weeks before the vote with personal appeals and follow-ups to politicians whose actions could make a difference. All the Congresswomen were personally called and asked to make speeches on the domestics issue in the event that a separate vote must be held. Congresswomen Abzug, Burke and Jordan all put inserts in the *Congressional Record* as a result of this action. Representative Chisholm also sent a personal letter to Representative Edith Green, who gave a powerful speech before

Congress on behalf of domestic workers. In addition, she personally relayed materials on the domestic issue to Representative Martha Griffiths, who made a powerful appeal to her colleagues. Although both Congresswomen Green and Griffiths are considered more conservative than Representative Chisholm, her aides recognized their value to the debate because of their excellent reputations, powerful committee positions (Green on Appropriations and Griffiths on Ways and Means), and long tenure in Congress, where political longevity and seniority count most in assessing a member's power and status.

A month before the debate was scheduled to come up the Chisholm forces inserted data on domestics into the *Congressional Record* of May 1, 1973. Two weeks later they called a meeting on the minimum wage attended by thirty-eight groups. Shirley Downs identified certain groups and leaders as indispensable to their efforts: (1) Kee Hall, an intern at NOW, who presented testimony before the General Labor Subcommittee of the House Education and Labor Committee. She also inserted data on domestics in NOW's newsletter *Legislative Alert*, and appeared on television on behalf of the bill; (2) Carol Burris of the Women's Lobby, who activated her own organization and got them to pass a resolution subsequently sent out to all their state delegations. She also conducted an extremely effective telephone campaign and oversaw four women working on the minimum wage on Capitol Hill who, among them, went to all 435 Congressional offices; (3) Alice Shabecoff, of the National Consumers League, who coordinated the resolution of support among thirty-two groups ranging from the AAUW and the ADA, to the National Council of Churches and the U.S. Catholic Conference. She too was able to circulate her material among all the Congressional offices; (4) Val Fleischhacker, an aide to Representative Don Fraser, working with Arvonne Fraser (Representative Fraser's wife and president of the Women's Equity Action League), was able to mobilize student and church groups, as well as women's groups.[4] Ms. Fleischhacker was also instrumental in working for the ratification of the Equal Rights Amendment in Congress; and (5) Ellen Sudow, who works both at the Democratic Study Group (an informal group of liberal Congressmen) and at WEAL, where she writes the newsletter.

Enlisting the support of diverse groups brought badly needed resources to a constituency too poor to compete with the well-heeled lobbies entrenched on Capitol Hill. These groups used their own communications networks to flag the issue and give it the widespread dissemination so crucial to successful lobbying efforts. Some groups, such as the Business and Professional Women's Clubs and the Hill Women's Caucus, put out special flyers on the issue. Others—the UAW, the United Church of Christ, the NWPC and NOW—included material on the issue in their regular newsletters.

In the privacy of their own office Ms. Chisholm's aides evaluated the condition of their troops before deciding to expend more of their energies training those unfamiliar with the terrain. "Depending on their level of sophistication about lobbying," recalled Shirley Downs, "we would run a little seminar on lobbying techniques." In many groups, she said, enthusiasm and dedication were the main resources, valuable in themselves, but badly in need of rechanneling to be effective: ". . . With women, minorities, youth and all the have-nots of society, it is important for them to understand the system and how it works, because most of the time they do not have money. All they have is the power of numbers and careful zealous organization."

The leaders involved in the domestics issue credited Representative Chisholm for her role in unifying such diverse groups on behalf of an issue whose time was long overdue. "She was a catalyst," Ken Young, the Capitol Hill lobbyist for the AFL-CIO, said of Ms. Chisholm. The previous year, organized labor had been virtually alone on the issue, having alienated the women's groups by its strong opposition to the Equal Rights Amendment. She punctured the myth that women's groups had a middle-class orientation, with its members more inclined to sympathize with the plight of the bored housewife or the working wife and mother than with the domestics she hired. "She has been the bridge in the women's movement between minority women and low-income white women, on the one hand, and the white middle-class women who have been the leaders of the movement," Ms. Downs said.

Still other leaders applauded Ms. Chisholm's efforts to bring clout to a woman's issue and to the women's movement. "The labor movement and the women's movement had never worked together before," said Kee Hall of NOW. "Last year NOW supported the bill, but didn't work on it. This year, we pushed to work on poverty issues." Carol Burris said that "without her [Representative Chisholm's] personal drive, there just wouldn't have been the kind of support you saw on the floor. Her asking personally for other black women made it hard for other women to turn down." Richard J. Omata, special programs officer of the National Committee on Household Employment, a group funded by the Ford Foundation, said, "She was particularly instrumental in terms of livening up the support of the other women in the House. She more than anyone else was able to make it a women's issue, and she also was instrumental in getting the Black Caucus to support it to the extent that it did. At the very beginning of the debate she set the tone for the debate on household workers. It gave the impression to members of the House that that was one thing they didn't want messed with."

Working within the Congress, Ms. Chisholm concentrated on both black members and women members as two untapped sources of influence. Whip calls were sent to all Black Caucus offices to remind their Congressmen to appear for the vote and to ask them to be prepared to speak to the issue. In the three to four weeks before the vote Shirley Downs met twice with Black Caucus staff aides to outline the issue and to warn of expected opposition. Representative Chisholm's most visible tactics included two letters to Representative John H. Dent, chairman of the House Labor Subcommittee, describing the desperate plight of the domestic workers and explaining why it was regarded as a major women's political issue. One letter was signed by all thirteen members of the Black Caucus, and the other was signed by thirteen of the then fifteen members of the Women's Caucus.

The letter sent by the women members was one of their first collective actions and therefore of great importance to the women's political movement. In contrast to the unity of the black

Representatives, women in Congress lack any consistent solidarity on women's issues. Representative Margaret Heckler, who had valiantly tried to form an ongoing Women's Caucus in Congress, said that she did not sign Representative Chisholm's letter because she had been unable to obtain Ms. Chisholm's help in her efforts to have the Labor Department relax immigration standards to allow for the admittance of domestic workers. Ms. Heckler argued that there was a shortage of domestic workers and offered her support as a tradeoff. She ultimately voted for the bill, however, as did Representative Lindy Boggs, Louisiana Democrat, who had just arrived in Congress to take the seat of her late husband, Hale Boggs, former House Majority Leader. Ms. Boggs was the other woman Representative who had not signed the letter.

"Dear Mr. Chairman," the letter began. "We have heard rumors that your subcommittee is under pressure to drop the extension of minimum-wage coverage to domestic workers. As women legislators, this is of great concern to us. Although we represent a variety of political attitudes and approaches and do not normally vote as a bloc, we are all very disturbed about this measure.

"As you know, women are at the bottom of the economic ladder. According to the HEW Report *Work in America,* December, 1972 (p. 42), the income profile for American workers is as follows:

MEDIAN INCOME, 1969

All Males	$6,429
Minority Males	$3,891
All Females	$2,132
Minority Females	$1,084

"Contrary to popular opinion, women work not for 'pin money' but because they have to. They are either the head of the household or contribute substantially to their family's income.

"For example:

"According to the 1970 Census, 11 percent of all American households are headed by women. Among Black families, 28 percent are headed by women.

"Further, female-headed households are growing. In 1960, 25 percent of all marriages ended in divorce or annulment. By 1970, the figure was up to 35 percent.

"Among married women in 1970, 8 million earned between $4,000 and $7,000. In addition, the proportion of women and female-headed families with incomes under the poverty line is a clear reflection of their economic plight.

"According to the 1970 census, there were still some 25.5 million poor in the nation (e.g., incomes under $3,969). Only 21.5 percent of these families are on welfare. Of these female heads of households who work, over half worked as maids in 1970 and had incomes under the Federal poverty lines.

"The median income for domestics is $1,800. These women are struggling to make ends meet and keep their families together. They are proud hard workers who are doing their darndest to stay off welfare rolls and are getting precious little help for their efforts. Let's provide some help for those who are trying to help themselves. We ask that you do everything in your power to see to it that the extension of minimum wage to domestic workers is not eliminated. It is time that these hard-working women got some help and protection.

"Very truly yours, Shirley Chisholm, Marjorie S. Holt, Leonor K. Sullivan, Yvonne Brathwaite Burke, Patsy T. Mink, Julia Butler Hansen, Edith Green, Martha W. Griffiths, Ella T. Grasso, Bella S. Abzug, Elizabeth Holtzman, Barbara Jordan, Patricia Schroeder, Members of Congress."

The rather startling and depressing statistics in their letter make it all the more remarkable that the women's movement was so tardy in making this cause its own. According to Shirley Downs, Representative Leonor Sullivan was the first woman member to sign the letter, while Marjorie Holt, a newly elected Republican Representative from Maryland, was the second.

Shirley Chisholm also worked quietly behind the scenes to soften the opposition of the White House, a factor in the 1972 defeat. "They were really putting the arm on people," an aide to Ms. Chisholm recalled. "This year, because of Watergate, nothing was happening from 1600 Pennsylvania Avenue." Within the White House, staff women sympathetic to the issue were reported to have cooperated with the Chisholm forces, although the intensity of prior White House opposition forced them to deny their involvement.

The key labor lobbyists were crucial, not only because they published newsletters and performed lobbying, but also because they held firm and told House members that domestics could not be traded out of the bill. Domestics were a nonnegotiable item, insisted lobbyists Ken Young from the AFL-CIO, Jane O'Grady from the Amalgamated Clothing Workers, Evelyn Dubrow from the ILGWU, Arnold Mayer from the Amalgamated Meat Cutters Union, and Richard Warden from the UAW. Labor shared some of the lobbying coordination with Ms. Chisholm's office, along with the Leadership Conference on Civil Rights.

Still other groups, too poor to afford printing bills, performed what are called "telephone-tree" operations. This entails a visit to a friendly legislator's office and using the telephone lines after 5 P.M. (Congresspeople may make free telephone calls from their offices after 5 P.M.) Telephone calls went out to various members' districts, asking constituents to meet with, phone and write their recalcitrant representatives. "It is always nice if we can get to someone who has worked in the member's campaign or has contributed to his campaign, or is active in some way in his hometown," Ms. Chisholm's aide said. "The women lobbyists also reached members through their wives, daughters, grandmothers and aunts."

There remained only the strategy for the floor session, and here Ms. Chisholm sought speeches from two of the most esteemed veteran women members, Edith Green and Martha Griffiths. Both took their cue from Representative Chisholm's rousing curtain raiser.

Ms. Griffiths' approach, appealing to the fiscal conservatism of her colleagues as well as to their humanitarian feelings, was effective: "Mr. Chairman," she began, "I would like to point out to the members that at the present time, wages are really competing with welfare. For anybody in this Congress to vote against a minimum wage for a domestic worker is to say to that woman, 'Be our guest; go on welfare.'. . . That is exactly what they do," she continued. "In a recent survey, . . . I pointed out that a woman today with four children . . . who goes to work at three dollars an hour, is really only earning seventy-five cents. We are not going to change these setups very rapidly. For us to sit here today and to deny a domestic worker even two dollars an hour is the height of the ridiculous."[5]

Ms. Griffiths also underscored the sexist nature of failing to include domestics under the minimum-wage law. "For five years I spent my time in the Committee on Ways and Means every time we had a tax bill, trying to get it set up so that one could deduct the wages he paid to domestics," she told the House. "To fail to deduct those wages is in itself a sexist discrimination. What the gentleman really is saying is what that woman does in a home is of no worth. I should like to differ with him. What she does in that home is a thing that makes life livable. She is entitled to a decent wage and her employer, whether it is the gentleman or his wife, is entitled to deduct that before he pays his taxes. For anyone now at this late time in history, who knows something about how the welfare system works, to come in and say, 'Let them work for nothing; they are not entitled to a minimum wage' is a sort of sex discrimination that is beyond my imagination."[6]

Representative Griffiths underscored these tax inequities privately, commenting that while wages for domestics could not be deducted beyond a certain income level, the loopholes of tax law allowed businessmen routinely to deduct money spent on prostitutes by including these sums in their "entertainment" expenses.

The Black Caucus also came through for Shirley Chisholm, providing some dramatic moments during a colloquy between Charles Rangel, a New York Democrat, and Robert McClory, a Republican from Illinois. Representative McClory began with the argument that increasing the minimum wage would deprive people at lower economic levels of the opportunity to work, since fewer employers would be able to hire them. "I understand," he reported to Congress, "that among black students, the unemployment rate now is about 37 percent. Without this meddlesome and harmful legislation, opportunities for working at lower wages consistent with their talents and abilities or on a part-time basis or during summer vacations or on weekends would be greatly increased. To legislate them out of those jobs is about the most absurd legislation action we can take here today."

At this remark, Representative Rangel rose to his feet and said, "I do not know about that statistical data, but it seems to me that if one is going to believe that the lower the wage the more employment we will get among black youngsters, one might suggest that slavery would take care of full employment among American black youths."

It remained for Edith Green, however, to perform the coup de grace on the attempt to exclude domestics from the minimum wage. Like Martha Griffiths, she too tried a rational approach, designed to convince her fellow legislators that extending the minimum wage to domestic workers would fight real poverty in America in a more meaningful way than the government's antipoverty programs. "Later on, I understand, we are going to have a bill extending the 'war on poverty' legislation," she said. "I am going to vote against extending the 'war on poverty' bureaucracy, because I think it has wasted millions of dollars in this country and that the impact has been minimal. That does not mean that I am satisfied or that I think people ought to live below the poverty level. I just think it is very foolish for us as a nation to spend hundreds of millions of dollars for social planners and hundreds of millions of dollars for the professional poor to go out and try to plan other people's lives for them, and foolish to pour hundreds of millions of dollars into consulting firms for contracts and for entrepreneurs who are siphoning off the money intended for the poor.

"If we would just pay people a fair wage—a decent wage—they could manage their own lives. That is what they need—not social engineers to tell them how to do better in their poverty. I appeal to the members to do something for those people living in poverty which would be the most meaningful thing possible. Listen to these statistics:

"Domestic workers today form a group composed of one and a half million people. This is a group that is 97 percent female. This is a group which is 46 percent white, 52 percent black, and 2 percent other races. This is a group which enjoys a median—I repeat—a median income of less than $2,000 per year for full-time employment. This is a group which includes over 275,000 heads of households, 54 percent of which are living in poverty. This is a group where over 52 percent of the unrelated individuals exist below the poverty level. This is a group where two-thirds have dependent children, including one-fourth with four or more children in the family.

"This is a group whom the present system guarantees that they will continue to live in poverty, to work a lifetime of hard work and to reach the end of life still in poverty."

Ms. Green then repeated Martha Griffiths' argument about the work ethic, about forcing domestics out of the job market and onto welfare, and concluded, "So, my colleagues, I plead with you for one of the most depressed groups in this country, for one of the groups that has absolutely no voice in this Congress unless we as a body will defend them and say that they are also entitled to be under the minimum wage as well as agricultural workers or people who process tobacco or people who work in canneries or any other group."[7]

There followed a rather lyrical statement by House Majority Leader Thomas "Tip" O'Neill, who tried to enlist the sympathies of second- or third-generation Representatives by getting them to identify with today's domestics: "I could not help but think of the poor immigrant mother, whether she was your own mother or whether she was your grandmother, or whether she was Irish or whether she was black or whatever nationality or race she happened to be. For the most part, when she came to this country, she was a domestic. All through the years America owes garlands of flowers to the immigrant mother who came to this nation and worked as a domestic. Yet all through the years, nobody has ever thought to protect her or her equal or the women who took her place along life's line."[8]

Until June 6, 1973. Then, by a vote of 225 to 193, the House included domestics under the minimum-wage law. The Senate, which had approved the legislation in previous years, did so again, but President Nixon vetoed the entire legislation as "inflationary." But the die was cast. It was thenceforth impossible to conceive a minimum-wage bill that would not protect domestic workers, and in March of the following year, when Congress overrode the Presidential veto, domestic workers were covered by the new law. Most important, the struggle marked a new maturity for the women's political movement, and was to become the first in a series of efforts to gain a measure of dignity for their most exploited sisters.

Coalescing II: Credit Where Credit Is Due

"Shortly after my marriage I wrote all the stores where I had charge accounts and requested new credit cards with my new name and address. That's all that had changed—my name and address. Otherwise I maintained the same status—same job, the same salary, and, presumably, the same credit rating. The response of all the stores was swift. One store closed my account immediately. All of them sent me application forms to open a new account—forms that asked for my husband's name, my husband's bank, my husband's employer. There was no longer any interest in me, my job, my bank, or my ability to pay my own bills."[9]

This was typical of the testimony received in hearings on sex discrimination in 1972 by the National Commission on Consumer Finance, which was created by Congress to examine alleged abuses involving consumer credit. The reason the newlywed lost her credit cards, the reason for the credit companies' intense interest in her husband, is that under most state laws husbands are responsible for the routine purchases of their wives. Because husbands generally earn more than their wives, credit companies seek to attach husband's salaries and bank accounts in the event that a wife defaults on her payments. For a working wife, however, the unceremonious deprivation of credit cards in her own name is a bitter pill to swallow.

This deprivation is only one of the many ways in which credit companies routinely discriminate against women, according to the findings of the National Commission on Consumer Finance. The commission found:

- Single women have more trouble obtaining credit than single men.
- Creditors generally require a woman upon marriage to reapply for credit, usually in her husband's name.

- Creditors are often unwilling to extend credit to a woman in her own name.
- Creditors are often unwilling to count the wife's income when a married couple applies for credit.
- Women who are divorced or widowed have trouble reestablishing credit.
- Women who are separated have a particularly difficult time, since the accounts may still be in the husband's name."[10]

As domestic workers are outraged by their low wages, interminable hours and poor working conditions, their more privileged sisters are equally outraged by their inability to obtain credit—the lifeline to economic sustenance. It is a second-class status that affects them almost daily, whether shopping for groceries or children's clothing, a home appliance, a car, or a home.

As women in politics mobilized around the plight of the domestic worker, they also coalesced around the issue of credit discrimination, led by Representative Leonor Sullivan of Missouri. As chairperson of the Subcommittee on Consumer Affairs of the Committee on Banking and Currency, Ms. Sullivan pioneered truth-in-lending legislation, designed to inform borrowers of the exact cost of their loans. Coalescing with Representative Sullivan were the liberal wing of the House Democrats, led by Representative Abzug, NOW, NWPC, and Betty Furness, who achieved fame in Westinghouse commercials, worked in President Johnson's White House as a consumer aide and then became Commissioner of Consumer Affairs for New York City in the Lindsay administration.

Although much of the testimony before the national commission could not be independently verified—because credit institutions generally denied discriminatory practices, insisting they were the work of overzealous subordinates—some independent studies were conducted. One such survey of twenty-three commercial banks was conducted by the St. Paul, Minnesota, Department of Human Rights.

"A man and a woman with virtually identical qualifications applied for a $600 loan to finance a used car without the signature of the other spouse," the survey reported. "Each applicant was a wage earner, and the spouse was in school. Eleven of the banks visited by the woman 'either strictly required the husband's signature or stated it was their preference although they would accept an application and possibly make an exception to the general policy.' When the same banks, plus two additional banks that would make no commitment to the female applicant, were visited by the male interviewer, six said that they would prefer both signatures but would make an exception for him; one insisted on both signatures; and six 'told the male interviewer that he, as a married man, could obtain the loan without his wife's signature.' "[11]

The findings of the commission and its recommendation that the states be urged to review and amend their credit laws to eliminate sex discrimination were forwarded to Ms. Sullivan's subcommittee. Ms. Sullivan quickly found herself pressed for immediate remedial federal legislation, which she favored, although she was inclined to give the banks, credit institutions and the states an opportunity to work out the problem by themselves.

"I found that a thoroughly convincing case was made by the witnesses that discrimination against women was at that time widespread throughout the credit industry," Ms. Sullivan told the House.[12] "Much of it was based on plain, ordinary stupidity by credit-office personnel rigidly applying standards of creditworthiness based on outmoded concepts of women's role in the economy. But it was also established that some of the discriminatory practices were based, whether legitimately or not, on state laws still in effect, or recently repealed or modified, which as the commission later reported, 'hinder the admission of creditworthy women to the credit society.' "

Ms. Sullivan found that as a result of the hearings many major creditors who had been identified as maintaining archaic and indefensible policies in refusing credit to women in their own names, not taking into account a woman's creditworthiness in rejecting her application, immediately began to study and revise their policies. Noting this quick reversal on the part of many banks, finance companies, department stores, credit-card companies and others, the commission recommended immediate action in the state legislatures to analyze any of their laws that led creditors to believe they assumed special risks in extending credit to married or previously married women in their own names.

Ms. Sullivan accepted the commission's view, to the consternation of Ms. Abzug as well as many of the more liberal male legislators from urban areas, led by Representative Edward Koch, Manhattan Democrat. Ms. Sullivan countered that the Truth-in-Lending Act indicated that her committee worked best when it used great care to formulate "workable solutions to real problems." Resisting a stampede, she noted that eighteen months earlier not a single bill had been introduced in either the House or Senate dealing with sex discrimination—apparently Ms. Abzug had been asleep at the switch. "Now there are dozens of such bills, with many cosponsors," she said, "and we are being urged to act on this issue immediately, to the exclusion of anything else."

From the practical standpoint, Ms. Sullivan said, a bill that dealt only with sex discrimination would place the House at a disadvantage in a House-Senate conference, because of the omnibus Senate credit bill. Therefore, the House could bargain away only portions of the sex discrimination bill, whereas the Senate could bargain away portions of an omnibus bill.

Drawing on her considerable legislative skills, Ms. Sullivan recalled that in 1967, after the Senate had passed a very weak Truth-in-Lending bill, 92–0, a bill that was more title than substance, she had been under intense pressure to report out an identical bill immediately. Otherwise, she was warned, Truth-in-Lending would never get through. However, six subcommittee members instead introduced the bill that became the Consumer Credit Protection Act, including a Truth-in-Lending Title that not only went far beyond the Senate-passed bill of 1967, but included many provisions, such as regulation of credit advertising.

In other words, instead of going through the motions of passing a bill with a high-sounding title but no substance, she had worked on that legislation until they had something they could be proud of as a solution to real problems. "So I hope those who feel the solution of the problem of sex discrimination in credit is the paramount issue before us will be willing to see this problem tackled in the context of legislation which also deals with a wide variety of other genuine problems of all consumers in the credit field, including the millions of victims of unconscionable or abusive credit practices described in the report of the National Commission on Consumer Finance," Ms. Sullivan said.

Perhaps the most urgent call for immediate legislation was made by the National Organization for Women, in a well-researched, closely reasoned brief submitted by Sharyn Campbell, coordinator of NOW's National Task Force on Credit. The brief contained a twenty-five-page summary of unsolicited complaints, as well as complaints received in response to a survey conducted by the Women's Legal Defense Fund and the Women's Equity Action League. Here are some samples:

- An unmarried Arizona woman, living with a man, had to use his name in order to get credit. Applications submitted in her own name were denied.
- An Arkansas speech therapist with an unemployed graduate-student husband applied for a credit card with Sears and was told the card could be issued only in his name, even though it would be based on her income and credit history.
- A thirty-eight-year-old California woman with five children, separated for four years, could not get credit cards in her own name, despite stable employment with the Los Angeles Police Department.
- A single woman in Florida asked that her telephone-company account be transferred to her soon-to-be married name. She was told the account would have to be in her husband's name and that he would have to pay a $50 security deposit since he had never had service before.
- In Georgia a married woman who purchased a $30,000 home with a $20,000 down payment from her own money, and had the house registered in her own name, was refused a Sears credit card.
- A divorced woman in Illinois was told that she could not get a Lerner's retail-store credit card because she was divorced. She was not even asked for financial information to prove her self-sufficiency.
- A married woman in Indiana who supported her graduate-student husband and who owned many credit cards in her

own name was refused a retail-store credit card in her own name and told that only joint cards in the husband's name were issued to married women.

- A woman who was serving as mayor of Davenport, Iowa, was denied a BankAmericard because she did not have her husband sign her application. She did not consider his signature necessary.
- A divorced woman in Kansas was denied a Macy's credit card because her ex-husband was behind on his car payments.
- A married woman in Maryland with an income of more than $15,000 was denied a credit card in her own name at Garfinkel's.
- A New Jersey woman with a $15,000-a-year income and a seventeen-year employment history was denied a Texaco credit card in her own name because her husband was retired and pensioned.
- A Texas couple was unable to get a mortgage because the husband's salary ($9,600) was inadequate; the wife's salary ($12,000) was not counted because she was a stewardess and the bank would not consider this a career position. Their first objection—that she was of childbearing age—had been countered by her airline's policy of granting maternity leave with no loss of seniority or salary and by her admitted practice of birth control.
- A Virginia woman who specified on her application to Lord & Taylor that her credit card should be issued in her own name and not her husband's was told that despite her own substantial income it was "law" that the card be in her husband's name.
- A Washington, D.C., couple that jointly earned $22,400 a year made a $12,000 down payment and applied for a $37,000 mortgage on a $49,000 home. They had an additional $40,000 in savings and could have made a larger down payment if necessary but preferred to retain their investment options. The mortgage loan was denied because the wife was in her childbearing years and her income, which was the greater of the two, was discounted.

These are among the hundreds of cases cited by NOW in

testimony before the Subcommittee on Consumer Affairs. What can be done?

In New York City women have organized the First Women's Bank and Trust Company. "The bank is being formed in response to widespread instances of credit and employment discrimination suffered by women at the hands of the banking industry," said Councilwoman Carol Greitzer, a Manhattan Democrat and one of the bank's founders. "We are now establishing a financial institution in the center of the financial world which will pay special attention to the needs of women in banking." The bank, incidentally, includes men among its organizers and on its board.

For most women, however, the remedy can come only from Washington in the form of legislation that limits the range of inquiry on credit applications to matters of credit. "Hormones, birth control and wedding rings are not matters of credit," Betty Furness, former New York City Commissioner of Consumer Affairs, told the House subcommittee.

And Representative Edward I. Koch, a Manhattan Democrat, urged legislation to assure that women "will no longer have to suffer such inequities and indignities as automatically losing their creditworthiness immediately upon divorce, or, even worse, being required to provide evidence of practicing birth control as part of a loan application."

Proponents of immediate federal legislation marshaled an impressive array of statistics to refute the shibboleths they said had been used to deny women credit. One shibboleth was that although some women may work, they don't work for long. The fact is that 43 percent of all women work, making up some 38 percent of the nation's labor force. That equals some 35 million workers. The average work-life expectancy of single women is forty-five years, actually two years longer than the average men. The widowed, divorced or separated woman at age thirty-five can expect to work for another thirty-eight years, just six months less than the work-life expectancy of a man at thirty-five. Even the married woman with children who reenters the labor market at age thirty-five can anticipate another twenty-four years of work, which is just under four years less than a man of thirty-five.

Another shibboleth is that women move from job to job. A U.S. Department of Labor study conducted in 1968 found the difference between the quit rate for men and women factory workers was four per thousand. The factors determining layoff rates are not sex or marital status. They are such factors as seniority and skill.[13]

A Veterans Administration study of mortgage delinquency showed that most defaults occurred during the first five years, especially in the second through fifth year.[14] The study also showed that the average length of a consumer loan was eighteen months.

A lender would have to draw the conclusion from this report that he should not be as concerned with the long-term employment pattern of women as with the short-term credit-worthiness of this particular loan or mortgage applicant. In fact one of the variables used by Herzog and Early was marital status. They concluded that "marital status was not a statistically significant variable in any of the equations."

Some lending institutions testified they had no objection to legislation prohibiting discrimination on the basis of sex, but would object to marital status being included in the ban. But studies indicate that married women are likely to remain in the labor force. Fifty-five percent of all women maintain their jobs when the husband is thirty-five years of age, according to testimony of Josephine McElhone, economist with the Federal Home Loan Bank Board, before the National Commission on Consumer Finance. A survey done by *Bride's Magazine* and reported in *Merchandising Week,* May 15, 1972, found that 94 percent of brides-to-be planned to work after marriage, compared to an 89 percent figure five years earlier.

Divorced or separated women constitute 11 percent of the women's work force. The comparable figure for men is 5 percent. Divorced women who are working at age thirty-five can be expected to work another twenty-nine years. A widow working at age thirty-five can expect to work another twenty-seven years.[15]

These women work from necessity. As of March, 1971, 70 percent of all divorcees, including those who were not family heads, and 50 percent of all separated women were in the labor force. In fact divorced women with preschool children had twice the labor-force participation of married women.[16]

In more than 40 percent of all American families, both husbands and wives are working. Married women with no children are likely to be in the labor force—72 percent of all childless wives between the ages of twenty and twenty-four, and two-thirds of those between the ages of twenty-five and thirty-four.[17] Some 50 percent of all married women with school-age children are in the labor force.[18]

There is little truth, then, in the myth that divorced, widowed and separated women and married women with children are economically unreliable. The Census Bureau has reported that women between the ages of eighteen and twenty-four expect to have only 2.1 births, and that the length of time between the first and subsequent birth has increased from two and one-half to three years since 1965.[19] In 1969, 44 percent of all mothers with children under the age of six were working.[20]

Few issues have infuriated women of all classes more than their inability to obtain credit. Society was reminding women in no uncertain terms of their second-class status. Their dependence on men was incorporated into law and into the routine practices of banks and credit institutions. From anger many of these women progressed to activism, with credit discrimination a major target of their wrath.

"It is time that women exercise their right to take part in all aspects of American life," Bella Abzug told Ms. Sullivan's subcommittee. "There is no rational reason for any sort of obstacle to women in their use of economic power."

Meanwhile the pressures have mounted. Banks and credit institutions are under the gun to reform themselves, and states are on notice to repeal discriminatory legislation. If they cannot, there stands Representative Sullivan, a moderate Democrat, smack in the center of a coalition of angry women of all political persuasions, totally committed to enact federal legislation to end credit discrimination against women, and thereby enable half the nation's population to take its rightful place in the American economy.

CHAPTER VI

Bella, the Cutting Edge: Shock Troops at the Locker-Room Door

Her voice is a national voice that still communicates on the neighborhood level. . . . The things she is against, most decent people are against: killing, war, waste, the mutilation of our national priorities. . . . Bella can infuriate you, cause you to despair, and drive you to make novenas. But it would be a terribly lonely town without her.

—PETE HAMILL

I hope she wins, but just by a little.

—A MANHATTAN POLITICAL SCIENCE PROFESSOR

The Autumn of '72

Autumn lingered in New York City in 1972. The dappled leaves remained on the trees through November, nature's gift to a city girding for winter. It was a long autumn, too, for Bella Abzug, anxious to reach the end of a Congressional campaign as anomalous as the season—as unexpected in content and uncertain in outcome. Ms. Abzug had lost her hard-won Congressional seat to the shredder of redistricting, after serving only one term in the House of Representatives. A natural fighter, she opted for battle, ignoring the ominous portents and the cries of betrayal by male liberals; she embarked on a struggle of great symbolic value for women politicians throughout the country—who watched one of the leading exponents of the women's movement emerge victorious over the efforts of her colleagues to destroy her.

"I did not win election by making deals with politicians, and I don't intend to lose my seat in Congress by becoming the sacrificial victim of male deals," she announced with rage. "This outrageous discrimination is apparently being planned by politicians who don't give a damn about genuine representation of the needs of ordinary citizens, of women, of poor and middle-income communities." Putting the world on notice, she spelled out her intention to fight: "My presence in Congress has symbolized to millions of Americans that a woman who comes out of a popular movement for social change, peace and women's rights can become a force in government. Obviously, there are those who would like to stop me now because I am only the forerunner of more to come. And let me assure you, *more will come.* "[1]

With her district trisected and absorbed into three Congressional Districts, Ms. Abzug faced an unhappy set of options in choosing where to run. One hunk of her district went to Representative John Murphy's new 17th Congressional District in Staten Island, another to Representative Edward Koch's 18th Congressional District, and the third to the 20th Congressional District, represented by William Fitts Ryan. Staten Island was ruled out immediately—its politics were too conservative for her brand of liberalism. In considering the 18th Congressional District, two factors convinced her of the futility of running there: the small number of her original constituents in this district and the judgment of many experts that Representative Koch was unbeatable.

With her bases of support firmly rooted in Greenwich Village and Manhattan's Upper West Side, Representative Abzug settled on the 20th Congressional District, announcing her decision to challenge Congressman William Fitts Ryan in the primary that June. That meant a race against a liberal Congressman with impeccable credentials—indeed, Ryan was the first member of Congress to oppose the Vietnam War publicly—who was also seriously ill with cancer at the time. Although Representative Ryan easily defeated her in the June primary, he died the following September, three months after the primary and two months before the general election.

His widow, Priscilla Ryan, promptly announced her candidacy for her husband's seat. The outcome was eventually decided not at the ballot box, but by the Democratic County Committee, which voted Bella Abzug its nominee by an overwhelming margin. Ms. Ryan then became the Liberal party's nominee and both women embarked on a campaign marked throughout by hostility and rancor. Bitter over Ms. Abzug's campaign, which some said had hastened Ryan's death, Ms. Ryan waged a prim, ladylike campaign that contrasted sharply with Ms. Abzug's. Feelings ran high during the two-month campaign; few remained neutral in a battle uncomfortably like the Civil War in its separatist passions.

The intensity of the campaign increased each day. Its electricity coursed through the large crowd gathered to hear Representative Abzug speak at the Ninety-second Street "Y" five days before the election. Mostly middle-aged and well-heeled women, the audience ranged from Ms. Abzug's most ardent supporters to those who clearly favored her opponent.

Despite the threatening weather outside, the women wore bright new winter wools, a colorful mélange of elegance and chic. One elderly lady stood patiently at the door as the auditorium filled, hoping the ushers would find room for her after those with tickets had been seated. Her eyes lighting up, she explained she came just to see Ms. Abzug. "I've never heard her, except on the TV," she remarked. "I thought it would be interesting."

At eleven fifteen, when an announcement was made that Ms. Abzug, scheduled for eleven, would be detained another ten minutes, groans were heard in the audience, one woman loudly exclaiming, "I've got things to do!" A tall, elegant woman in white slacks with a gold chain belt gathering in her wine-colored sweater stood up and left the room in a huff, soon followed by others complaining of the heat and the noise. The old woman, sighing with relief, was finally seated.

Surrounded by her staff and admirers, Representative Abzug finally appeared and strode quickly to the rostrum. To the surprise of her audience she began her speech talking in flat, monotonous, barely audible tones, the voice of a speaker who has given the same lecture too many times, and one determined not to be strident. As she warmed to the subject, she began to punctuate her speech with partisan jokes, using well-timed pauses that would have done credit to a professional comedian. "Nixon decided women had a role in politics," she said, with a twinkle in her eye, "so he took a few to China: Pat and a few secretaries. Pat to inspect the kitchens." Referring to the President's recent failure to appoint a woman to the Supreme Court, she surmised, "The reason Nixon couldn't find a woman appointee was that he couldn't find one bad enough."

Aware of her audience—comfortable upper-middle-class women glowing with an East Side patina—Representative Abzug remained low key throughout, stressing her effectiveness in Congress and the positive features of the women's liberation movement. Doing her part to "deodorize" popular stereotypes of women's liberationists, she talked about her own family life as the major force behind her interest in social reform. "I have yet to see a bra burned, or a man exorcised," she chided her listeners. Reminding them that 40 percent of the delegates at the Democratic national convention were women, she emphasized her own role in encouraging young people and women to participate. Only in the last fifteen minutes of her speech did she exhibit some of the passion for which she was so well known, exhorting her audience to share some of her commitment. "Do you think we would have had war," she asked, "if women and youth had participated?

"I have sat in Congress and have worked—and screamed, as some of you think—and seen lots and lots of bills killed by a coalition of conservatives and southern Democrats," she continued. "I have watched the President mine the harbors of Haiphong," she intoned, her voice building with anger and bitterness. The color rising in her cheeks, she berated her audience, reminding them that they had an obligation to participate, not just in lectures and question-and-answer periods (indeed, like the one they were attending) but in real political activity. "I always tell the young people," she added, becoming gentle again, "look, while you're waiting for that other thing, that revolution of yours, pick up a piece of political power and do something."

Her efforts paid off. As she left the room, a woman extended her hand and said warmly, "You've changed my vote. I was going to vote for Mrs. Ryan." Others flocked around her and wished her well, until she finally made her escape about twenty minutes later.

In the car going back to her home territory on the West Side, where she faced a full schedule of afternoon campaigning, she slumped over in the seat, the vitality draining as she let fatigue take over for a spell. A heavy chest cough wracked her body, a condition not at all apparent during the morning except for the hoarse, strained quality of her voice.

Pouring out the anger she had felt throughout the campaign, she catalogued the odds against her—all bound together by the threat she presented to male elites, reformers and conservatives alike. Fellow reform Democrat Edward Koch failed to support her, she charged, "because he is afraid of women in politics. He feels threatened."

"They're all threatened," she continued, referring to the Republicans. "That's why they put up women like Jane Pickens Langley,[2] as setups by the Nixon administration to defuse the women's issue." Others threatened by her and by her politics quietly funneled money to her opponent: "Mrs. Ryan is being supported," she charged, "by Nixon union money . . . Ray Corbett from the AFL-CIO. Al Shanker [president of the UFT] gave her $100,000."

The unkindest cut of all came from the press. Why? "Because it's all-male, baby . . . and they feel threatened by me." The press should have reported that Representative Ryan had cancer, she argued; everyone knew. But everyone did not know; Mr. Ryan's physicians publicly denied it. "How would you feel if you picked up the New York *Times* one morning and read that you had cancer?" asked a devil's advocate. No answer. To Ms. Abzug the most flagrant insult was the press treatment of Priscilla Ryan and herself as equals. "I don't consider Mrs. Ryan qualified," she said disdainfully. "I was very friendly with Bill, and I never saw Priscilla around in all the years I've politicked around New York."

Some critics felt that Ms. Abzug's view of the press bordered on paranoia, especially when *Life* magazine weighed in with a cover story—including a magnificent cover photograph of her headed WOMEN IN POLITICS—the weekend before the primary. Many of her male colleagues, jealous of her ability to attract press coverage, regard her as a creature of the media, more interested in showboating than in doing the hard, anonymous behind-the-scenes work.

Back again on the campaign trail, her juices continued to flow. In the West End Bar, near Columbia University, young men and women with books under their arms thronged her table as she lunched, trying to shake her hand and wish her luck. Farther uptown, as she began street campaigning, all signs of exhaustion had disappeared, and she forged ahead with vigor to finish the day's grueling schedule. Although difficult to relate to on a one-to-one basis, she seemed to undergo a metamorphosis as she warmed to the adulation and support heaped on her by the crowds on the street; clearly more at home among the street people than among the women on the East Side. "How are you, baby?" asked a young Puerto Rican boy. "Go home and get some rest," yelled a sanitation foreman stepping out of his car. "You've got it made." "I seen you so much on television. I gotta tell my wife," an old Jewish man told her, with tears in his eyes.

Reciprocating the warmth she communicated to them, people showered admiration on her, particularly those toward whom she had directed her programs: the young, the poor, the old, racial minorities and women.

Marching well ahead of her staff, Representative Abzug rushed into stores, ferreting out people to tell them to be sure to vote Row B. She wasted no time and missed no one. Even as her car was being driven around the corner to take her to another location, she plunged into the Pizza Food Shop seeking more people, as if every vote counted in a contest lacking a predictable margin of victory. Her staff also operated at a frenetic pace, though not half as vigorous as hers, passing out leaflets in Spanish and English, as well as shopping bags bearing her name. Even the driver, an adenoidal-looking college student with bulging eyes and Adam's apple, was pressed into service; however, the campaign pace was evidently too much for him as he verbally assaulted an observer who refused to help him: "Ya gotta participate!" he shrieked. The other volunteers were somewhat calmer; one weathered but pleasant-looking older teacher explained why she had taken the term off to campaign for Representative Abzug: "I had to do it, just because of what the UFT is doing to her."

Genuinely touched by the response she was getting, the cares evaporated from Ms. Abzug's round, high-cheekboned face as a black man finished telling her, "I want you to know I've never voted before in my life, and I'm voting now for the first time because I want to vote for you." Very much an urban populist, Ms. Abzug's dazzling performance vividly demonstrated how she had earned her reputation as an effective street campaigner and why so many attributed her first victory over Representative Farbstein to that talent.

Priscilla Ryan's campaign contrasted almost too perfectly with Ms. Abzug's to ring true. Billed by press wags as "Priscilla *versus* Godzilla," the most marked differences in the campaign emerged in terms of style. (Ideologically they agreed on most issues.) Unlike Ms. Abzug, who generated her own momentum and dragged her staff along with her, Ms. Ryan hung back, shy and tentative in her approach to voters. Preceding her, more than half a dozen volunteers followed a bushy-haired man named Jules Rothstein, who shouted through a bullhorn like a carnival barker at a fair: "Step right up. Priscilla Ryan is here and wants to meet you." People were then led over to Ms. Ryan, her eyes glazed with fatigue, as she reminded voters to vote for her on the Liberal line. "The election is going to be a close one," she told prospective voters as she proceeded slowly up 181st Street.

Compared to Bella Abzug, who came to life on the streets, Ms. Ryan showed genuine discomfort in the role of street campaigner. Tall and delicate-looking, with darting blue eyes and white porcelain skin, she spoke in soft, professorial tones, more suited to the seminar or drawing room than to the harsh pace of life in Washington Heights. In contrast to Representative Abzug, who told voters authoritatively, "Vote for me on Line B," Ms. Ryan requested votes: "You've got to remember I'm running on Line D." While some of Ms. Abzug's staff acted sullen and downtrodden, pressed by their candidate beyond their capacities, Ms. Ryan and her staff enjoyed warm personal relationships, marked by mutual consideration and affection, apparent even during the impersonalities of street campaigning. Concerned for their welfare, Ms. Ryan kept asking her workers whether they were warm enough, whether they were getting too tired; at one point she gave her own coat to a staff member who seemed chilled by the early gusts of night air. Her kindness was contagious; her staff showed the same concern for her, with a protectiveness sometimes bordering on the officious.

To a marked extent street campaigning in the Ryan camp assumed the character of an extended wake. Running for her husband's seat scarcely two months after his death, Ms. Ryan displayed great courage and emotional stamina, particularly as she withstood the well-meaning but constant reminders of her loss. Many of those who stepped up to shake her hand had tears in their eyes; many told her how wonderful they thought her husband was. "I liked your husband," a Puerto Rican man told her. "I'm sorry for the death. He was a big man." "I'm sure your husband's ability will rub off on you," an old Jewish lady assured her. Clear-eyed, Ms. Ryan gracefully accepted their condolences, everyone around her wondering how many well-wishers would cast their votes for her the following Tuesday.

This was a neighborhood close to the immediacies of death, where the people, themselves the victims of much struggle and grief, responded with compassion to tragedy. Nestled in the shadow of the George Washington Bridge, their community, once proud, now fought the onset of poverty and decay. A disproportionate number of old people crowded the streets, going from store to store searching out the best bargains at butcher shops featuring fresh chitterlings at fifty-five cents a pound and pork stomachs at thirty-nine cents. A striking example of symmetrical if reluctant integration, signs advertising spareribs and chicken fat shared the same glass pane in a grocery-store window, while Greek, Italian and Spanish could be heard on the streets.

The most serious problem affecting Ms. Ryan's campaign was that it seemed hydra-headed; little leadership existed beyond what staffers themselves assumed. Staff aides leading Ms. Ryan from place to place were thrown into a state of confusion when asked their function or the title of their staff positions. Were they press people? Public relations aides? Repeated calls to Ms. Ryan's headquarters failed to produce either a public relations director or a campaign director, although such personnel were known to exist. On the campaign trail the leadership that had surfaced showed no evidence of a plan or much direction—again in marked contrast to Ms. Abzug, whose presence dominated everything. At one point a staff aide materialized from nowhere to pull the candidate away from a crowd, announcing to all that he was going to see to it that she got some rest and some dinner. He, too, was unable to answer questions about his role.

The staff's strongest suit was their loyalty to the late Congressman Ryan, although personal loyalty and affection for his widow was also very much in evidence. Several staff members worked for Ms. Ryan out of hatred for Bella Abzug, a recurring negative factor throughout the campaign. One heavy-set photographer named Alfred Perlen boasted that he worked for Ms. Ryan mainly because he "hated Bella so much." Needing little encouragement to express his feelings, he recalled, "I worked for Bella in the Barry Farber race. She's a nonperson. She uses words I wouldn't repeat to you. . . . If I gave her a color scheme she didn't like, like orange on lilac, she'd say, 'Fuck you.' "

Hatred resounded among Ryan loyalists and among a substantial segment of the community as well. Many vocalized their revulsion toward Ms. Abzug's decision to challenge Representative Ryan; their emotion rose with each public appearance by Mr. Ryan, his face swollen and disfigured, and his voice barely audible. A chord of sympathy among the voters translated into a rousting at the polls in the first primary.

There was no doubt that despite her callousness in challenging Mr. Ryan, Ms. Abzug suffered much heavier public censure than a man would have experienced under similar conditions. The public reaction could be described only as an intense culture shock, as people tried unsuccessfully to cope with a woman cast in the role of attacker; they were accustomed to more traditional images of the woman as nurturant, Florence Nightingale healing the sick and the wounded.

Paradoxically, random sampling revealed men more shocked

than women by Ms. Abzug's challenge, although not so shocked as they would have been if a man had challenged Representative Ryan. "What if Ed Koch or Ted Weiss had run against Representative Ryan? Would you feel the same way?" brought looks of incredulity, often followed by some soul-searching and the reluctant admission that no, they would not have been as averse to a male candidacy against Mr. Ryan. The first defeat, however, served as a sufficient cathartic. Tough but forgiving New Yorkers felt they had adequately chastised Ms. Abzug; they were unlikely to repeat the experience, particularly when the opponent was different.

One month after the election, as she packed up her Riverside Drive apartment, Ms. Ryan talked about the election, clearly indicating that her entry into the race also contained a "Stop Bella" element. At first, she recalled, many constituents telephoned and wrote to her, urging her to run. "They wanted an alternative [to Ms. Abzug], very much so."

Other candidates were considered and approached, but they "just wouldn't do it," she continued, referring to such well-known West Side reform Democrats as Jerry Kretchmer, who refused to run against Bella Abzug. The determining factors behind her final decision to run, she said, were the offers of support from two of the city's key influentials: Albert Shanker, president of the UFT, and Alex Rose, the leader of the Liberal party, both of whom considered Bella too far left for comfort.

In a paid advertisement in the New York *Times* Mr. Shanker assailed Representative Abzug as a fringe candidate: "There is a fundamental difference between these candidates [Ms. Abzug and Ms. Ryan], and in that difference lies the answer to whether the Democratic Party can once again put together a majority coalition, including labor unions, minority groups, the ethnics, liberals, and urban dwellers—a majority which rejects, with equal vigor, the Haynsworths and Carswells on the right and ethnic-quota proposals, community control and antilabor bias on the extreme left."[3]

Ms. Abzug had earned Mr. Shanker's eternal enmity when she crossed the picket line during the 1968 teachers' strike. "I was appearing at Music and Art High School," she later recalled, "and most of the parents were very friendly with the teachers. We were talking and saying this thing has got to stop. What would be solved by the strike? We've got a million kids in the streets. We should go in and find the ways in which we can work together. I was a parent who agreed with other parents it was time to end the strike so the teachers went in the school. We agreed for the district superintendent to open the school."

She believes Mr. Shanker's opposition to her ran deeper, however. "Basically I think Al Shanker is a hawk and was always a hawk, and I was a leader of the peace movement and always took a strong position on that, and I think his objection to me is more based on that than anything else."

An ugly whisper campaign smacking of McCarthyism also circulated linking Representative Abzug to unspecified leftist elements in the distant past. The origin of the rumor was untraceable—although some accused a splinter group within the Women's Political Caucus[4]—but they dogged Ms. Abzug's campaign nonetheless, while no one of any credibility stood up either to claim or to denounce them.

Did Ms. Ryan personally blame Ms. Abzug for hastening her husband's death? She says not. Reporters tried to extract such statements from her, but she denies ever commenting on the subject of Ms. Abzug's responsibility for aggravating his illness. What angered her most was Ms. Abzug's claim to fame as an ideologue, which was false, she charged, in the light of her tendency to operate as pragmatically and as ruthlessly as those who made no claim to moral superiority. "She took on Bill purely because she thought she could win," said Ms. Ryan. "She decided on pragmatic decisions, not on issues. . . . I was furious with her for running against him on the hawk-dove thing. . . . She had a chance to run against Murphy [Representative John Murphy of Staten Island] on the Vietnam issue. She was afraid she would be beaten, which she probably would have. . . . Sure there were people who supported me who were hawks. But that didn't mean that I was. Which is what she [Ms. Abzug] tried—guilt by association."

Ms. Ryan's observation was well taken. Representative Abzug, who portrayed herself as an ideologue, showed in the two Ryan campaigns that she was as tough and practical as any machine politician. Take the issue of seniority, for example. When Mr. Ryan, a veteran of ten years in the House, pointed out that, all things being equal, he enjoyed far more seniority than Ms. Abzug, a freshman, she replied, "I have found that seniority is not helpful, and to use that is a way of saying that there can be no change. Every time you run against somebody who has many more years, if that's the consideration, you don't run and you have no change. If you want to have a seniority system, then you have a static system with no change. There can be no new people. . . . We have to be able to bring people in who are new because they're good, because they're able, because they're good legislators, because they can create legislation and help to fight it through and create the pressures in the country to get this legislation through. So that I don't believe that should be an issue. As a matter of fact it's a way to stifle any kind of change in the Congress which is so desperately needed today."[5]

But when Ms. Abzug ran against Representative Ryan's widow, what did she cite as her major qualification? "I'm seeking the election as an incumbent Congresswoman," she said. "I think that's a difference. I am one who has lived and worked in this district and gone to school on the West Side, a graduate of Columbia Law School. I know the people here and in the Bronx where I have lived, where I was born. I know their problems and I think in my first two years of Congress I've shown that I know how to represent people effectively.

"I believe that I have had a very effective relationship with my constituents," she continued. "I've maintained a very active district presence with two district offices, in which more than half of my staff and a large group of volunteers not only service the problems of constituents but also help doing community organizing with tenants and veterans and elderly citizens and that sort of thing."[6]

Then, with the flair of veteran politicians, she ticked off the accomplishments that only incumbency can provide. "I feel very proud of the fact that I have been able to see the passage of legislation in such fields as rent and housing, and development in the area of discrimination against women, and federally assisted employment in the area of economic development, in the area of water pollution, in which I played a major role in development, and in many other areas. I feel particularly very proud of the fact that I have been able to secure funds for various important areas in my district in connection with expansion of health facilities and recreational facilities, bilingual education and programs of that kind.

"The issue in this campaign is one of qualification," she added. "None of the candidates who oppose me have had any deep community involvement on the issues that concern the community or these many communities in the district. They have themselves no record of their own."

Ms. Ryan's reasons for running stemmed from her reaction against what she regarded as Bella Abzug's betrayal, as well as her desire to give her late husband's constituents an alternative. "I was furious with her for running against him. . . . It is incredible that somebody who would ape everything he did—and I know for a fact how often their office would call and ask, 'How is Bill going to vote on this?' or 'What should I do about this?'—and then to run against him. . . . He [Representative Ryan] was the one person in the Congress who really tried to help her and show her the ropes.

"She never did her homework," she continued. "In the first place she is always running off making a big speech . . . she is a creature of the media. She doesn't do any work in Congress . . . and she can't keep her staff. . . . You can't run an office with a constant turnover like that." Ms. Ryan also feared her opponent would not be able to provide the individualized constituent services her husband had prided himself on delivering. "Another thing people here felt very strongly about was the constituent services which Bill had provided. He was unique. I don't think any other office does this. People in this area have forgotten what Congressional offices were like before Bill."

Tarnished with bitterness at every point, the campaign mercifully ended with Ms. Abzug winning by a margin of almost two to one. (Ms. Abzug drew 85,558 votes against 43,045 for Ms. Ryan. The three other candidates shared the remaining 28,735 votes.) Many district leaders who had supported William Ryan in the June primary found it easier to transfer their support to Ms.

Abzug than to Ms. Ryan, whose links in the New York political community were weak at best.[7] One district leader, Sara Kovner, explained her feelings: "I supported Bill in the primaries," she said. "In the general election I supported Bella. My feeling was before the primary got under way that Bella and Bill were people that I and a lot of people around here had supported and wanted to see in Congress. I had worked for both of them to be elected, and I felt that it was unfortunate that we had to make a choice. I wanted to support Bill. I felt that he earned that support over a period of time. He wasn't liked any more than Bella was when he first went to Congress. The thought that Bill Ryan was the kind that went along with the Congressional establishment was a joke to me, because I remember when he got elected, how irascible he was and how difficult he was with the Congressional leadership. . . . I had supported Bella when she first ran in 1970, worked hard for her and raised money for her. . . . Once he [Representative Ryan] died, I certainly didn't feel that we shouldn't have either one of them."

The key variable influencing Ms. Abzug's success was the support of Mayor John Lindsay, which brought the help of many of his key aides, including Deputy Mayor Richard Aurelio and patronage dispenser Sid Davidoff.[8] Their troops weighed most heavily in assuring her easy victory in the special balloting October 1, 1972 at the County Committee, where in a tumultuous session at New York's Commodore Hotel, Ms. Abzug defeated Ms. Ryan on the first ballot by a vote of 553 to 333. Thus the crucial decision on Ms. Abzug's reelection was made, not by the public at the ballot box but by fewer than a thousand politicians in a large ballroom. Winning the Democratic nomination was crucial in the 20th C.D.,[9] where it was virtually an electoral impossibility to change the lifetime habits of habitual Democrats—particularly in a Congressional race, and for a candidate almost unknown to them.

In one sense Ms. Abzug's victory could be read as a victory for the women's movement, the constituency she had helped build and had worked so hard to maintain. The existence of a woman candidate opposite Ms. Abzug failed to defuse the women's issue; instead, it worked counterproductively, eliciting anger from women's groups who attacked Ms. Ryan's candidacy as "dynastic."[10]

Miscalculating its appeal, Ms. Ryan underplayed feminism and abandoned her chances to cut into its electoral benefits. In the only real ideological difference between the two candidates Ms. Ryan clearly departed from the feminists' stance on the subject of women in politics. "I differ from extreme attitudes of having women run," she emphasized. "I think they ought to be able to run on an equal basis with men, but not just because they are women. . . . I disagree with her [Bella Abzug] on this thing. It is paranoid to have to support a woman."

In contrast, Bella Abzug wedded her candidacy to the survival of women in politics. Women, she felt, owned a vested interest in her victory, a forecast of their future survival in the political arena. Even those who objected to her on other grounds admitted she was right on this issue and suppressed their misgivings. "I hope she wins, but just by a little," said a Manhattan political scientist with feminist sympathies.

But many others rallied to her side, supporting her candidacy with enthusiasm and fervor. Well-known activists in the women's movement helped strengthen Representative Abzug's image as a women's candidate, among them: Gloria Steinem (editor of *Ms.* magazine); Muriel Fox (National Chairwoman, NOW); Ronnie Eldridge (her campaign manager, now on the staff of *Ms.* magazine); Eleanor Holmes Norton (Chairperson of the City's Human Rights Commission); Assemblywoman Carol Bellamy; Susan Rosenfeld (a leader of Women in City Government United and a deputy commissioner in the city's Economic Development Agency); Beulah Sanders (National Welfare Rights Organization); and Letty Cotton Pogrebin (a well-known writer and feminist).

Feminist supporters regarded Ms. Abzug as a candidate who had proven her ability to project women's issues onto the national consciousness, promoting in Congress and on the lecture circuit such issues as equal rights, abortion reform, comprehensive child care, tax reform, the elimination of sex discrimination, and the prevention of sex discrimination in programs receiving federal money. "Child care and women's rights took a giant step forward when Congresswoman Abzug came to Congress," affirmed Representative Shirley Chisholm. "Working together we've initiated some solid achievements. . . ."

A great rhetorician, who was one of the first to formulate peace as a women's issue, Representative Abzug shared equal billing with Gloria Steinem and Betty Friedan as one of the original leaders of the women's political movement. Through their efforts to spread the message, the idea of women in politics gained national exposure, providing the basis for the founding of the National Women's Political Caucus in 1971. "We are here to serve notice," Representative Abzug told a meeting of the NWPC, "that . . . we will no longer take second place or last place to anyone. We are going to demand and win equal status in politics, equal pay and recognition in our work, full equality in our civil rights and in every aspect of our lives."[11]

Many others began to lend their support to Representative Abzug, their numbers swelling with greater speed as it became apparent she was headed for victory. Her roster included the major Democratic city councilmen, assemblymen and state senators, as well as influential labor leaders, rabbis, good-government types, and a host of other elites identified with local interests and interest groups. Gathering the best from all possible worlds, Ms. Abzug was also able to rally stars from Broadway and publishers' row; her list of supporters boasted writers and editors (Jules Feiffer, Murray Kempton, Jimmy Breslin, Nat Hentoff, Nora Ephron, Jason and Barbara Epstein); actors, playwrights and producers (Hal Prince, Sheldon Harnick, Neil Simon, Jerry Orbach, Joseph Bologna and his wife, Renee Taylor, Estelle Parsons, Rita Moreno, and Shirley MacLaine); and many others associated with New York's glamorous intellectual and artistic world.

Although the outcome of both the party and the electoral races was doubtful at the beginning,[12] it soon became apparent that Ms. Ryan's campaign stacked up as frail competition for Ms. Abzug's well-projected identification with such issues as peace and women's rights, both wildly popular causes on Manhattan's West Side. Added to this was the canny decision credited to campaign manager Ronnie Eldridge to keep Representative Abzug's campaign low key, the idea being to counter the candidate's widespread reputation for abrasiveness. "We made the decision," recalled Ms. Eldridge, "to keep the campaign low key . . . that she [Ms. Abzug] shouldn't be loud or harangue at the microphone or on streetcorners; that she should act like an incumbent Congresswoman; and that basically she should meet as many people as possible, because she is prettier than people think she is."

Working with an undramatic scenario, Ms. Eldridge successfully downplayed her candidate's attraction for publicity, concentrating instead on the more mundane tasks of telephone canvassing and extensive mailings. Her efforts and strategy paid off, as Ms. Abzug climbed from an outcome that began as "undecided" to a victory of almost two to one. And from under the dark cloud of a strange and unhappy campaign marking the nadir of her popularity, she reemerged to reclaim a seat in Congress.

The Character of Charisma: Who Bleeds From the Cutting Edge

Neither a political fluke nor a slip of the computer caused Ms. Abzug to be redistricted so unceremoniously out of her Congressional seat—the origin of her fight against the Ryans—even though the redistricting took place in the best tradition of ladies first. But Ms. Abzug was not merely a woman; she was a difficult woman, her personality compounding her political problems throughout both terms in Congress.[13]

Few politicians of either party were less cooperative than Bella Abzug. Unpopular with the party leadership, she also was one of the least popular freshmen in Congress, a "loudmouth" continually in the vanguard of unpopular causes, as far as the leadership was concerned. Long before serious talk of impeachment began, for example, Ms. Abzug's office boasted leaflets calling for President Nixon's removal for "high crimes and misdemeanors in conducting a war against the peoples and nations of Indochina in the absence of a Declaration of War as required by the United States Constitution."[14]

On other issues Representative Abzug also raced ahead of the flock in much the same way she sped ahead of her staff on the campaign trail. She communicated a sense of urgency and mission to some, while others found her truculent and threatening, an aberration to those accustomed to respectful silence from newcomers. Reacting to their criticism of her style, Ms. Abzug emphasied that their criticism was more basic. They opposed her, she said, for her leadership on issues of social justice and discriminated against her because of her sex. "I'm a target because I'm a woman. I've been a leader of the peace movements, a leader of movements of the underrepresented, a leader in the woman's movement, yes, and in the demand of women for more representation, politically as well as economically, for equal pay for equal work, a leader in the fight for child care . . . and a woman who has furthermore been probably one of the most outspoken challengers to Mr. Rockefeller and Mr. Nixon.

"I think that there is a resistance to accepting women yet in politics," she continued. "And I think that it's like the last elected and the first to be dismembered or the last hired and the first to be fired. And I think that as we seek more political power and more economic equality there will be more resistance to us."[15]

As her ideas and her sex alienated her from her peers in Congress, so did her style, the style of the movement politician, rich in charismatic appeal and miserly in its attention to personal needs. Like many in public life who find themselves increasingly dependent on the adoration of others, she is easily wounded by criticism, both real and imagined; her insecurity takes refuge beneath an ever present floppy-brimmed hat, clouds of cigarette smoke, and a derisive manner. In her abrasive cycle she has been known to level insults at foes and admirers alike; her penchant for Anglo-Saxon expletives has become almost legendary around Capitol Hill, where anecdotes revealing her pungent speech abound. One famous incident recalled her response to House Doorkeeper Fishbait Miller, whom she allegedly told to "perform an impossible act" after he requested that she remove her hat.[16] Another story told how after losing an antiwar amendment she reportedly told Carl Albert and several other leaders who came over to console her, "Fuck off."

Ill-tempered and impatient, she antagonized many of her close

supporters and found it difficult, once elected, to retain a
Congressional staff. A former aide recalled her association with
Ms. Abzug as "the worst time of my life." Others also reported
difficulties in their personal dealings with her, sensing in her a
contempt uncharacteristic of other politicians. "How can you be
so stupid?" was her common response to questions eliciting
information. "You obviously don't know anything about housing," she told a reporter asking a neutral question about her role
on a housing bill. "It's clear you know nothing about the Liberal
party," she answered a political scientist researching her
campaign.

Derision under normal circumstances is generally regarded as
an undesirable way of doing business; in an occupation relying
heavily on personal relationships, it is plain suicide. At the very
least it is unproductive to deride people who treasure their
self-respect and who are bound to react negatively to assaults on
their egos.

Armed with egos and ego problems of their own, Ms. Abzug's
colleagues responded in kind and subjected her to their own
methods of hazing. By the end of her first term she had alienated
so many Congressmen that the Ralph Nader report on Congress
concluded, "Whenever Abzug offers a measure, it gets twenty to
thirty fewer votes than the same bill would under someone else's
name."[17]

Her fellow legislators sabotaged her at every turn. At one point
the leadership scuttled her in a prank worthy of fraternity pledges
on a college campus. The House, acting with unusual speed after
convening at the stroke of noon, called up a resolution of
Representative Abzug's and quickly tabled it—killing it, for all
practical purposes—without debate, while she unknowingly
chatted with an aide at the entrance to the chamber.[18] On this
particular occasion Representative Thomas E. Morgan, Pennsylvania Democrat and chairman of the House Foreign Affairs
Committee, was recognized and quickly called up Ms. Abzug's
resolution. "Mr. Speaker," he declared as he glanced around the
chamber, "I intended to yield to the gentlewoman from New York
ten minutes for debate only, but I do not see the gentlewoman on
the floor." Mr. Morgan said that he had "certainly notified the

gentlewoman's office I was going to call this up first," and as chuckles were heard from the Republican Representatives, Mr. Morgan succeeded in having the resolution tabled on a voice vote.

To a certain extent Representative Abzug's problems in the realm of interpersonal relationships can be explained by the distorting effects of fame. Without question one of the bona fide heroines of the women's political movement, she is engulfed in adulation whenever she addresses women's groups and is besieged for autographs by a nationwide network of supporters, many of whom have contributed to her campaign even though they live outside her district. Even the more conservative women speak admiringly of her. Representative Margaret Heckler says, "I would never criticize Bella." Genuinely charismatic in her own right, she responds to crowds as positively as they respond to her, each side hungry for ideas still outside the mainstream of American public opinion. In this context she became accustomed to relating to crowds, finding it difficult to acclimate to the workaday world of American politics, the fabric of which is woven around close attention to detail, personal ties, mutual agreements of support—in short, one-to-one relationships that lead to concrete political action.

With an impatience endemic to movement politicians Representative Abzug made it clear she had little use for those outside her ideological framework, and little respect for the norms of a slow-moving and tradition-minded Congress, unresponsive to issues she considered national emergencies. Frustrated in many legislative attempts, she berated House leaders impeding her progress and, to her credit, publicized facts about the legislative process normally restricted to political-science classes. "Both houses," she said in a speech at the beginning of her term, "are dominated by a male, white, middle-aged, middle- and upper-class power elite that stand with their backs turned to the needs and demands of our people for realistic change to create a society with humane and healthy values."[19]

In view of rhetoric like this, representing her genuine commitment to the advocacy of women candidates, it remains a mystery just why Ms. Abzug has been reluctant to endorse and promote women candidates within her own citywide party organization. Ross Graham failed to win Ms. Abzug's endorsement in that short-lived West Side campaign for the state legislature. Although Representative Abzug said Ms. Graham never formally requested the endorsement, apparently she was loath to antagonize the West Side's male power structure, which was supporting the incumbent Richard Gottfried. Nor did Ms. Abzug endorse Elizabeth Holtzman in her successful campaign to unseat Representative Emanuel Celler. Such a bare acquaintance with the necessities of the protégé system doesn't quite jibe with the movement's goals of helping women achieve meaningful positions of power.

Nor did Ms. Abzug endorse Shirley Chisholm, the first woman to seek the Presidential nomination of a major party. Ms. Chisholm describes Ms. Abzug's ambivalence and reluctance to support her in her book: "One surprise came from my sister Congresswoman from New York, Bella Abzug . . . five minutes before the Washington press conference [announcing her candidacy] started I had a call from an Abzug aide asking whether Bella could appear with me and my supporters at the event. I could not discover whether she intended to endorse me, or what she had in mind, but I said yes because I could see no reason to say no. After my statement, Mitchell and Dellums spoke; they gave me strong and moving endorsements. Then Bella made a strange statement, largely about movements and the under-privileged in politics. She said little about my candidacy, except that it was 'an idea whose time has come,' if I remember it correctly.

"Later a reporter asked her whether she had endorsed me or not. Bella hedged. She said she supported 'the idea' of my candidacy and would support me in those states where I was running. At the time she appeared to think I was going into only three or four primaries. Bella never offered to campaign for me in Florida, North Carolina or even New York, for that matter. It was a letdown, and also bewildering. If she intended to sit on the fence, why did she ask to appear with me when I made the announcement for the Presidency?"[20]

With a lawyer's penchant for adversary relationships, Bella Abzug's politics are exciting, conflict-oriented, mercurial and often aggravating to those who have to work with her, and to those whose expectations she has raised. Aware lately of how badly women need her representation in Congress, she seems to have become more flexible, responding to the socialization processes of the House, and more accommodating to some of its idiosyncrasies, lest the cutting edge hurt the movement she had built and nurtured.

The New Pragmatism: The Blunting of the Cutting Edge

Her legendary profanity is now muted. She takes the floor of the House less often nowadays, and when she does, her words flow more slowly and more softly. She works more quietly in committees, introduces fewer amendments, and takes an unaccustomed seat in some important legislative battles.

Has Bella Abzug mellowed? Has the controversial, larger-than-life feminist been caught up in the socialization process of the House of Representatives, which biannually receives dozens of feisty freshmen heady with victory and transforms them into subdued sophomores? Is the change more illusion than reality, a change of heart or a triumph of Miltown?

"I would say she has mellowed, at least on the surface," said Speaker Carl Albert of Oklahoma, with whom Ms. Abzug tilted during her freshman year. "She measures her activities more than she did at first. She's learned that she doesn't have to get out in front on every issue." But Majority Leader Thomas P. "Tip" O'Neill of Massachusetts disagreed. "She's the same old Bella," Mr. O'Neill said. "She hasn't changed a damned bit. The first call I get every week is from Bella, trying to tell me how to run the place." To Representative Mario Biaggi, the Bronx Democrat and unsuccessful Conservative party candidate for mayor, "She's a different person." But to Ronnie Eldridge, a former aide to Mayor Lindsay and the late Senator Robert F. Kennedy, and one of Ms. Abzug's closest friends, "She's overwhelmed with work, so she doesn't have too much time to be extraneous, but Bella hasn't changed."

Those who discern a change point to the fact that Ms. Abzug allowed others to take the lead in the debate on the Cambodia bombing halt and was persuaded by legislative leaders not to introduce an amendment to the mass transit bill for fear the amendment might lead to the bill's defeat. Perhaps most uncharacteristic, in the eyes of her colleagues, was Ms. Abzug's teamwork on the impeachment resolution. "Don't you think I wanted to drop an impeachment resolution in the hopper?" she asked during an interview, fingering a lorgnette that dangled on a gold necklace beside a brown silk scarf. "I spent all this time talking, educating. Finally I cosponsored the resolution, as one among many." Ms. Abzug's restraint contrasted with the action of Representative Robert Drinan, a Massachusetts Democrat and Jesuit priest, who, like Ms. Abzug, is an ultraliberal looked on with suspicion by many liberals and conservatives alike. Father Drinan yielded to temptation and introduced an impeachment resolution, which was promptly tabled.

"I use all the tactics that everyone else uses of compromise and vote getting," Ms. Abzug says. Others disagree, however, and say that her West Side constituents simply will not tolerate compromise on the part of their representative in Congress and that Ms. Abzug's other constituencies—women, minority members, early peace-movement supporters—would also tend to regard a compromise as a cop-out.

Whether or not she has mellowed, Ms. Abzug remains a distinct presence, a large woman of great vitality, seemingly ubiquitous, striding into committee rooms and cloakrooms beneath her omnipresent floppy, broad-brimmed hat, in a wardrobe that owes much to Loehmann's and Alexander's. She seems to be more at home in the House than last year, however, and banters more with colleagues of all political persuasions. The House seems to be more at home with her, as well. No longer do conservative members post themselves at the entrances to the chamber to inform incoming Congressmen that a vote is on an "Abzug amendment—vote no."

Ms. Abzug herself feels that she has not altered. Instead, she believes she contains multitudes, and that colleagues who had previously seen only one side of her are now beginning to appreciate her complexity. "I was originally a pressure force on these people," she said, recalling her days as organizer of

Women's Strike for Peace, which she served as a lobbyist. "It takes time to get to know a personality, especially one that has a lot of nuances, and is prepared to show them all," she said. "They're getting to know me, and I'm getting to know them."

Some of her colleagues in the city's Congressional delegation contend that Ms. Abzug would have encountered hostility among some of her Congressional colleagues regardless of her personality, simply because she is an articulate, liberal, New York, West Side, Jewish woman. They say that any of these qualities alone would have raised eyebrows in some quarters. "She could be a combination Helen Keller and Joan of Arc, and some of these people still wouldn't accept her," one colleague said.

To Ms. Abzug, on the other hand, "Most of the people here are from one grouping: white, middle-aged men, lawyers and businessmen. The style is conservative," she said. "They don't really represent America. Congress needs more women, some trade unionists, city planners, younger people and minority members." She is most heartened by the surge of women in politics, she said, because "they're fresh and new and have no commitments. That's why it takes so long for this body to respond—they have commitments." But even though she feels that her colleagues do not represent America, Ms. Abzug has learned that she must deal with them. "The first year she didn't know what she was doing," a former aide recalled. "Now she knows that there are certain people she has to swallow."

Ms. Abzug deliberately relinquished a leading role in the debate on the Cambodia bombing halt, which was led by two more moderate Democrats—Representatives Joseph P. Addabbo, of Queens, and Robert N. Giaimo, of Connecticut. "I worked hard getting other people to take leadership," Ms. Abzug said. Representatives Addabbo and Giaimo agree. "She realized that if you push too hard, you scare people away," Mr. Addabbo said. "She agreed to work more in the background than up front leading the charge." "She had an image problem to overcome," Mr. Giaimo added. "She's earned respect from more people than she used to have. Mainly she does her homework, she's very knowledgeable. She's aware of the issues and of the parliamentary proceedings. She's developing the ability to cooperate with other members."

On the mass-transit legislation, Representative Joseph G. Minish, New Jersey Democrat and chairman of the mass-transit subcommittee on banking and currency, said, "I pointed out to her that I knew they were going to zero in and make it look like a big-city bill. There were a lot of people from New York who were interested in putting in amendments," he continued. "I said, 'We're having enough trouble selling this bill.' Bella came to me and said, 'Joe, if you think it'll hurt the bill by me offering it, I won't offer it.' I talked to her, and she was very gracious."

Ms. Abzug's increased sensitivity stood her in good stead in her role as New York City's representative on the House Public Works Committee, where she has succeeded in gaining approval of projects that helped the city. One such project involved the U.S. Army Corps of Engineers, which was directed to clear debris and sunken vessels from New York Harbor. Another directed them to conduct erosion control projects in the Rockaways. "She was extremely effective in the Public Works Committee," said Edward R. Skloot, the city's deputy administrator for parks, recreation and cultural affairs. She also succeeded in persuading the Public Works Committee to relinquish federal air rights above the Morgan Annex Post Office, enabling the city to build low and middle-income housing on the site.

These victories reflected Ms. Abzug's newfound skill at working with the committee members. "In my committee, some of the members from the South and West saw me as a very strange being," she said. "They didn't see me as interested in marriage, a family and a home. Now they understand that a lot of my passion comes out of a deep commitment. I don't wait and examine and test and feel—and I think this was a shock even to some people who shared my views. They began to see, I believe, that I could subsume. They began to understand what I was all about, not to grab off a headline, but acting out of my commitment."

Does Ms. Abzug acknowledge the effects of the socialization process of the House? "Very definitely," she said. "But since it's a club—essentially a male club—it affects men more than it does women." Did she want peer approval? Ms. Abzug smiled broadly, and looked wistful. "Everybody likes to be loved," she said.

Chapter VII

Winning Clout: Victory at the Ballot Box

You can't win on ideas alone.

> —AUDREY BECK, Connecticut
> state representative

*Women need a longer lead time. They need expertise. . . . They
need a wide support crew behind them. . . . They have learned
that you really have to have a plan.*

> —NIKKI BEARE, a political
> consultant from Florida

Taking on the Odds

They are a new breed of women, nurtured by the women's
movement, eager to invest the time and effort to master the basic
tactics of winning elections. Their ultimate ambitions are as
diverse as their backgrounds, but they share a quiet seriousness
and singularity of purpose: to win and hold political power. For
many, the dominance of charisma and rhetoric has bent to more
pragmatic considerations; now the hard realities of canvassing,
fund raising, media training, organization building, graphics
presentations and the myriad nuts-and-bolts tasks involved in
running for office occupy the lion's share of their time. Ideology
remains the moving force, but it is now grounded to an action
base, as women have finally become convinced that without
expertise in such minutiae they stand little chance of winning
elections.

"Some people have professional polls; I have bookies," Barbara Mikulski, a short, feisty woman elected to the Baltimore City Council, told the hopeful women candidates convened in Houston. "And the bookies in my community, whom I always consult, gave me two hundred-to-one odds that I couldn't win. They said I couldn't win, number one, because I was a woman. And in a community such as mine, all the women always vote the way their husbands tell them. And I did not belong to a political machine, and we were dominated by a political machine for the past forty years. And also the fact that I didn't have big money . . . and I had the reputation of being a liberal. Do you know what being a liberal meant? That I was a social worker, that I worked with civil rights, that I tried to help people get opportunities to improve their life."[1]

With all these "strikes" against her Ms. Mikulski ran an energetic, well-planned campaign, designed to prove the bookies wrong. In one of the most methodically conducted campaigns in the history of councilmanic politics, Ms. Mikulski's army of volunteers personally spoke to 50,000 voters, while the candidate herself spoke to 15,000. Personal contact, she stressed, was the key to her success, particularly in the neighborhoods where traditional fraternalistic values still prevailed. What she and her workers tried to communicate to the voters was that she cared about them in a genuine way. "We didn't see them [the voters] as blocs to be manipulated," she said emphatically. "We saw them as people to be reached out to, and that's what we did. . . . In our campaign we tried to have the word 'respect'—respect for the voters and for volunteers. . . . The basic technique of our campaign was to go door to door to door. I would start at nine o'clock in the morning and campaign until lunchtime, and then go back at night."

A grueling schedule, to be sure, but very important to the lower-middle-class ethnic community in which Ms. Mikulski conducted her campaign. She campaigned in the black community, the Polish community, the Greek community and the Italian community, passing out literature in the language of each neighborhood as part of her overall theme of emphasizing the needs of the forgotten ethnic Americans. In the Polish community she campaigned with members of her family who were descended from Polish immigrants. At a Polish hall, where generations of her family had married and held their christenings, Barbara Mikulski announced her candidacy in a ceremony she referred to as "mini-Polish wedding," a celebration of her ethnicity. "In one breath," she reminisced, "I informed everybody, 'I announce my candidacy for City Council.' Then I reminded everybody how my great-grandmother came to this country with sixteen dollars and a bed and a mattress looking for the American dream. And through efforts of women like her, that American dream could come true for people like me, her great-granddaughter."

Door-to-door campaigning was no easy chore, she warned, an occupation attracting the same hazards that beset mailmen and Fuller Brush salesmen. Dogs threatened her, people slammed doors in her face, and one group of old men in a laundromat asked her why she wasn't out doing her wash. Recalling Shirley Chisholm's advice not to be put down, Ms. Mikulski grabbed back her literature from the old men, telling them she didn't want their vote anyway.

A major problem for Barbara Mikulski was how to use issues that concerned her constituents, without pandering to their fears and prejudices. These people were accustomed to candidates who had appealed to them as the "new majority," using such code words as law and order to communicate race polarization. "We never played to the fears of people," said Ms. Mikulski. "We always played to the hearts of people. Everybody is concerned about drugs. Everybody is concerned about schools. Everybody is concerned about health care. We tried to come up with constructive solutions. I wasn't going to announce my candidacy by sitting on the back of a garbage can and saying, 'I'm going to clean this mess up.'" When potential voters disagreed with her, as they often did, she preached mutual tolerance and respect. "What we were saying was that we respect you," she told her audiences. "Here are the issues that are the same for all of us in the city. But because we all have diversity and our own identity, we respect that."

In the end her struggle paid off, and Ms. Mikulski claimed her well-earned victory against formidable obstacles: an entrenched machine, a well-financed opposition, a district of extreme heterogeneity, and all the prejudice normally confronting a woman in politics, particularly an unmarried woman. She won—to the surprise of the bookies—because she was able to mobilize an army of volunteers drawn from the community and from community groups. "They came from the community," she said, "not from those hotsy-totsy political things. They came from the Hudson Street Improvement Association and the Southeast Expressway Coalition."

Ms. Mikulski's rise in Baltimore politics led to her rapid advancement in the ranks of the national Democratic party. She was invited to head the party's Delegate Selection Committee shortly after her election to the City Council, a post that sorely tested her political skills and equilibrium. After many stormy sessions her final report, which will determine the composition of the delegate body chosen to select the nominee for President in 1976, was accepted, elevating Ms. Mikulski to a position of national prominence.

Mastering the Dynamics: Successful Game Plans

Women candidates can live without bookies, but they have found other forms of professional aid indispensable. When they can afford it, they hire political consultants, whose expertise in systematic campaign management often increases their chances of success. One such consultant especially interested in women candidates is Nikki Beare, who operates out of Dade County, Florida. Ms. Beare, a board member of NOW, has managed several successful campaigns for men as well as women, and in 1974 announced her own candidacy for the state Senate. She ran the campaigns of Gwen Cherry, the first black woman elected to the Florida state legislature, and Elaine Gordon, a talented young woman elected to the lower house. Both women had been active in the women's movement, both ran on low budgets, and both recruited their own organizations outside the party, from the ranks of their local Women's Political Caucus.

Discovered and encouraged by Nikki Beare, Gwen Cherry rose

to prominence as one of the first women candidates in Florida. Representing an effective political identity for both black and white women, Ms. Cherry achieved what she herself had once thought impossible: She managed to beat a well-funded, popular and extremely influential black minister, the Reverend Temperance Wright, by a margin of two to one.

At the time she decided to run, Gwen Cherry worked as a practicing attorney, active in the civil rights movement and deeply involved in several sex-discrimination cases. Ms. Cherry found herself propelled into practical politics as a logical consequence of her activities in movement politics, a route similar to Bella Abzug's progression from the peace movement to Congress.

She knew she faced an uphill battle, but convinced by Ms. Beare and others close to her that she had a chance to win, she finally decided to run. In the past, she admitted, she had been approached by groups in the black community to run for office, but had never felt sufficiently secure to launch her own campaign. As her strategist, Nikki Beare structured Ms. Cherry's first campaign around what she considered her candidate's most serious political problem: making herself known. "It was simply a case of educating the public to her [Gwen Cherry] as a viable political person," she explained. Once she achieved higher visibility through intensive campaigning, contributions and workers became easier to attract. "In her first campaign for the state legislature," Ms. Beare recalled, "Gwen Cherry didn't have any major funding from any one particular group or individual. The contributions ran mainly fifty dollars or less, and she never spent more than ten thousand dollars." All this considered, Ms. Cherry's victory came as a surprise to some seasoned political observers.

Adding to the inherent difficulties of the race, Gwen Cherry also found herself challenging both the regular party organization and influential segments of the black community. The real race in this election was the primary, where substantial opposition presented itself. Her most formidable opponent, Reverend Wright, entered the race as the favorite, benefiting from the fruits of his incumbency as the chairman of the Miami Planning and Zoning Board. When he neglected to resign his position on the

zoning board before running for office—as required by law—
Gwen Cherry challenged his qualifications as a candidate. The
attorney general of Florida took up the challenge on her behalf
and on behalf of the other candidates. The case was appealed all
the way up to the state Supreme Court, which ultimately decided
in the Reverend Mr. Wright's favor. He had intended to resign,
the court said, and therefore was still eligible to run.

Gwen Cherry then faced running against the Reverend Mr.
Wright without the support of party regulars, and without the
support of some members of the black community, who accused
her of not being fair to a minister by portraying him as a liar. "She
had to fight the battle of women's liberation and also black
liberation," said Nikki Beare.

Originally in business for herself as Nikki Beare and Associates,
Ms. Beare's consulting firm is now nationally based, having been
recently acquired by the financial public-relations firm of
Chancel, Caroll, and Holzer. Emphatic about her status as a
political professional, Ms. Beare charges candidates for her
services, her fees dependent on the amount of work needed.

Drawing on her skills in political management and her
background in feminist activities, Nikki Beare has developed a set
of strategies geared to women running for office. She is most
emphatic about the point that women need much more "lead
time" than men, lead time being the allotment of time set aside
before an election to conduct a campaign. Nikki Beare allowed
nearly two years lead time—nearly the same time span calculated
for a Presidential or Senatorial campaign—to build up the
candidates of Gwen Cherry and Elaine Gordon. "Women need a
much longer lead time," she said. "They need expertise. They
cannot do it themselves. They need a wide support crew behind
them. . . . A number of women who ran and didn't make it for
various reasons are going to run again. They have learned from
their mistakes. They have learned that you really have to have a
plan. You just can't say the day before the end of qualifying, 'Hey,
I am going to run and get elected.'" Convinced by her early
successes that her lead-time theory was right, in 1972 Nikki began
designing campaign plans for women planning to run for the
state legislature in 1974. As a result more women from Dade

County reported plans to run for office in the 1974 elections than in any other section of the country.[2]

A longer lead time helps women candidates compensate for their three most serious difficulties in running for office: lack of recognition, inadequate financing, and weak party ties.[3] It gives them time to accomplish through tenacity what their competition may be able to achieve through expensive television advertising, a high-priced campaign staff, or well-disciplined party workers. Early successes have worked well in terms of encouraging women who had previously been discouraged from seeking office by the well-heeled character of the "new politics." Indeed, it was in Florida, where the well-financed Presidential-primary campaign of John Lindsay attracted a mere 7 percent of the state's vote, one of the first times in recent history that the voters reacted against the conspicuous use of political money.

To ensure victory, women strategists agree that they must spend most of their time developing their own organizations, finding workers who will slowly and meticulously plod through their districts, recruiting votes, supporters, money and more workers. Absorbing the lessons of organizational politics, women have learned that insurgents can exercise very few options, the best of which lies in developing an independent army, ultimately challenging the party to accept women on the basis of their support in the community.

Coping: The Mothers of Invention

1. Politics and Money

The impulse to run for office became contagious. It led to other victories on the part of women who had run against entrenched party organizations without the benefits of fat purses or readily available workers. Young Sarah Weddington, a twenty-six-year-old attorney from Austin, Texas, ran for a seat in the state legislature without money and without a party organization, backed only by her local Women's Political Caucus chapter. Digging into her own savings for the hundred-dollar fee required of candidates who file for office, she registered her candidacy with the county chairman. "That was my first contact with organized politics," she recalled, describing her visit to party headquarters. The chairman himself never emerged from his office to meet the new candidate, an indication of how seriously he regarded her candidacy.

No matter. Sarah Weddington, like Barbara Mikulski and many others, developed her own machine, recruited from members of the caucus, from the community, and from personal friends and politically involved women, many of whom welcomed the chance to run a campaign. Two of her workers had worked for elected officials, one for a Congressman, another for a Senator. A third, Ann Richards, was referred to by the Texas *Observer* as the campaign's "political brain trust," a high compliment for a woman who had worked in many campaigns and was already well-known by the community as politically knowledgable, but who had never before been given the chance to assume the responsibility of a campaign. "She was so happy to be referred to as a political brain trust, not just a housewife," said Ms. Weddington, discussing the new dignity given to women in politics. "Ann came out with the idea of cheap paper bags with my name on it, and my autograph. Then everybody had something to put all this junk in."

Like most women candidates, her campaign was short on money and long on workers, but unlike others who bemoan their empty pockets, Ms. Weddington turned this into a virtue. Political money, she said, meant obligating herself to political interests whose projects she might not want to promote in office. "We took the attitude during the campaign that we wouldn't spend money we did not have. I never owed anybody any political money, and the day I won, I owed nobody anything. It's a feeling of independence that few people have."

And realistically it's a feeling of independence few can afford, since funding remains the most serious problem facing women candidates today. The higher the office, the greater the challenge. Betty Friedan, who wanted to challenge the Senate seat of Jacob Javits, calculated the cost at $2,000,000. Realizing she couldn't raise anywhere near that sum, she abandoned the idea of her candidacy.[4]

Regardless of region, women who have taken the plunge into

politics bemoan the financial problems impeding their ambitions. Sissy Farenthold reported that her 1972 race for governor cost $600,000 and that she was still $60,000 in debt. Campaigning in Texas, she pointed out, is especially expensive because of the size of the state, where door-to-door campaigning is an ineffective substitute for television advertising and the easy access to fast, but costly, air travel. Without the funds to mount an expensive television campaign (or a fleet of helicopters and jet airplanes at her disposal) Ms. Farenthold tried her own brand of grass-roots campaign, also expensive, but not as expensive as television. It involved stumping the state in an aircraft of dubious usefulness, which she dubbed an "airborne camper."

"It was a DC-3 that was used in 1962," she recalled. "It was so slow that during a windstorm some reporter looked down and said he saw a car passing us." Toward the end of her campaign some money started coming in, but not nearly enough to compete with the two million dollars she claimed her opponent, Dolph Briscoe, had spent. She was lucky, she said, because her family helped her out; she didn't want the "big money." "The thing about the big money is that I want to know what kind of big money it is, because I don't want strings," she said. "I don't want to be in office with strings."

In 1974, after she announced again for the gubernatorial race in her state, her strong feelings about political money surfaced as she called for all women candidates to adhere to model campaign-finance disclosure practices and to disclose statements of their net worth, assets and liabilities, sources of personal income, and income-tax returns.[5]

Most women agreed that attracting money was much harder for women who are proven political quantities than for men. "Money was a super pain," said Pat Schroeder, who complained that too much of her time had to be spent soliciting contributions. "We just fought for nickels and dimes. The big money didn't come in until the last few weeks. Our average contribution is $7.50, so you can just imagine what time it takes. . . . You just spend hours. . . . You feel like you're begging. If you can just get away from that, you could do such exciting things."

Ms. Schroeder said she spent $85,000, an exceedingly low

figure for a primary and general election run in a densely populated heterogeneous district. (Representative Elizabeth Holtzman, who also felt money was her biggest problem, says she spent $36,000 on her primary election alone, and then had to contend with the expenses incurred by a costly lawsuit initiated by Emanuel Celler, who had lost the primary.) "No one believes a woman can win," Ms. Schroeder said. "Most any kind of money comes from people who want to see someone win . . . especially your institutional money, the groups that back candidates. They're looking for winners, and the minute they see that you're a woman and a young woman and you're running against a Republican incumbent, they just think, 'Ha!'"

In the end some groups came through and channeled money to Ms. Schroeder's campaign. In the last few weeks of her campaign, for instance, the National Committee for an Effective Congress and the Democratic Study Group, came to her rescue with some money, although she charged the amount was not nearly in the same league as their contributions to male candidates. "The Democratic Study Group finally gave us $1,000 after everybody just beat them over the head," she said, recalling her surprise at meeting freshmen male members who had been given a lot more money from this group. Other groups applied the same double standard. The Democratic National Committee, she continued, gave her $1,500 although their contributions to congressional candidates averaged $3,000. The AFL-CIO, whose average contribution to new candidates ranged from $15,000 to $20,000, donated only $1,000 in the last week of her campaign. "I remember having breakfast with a young man [also running for Congress in Colorado] after our September 12 primary," she recalled. "He said, 'I guess I'm going to have to appoint a finance chairman. I went back East and we raised about forty thousand.' We didn't get a dime. He didn't have to worry about money."

Elaine Gordon experienced the same double standard in her efforts to attract money. "If you go up to a man," she said, "and ask him for a contribution, he'll give you ten dollars. And when I looked at other contribution reports, the same person gave thousands of dollars to other candidates.

"I got nothing from the unions," she continued, "although I

was strongly pro-union in my campaign. I got nothing from any kind of organized effort." In the end, she admitted, she had to go to men for money, not only because they had the money, but because they were the ones who were able to get other men to contribute to her campaign. "Most of the money besides my own that I got from men," she said, "came from men who were interested in seeing women get elected. Like my boss. My boss encouraged me to run. And he went out and got money and twisted the arms of men who would say, 'A woman?' And he would say, 'Give *me* the money.' These were the people I depended on. I am in a man's world all the time. [Ms. Gordon sells industrial machinery.] These were the men who know me, to whom I had proven myself already, who were willing to support me." The total cost of Ms. Gordon's campaign ran $13,000—$7,000 of which came from her own personal funds.

Traditional ways of raising money that have succeeded for men often become grounded when applied by women candidates. A testimonial dinner, for example, which can raise anywhere from $5,000 to $20,000 for a man—and more for Presidential and other high elective campaigns—has proven an ineffective resource for women, many of whom consider themselves lucky to break even after fund raisers of this kind.

These techniques fail primarily because women themselves, unconvinced of the necessity to use money to translate ideals into public policy, do not open their checkbooks for political purposes.

Women candidates say it is hard for a woman to write a check for more than four or five dollars for a campaign. Even rich women find it difficult to invest in politics; and when they do, their money generally goes to male candidates. "Older women are very hard to convince," said Ronnie Feit, the finance chairperson of the NWPC.[6] "We had a fund-raising luncheon that Jane Pickens Langley helped put on . . . with really moneyed women, quite social . . . married to important business and professional people. These women heard us and never gave a nickel. They could each have written checks for ten thousand and wouldn't have felt it. . . ." She added, however, that the caucus had been fortunate in receiving large grants from Stewart Mott [$25,000 for the Women's Education Delegate Selection group] and smaller ones from some small companies, the Avon corporation, for instance. Gloria Steinem, who corroborated Ronnie Feit's accusation that rich women tended not to contribute to the women's political movement, added that two notable exceptions were Carol Hausman and Geraldine Stutz.

The party often picks rich women to run on the basis of the money they can bring in to the party—an avenue of success open to men as well. Martin Gruberg cites an example of such a woman, a kind of political ambassador for the party: "Mrs. Ruth Watson of California, vice-chairman of the Republican Central Committee, must deserve commendation from the men for her selflessness. . . . Mrs. Watson does not accept expense reimbursements, not even for traveling. When asked how much her job cost her, she . . . said: 'I have probably spent between ten and twenty thousand dollars in the last four years, traveling in the state and going to Washington.'"[7]

Women who can't bring in money, who contribute only service to the party, lose out, finding themselves permanently relegated to the lower ranks of the party. Many now see the connection between money and influence and resent their position outside this orbit. "I'm the one that does the walking in the precincts because I can only put in my time," said Donna Meyer of the Oklahoma Women's Political Caucus. "I can't go to a fifty-dollar dinner. And this is where you are going to see people like La Donna and [Senator] Fred Harris, at fifty-dollar dinners. This is where you are going to see your big wheels, and I am not on a first-name basis with them because I'm the peon down at the bottom."

"I feel that women like us, who have done the walking, have done the crap work, should be given tickets," chimed in Marilyn Kalbach of Tucson, Arizona. "We've earned it. They couldn't afford the salaries we are worth."

Women who have gotten a great deal of publicity, who are well known on the national level, have an easier time attracting money. Bella Abzug says money now presents no problem for her. "I get a lot of mass support both here and across the country in terms of funds, and so on. People raise money for me in different parts of the country . . . women, and peace people, and people interested in my issues. I don't go to lobbyists for money, because I don't respond to lobbyists. I run a mass campaign and [average] from $3 to $50 contributions. . . . I had a $3 event, a $5 event, a $25 event and a $50 event to raise money. Then I had a direct mail for people who were on my national constituents list, a list I have of people who write to me from all over the country who want me to represent them and keep them informed. There's a group of people in Washington who run out a newsletter of all the things I do, and they raise money and funds in small doses."

Similarly Martha Griffiths disclaims any problems about money. She raises money through pancake suppers costing $1.50 a plate and promises "all the pancakes, applesauce and sausages you can eat." The Democratic party, she chuckled, assumes that she collects $500 from these suppers; not so, she raises thousands.

Challenging the traditional wisdom, Esther Newberg, executive director of the New York State Democratic party, advises that there is a lot of money around available to women of liberal bent. "Liberal money will go to men as well as to women," she said. "Stewart Mott will give to women and men as long as they're issue people. The same is true of Marty and Ann Peretz, the Singer Sewing Machine heirs in Boston. They give to liberals. Ella Grasso never hàd any money problems. Since 1968 this has been true. Gene McCarthy tapped money no one had ever tapped. So did Bobby Kennedy. Before the money would come in only for patronage: judgeships, no-show jobs in Albany, nonpaying jobs on commissions. Now it's coming in for issues."

2. *Getting out the Troops*

The success of women like Sarah Weddington inspired other candidates. Ms. Weddington had been urged to run by members of her local caucus, many of whom had lobbied with her in Austin on behalf of feminist issues: equal rights, abortion reform and family planning. Meeting with uneven success, they were appalled at how difficult it was to find sympathetic legislators who were willing to face and deal with these issues; they finally decided the time had come to promote their own candidates.

"Never again will I give my heart to a party and another male candidate, never," said Helen Cassidy, one of the leaders of the

Texas Women's Political Caucus. "I have a limited amount of time and energy and money, and I am going to start giving it to women. I don't think that Sarah Weddington is going to disappoint me, and I don't think Chris Miller [another woman who, aided by the caucus, won a seat in the state legislature] is going to disappoint me. I think they are going to come through for us."

Starting with Sissy Farenthold's campaign, which pulled women together across the state, the caucus organized its troops, to the benefit of candidates like Sarah Weddington (whose husband had worked for Ms. Farenthold). Women who had never actively participated in partisan politics were drawn to the caucus, yet they moved right into the party structure once they learned the mechanics. They learned about precinct organizations, how to canvass a precinct and how to have an impact on precinct conventions. They appeared as delegates at senatorial district conventions and at the state party convention. With the caucus as their training ground they learned how to organize precincts, how to take over precincts, and how to take over precinct conventions, many of which, Ms. Cassidy said, caucus members were able to dominate. Most important, they discovered how vulnerable the party system really was, and how to conquer this system by mastering its mechanics.

Pat Schroeder also circumvented the party by organizing her own troops, many of whom were recruited from the local universities[8] and from what she called the "great reservoirs of dedicated, talented women who will really work for another woman." (The WPC was not as cohesive in Colorado at that time as it was in Texas.) As Ms. Schroeder tells it, she originally had no intention of running for office. Instead, she and her friends tried to get someone they felt was more representative of the district to run an issue-oriented campaign against the incumbent, whose record boasted a "hundred-percent rating from Bill Buckley."

"Everyone said they were not going to spend the money or the time, because they thought they couldn't win," she recalled. "Since I had been telling everyone else to run, they all turned around and said, 'Hey, you with the big mouth.' I kept all my jobs, and in November, when I had won, I was still teaching. . . . Jim and I ran the campaign from home. We had no campaign manager. We were outspent three to one. The guy bought every billboard in town. He bought all the radio and TV."

Pat Schroeder overtook her opponent with a strong well-developed grass-roots organization. The Schroeder talent pool consisted primarily of older retired women, as well as younger women—students and working women—many of whom were tapped from among her extensive professional contacts. Utilizing her contacts from the field of labor law, she was able to obtain organizational and financial support from several unions, while her teaching contacts in three local universities brought additional volunteers. The stronger the volunteer army, she emphasized, the greater the candidate's chances to put her "scarce dollars into essential items like printed materials and media time."[9]

Representative Elizabeth Holtzman, founder of the Brooklyn Women's Political Caucus, also saw women as the backbone of her organization. She knew what kind of help she could expect from the conservative, male-dominated Brooklyn Democratic organization—"I didn't ask for his support and didn't get it," she said of Meade Esposito, the powerful Brooklyn county leader whose support provides the lifeblood of practically every candidate from his domain, indeed to many candidates seeking city, state or national office as well. Neither did she ask for or receive the support of New York's liberal Mayor John Lindsay, her former boss; he had developed his own citywide organization but was apparently no more receptive to women candidates than the party.

Although individual women played large roles in her campaign, Ms. Holtzman received no help from the women's political movement, a surprise to her in view of her previous involvement with the caucus.

"Did Bella help you?"

"No."

"Shirley?"

"No."

"You're a real loner."

"Yup."

"Did any nationally known women come in?"

"No. The National Women's Political Caucus at the end was going to do a calvalcade," she said bitterly, "but I guess it was too much of a problem to get across the East River. We got very little support from the Women's Political Caucus because nobody thought it was a credible race. They thought there were more important races to support elsewhere. I can't quarrel with their judgment."

For their part the NWPC explained they had no control over where their members decided to work and admitted that the movement was still somewhat afflicted with a "star syndrome." "We got twenty to thirty people up there [New York]," said Jane McMichael, the new executive director of the NWPC. "On Saturday they worked for Bella and Shirley, and by Sunday there were very few people left. It is hard to get people to travel to campaign for candidates, especially since we're so understaffed ourselves."

3. *Training Political Troops*

Convinced that a volunteer army is the key to their success, women politicians have initiated training programs throughout the country, geared to professionalizing the activities of women in politics. "When I ran for mayor of Syracuse," recalled Karen De Crow, "I realized that I had been completely unschooled in the kinds of skills that people need to run for public office. These are skills that a lot of men get in business . . . public speaking, debating skills, the ability to handle the media without quaking in your boots, and the ability to handle a hostile situation." Then a thirty-one-year-old first-year law student, Ms. De Crow, as the Liberal candidate, faced two male opponents, both in their late forties and both incumbents, one a district attorney, the other a member of the City Council. The campaign lasted three months and cost Ms. De Crow her law-school scholarship. The dean of the law school, said Ms. De Crow, did not approve of students running for political office.

"I learned a million things," recalled Ms. De Crow, of her fifteen-hour days on the campaign trail. "I learned them under fire. But I had the feeling that women could be taught these things, not under fire, and then could use them to run for office." To help other women avoid some of the pitfalls she experienced, Ms. De Crow set up a nationwide series of courses called "Schools for Candidates." Although she teaches all the skills needed to run for office, her course stresses methods of handling the electronic and print media. Based on her own experience, Ms. De Crow strongly urges her students to learn to cope with a press that is "ninety-nine percent very hostile or teasing," a press that may regard their campaigns—as it did hers—as "funny." Within this environment she tries to teach women how to project their candidacies as serious, how to convert a silly question into a serious response. "They will try to make you look like an idiot," she warns her students, "especially if you are young, and especially if you are reasonably attractive." Using a videotape machine, she teaches techniques of handling the electronic media, so that women will learn the nitty-gritty skills—how to evaluate a two-minute spot, a thirty-second spot or a one-minute spot, to maximize the time allotted. Even minutiae—such as when to take a breath when being interviewed—can be significant, cautions Ms. De Crow: "If you are giving a statement and you pause after every sentence, they can splice the tape so you don't make any sense. If you take your breath in the middle of sentences, they can't splice the tape, so they have to put in your whole statement."

On a broader canvas Ms. De Crow encourages women to develop better ego tools, the strength and self-confidence to confront men on their own ground. On substantive issues, she warns, women still fail to assert themselves. "If a man says, 'Solid waste is the solution,' and it's not, women just aren't inclined to say, 'That's not true.' They have to learn how to confront men on substantive issues and disagree with them. There's nothing very mystical about all of this; it is part of a mind set, which can be changed and relearned to maximize women's future success in politics."

Nikki Beare, in addition to her consulting firm, has constructed a program called "Women in Politics," designed to train women interested in becoming legislators. Operating out of the local Women's Political Caucus, the program teaches women how to function in campaigns, with the goal of sending them out later in an organized way to run for office and to manage campaigns. As part of their training, they spend a week in Tallahassee as interns, learning all the ramifications of what being a legislator means:

how the committee system works and how to run for office. Ms. Beare's group also attempts to pay for those women who otherwise could not afford the transportation and other expenses entailed by the program. "We are trying to turn them [women] on in many ways to go into public office," said Ms. Beare.

So far, training programs have been successful but have failed to reach out to the whole community. In an attempt to mobilize women on a more systematic basis, a group known as the National Women's Education Fund was formed by Betsey Wright, former assistant to Sissy Farenthold, to help women collectively in all parts of the country. With seed money from contributors Stewart Mott and Heather Hess—as well as an unsolicited contribution from the Playboy Foundation[10]—the group plans three workshops for 1974, each to last three days, concentrating on congressional and state legislative races. They hope to expand to eight regional workshops by 1976, all of which will encompass elections on each level of government.

4. *Political Ecology*

Many advocates of womenpower argue that instead of running indiscriminately, women would be wise to concentrate their sparse resources on seats that are winnable. The Florida Women's Political Caucus, for example, plans to run a woman for every seat on the Miami Beach City Council except the mayor's, "because he is pretty strong and pretty good," according to Monna Lighte, one of the caucus' wealthiest and most active members. Is he a feminist? "Oh, no," replied Ms. Lighte, "but you have to recognize your power bloc, and nobody wants to spend money foolishly. Even a man who might run against another man could be foolish in doing so. Also in the caucus we have taken a very strong position for now that we are not going to run a woman just because she is a woman. There could be a perfectly great guy and a lousy woman." On the statewide level, added Nikki Beare, they plan to follow the same principle of not running a woman either against a very powerful figure or against a man who has been particularly sympathetic to women's issues. Neither would they ever run a woman against the attorney general, for example, who ran with the backing of the state's feminists in 1970 on the basis of his stand favoring abortion reform. "He has kept that vow," said Nikki Beare, "that he would be supportive of the repeal of the abortion laws. It hasn't happened, but he did everything he could to implement the law that did pass. He also appointed a woman in the attorney general's office as assistant administrator, and that has never been done before. She is the resource person whom people go to for women's issues and laws."

The real hope for equality lies in annexing the weak flanks: the rotten boroughs in the system, whose leaders remain in office propped up with barely marginal support. Bella Abzug's first Congressional campaign provides a striking example of this tactic, showing how a virtually unknown woman could wrest control from an undistinguished Congressman who had managed to stay in office despite his lack of support from the party's reform wing.

On lower levels as well, women are seizing political options of this kind. Encouraged by the women's movement, Ruth Harper challenged her local committeeman in Philadelphia and beat him handily. Much to the surprise of local Democrats, Ms. Harper led the district ticket with the highest number of votes, even though she ran for the lowest office. In a related coup she managed to pull another woman along on her coattails, the net result bringing two women into party office where before there had been two men.[11]

A tall and statuesque black woman who runs her own cosmetics firm and charm school, Ruth Harper turned to politics as a logical extension of her activities in the community and in her local Women's Political Caucus. On the basis of her experience in the community, she decided that the local committeemen were doing very little for their district, and even less for the party. At first the incumbents laughed off her challenge, as she and her running mate, May Hall, handed out their pamphlets throughout the community. The incumbents were so complacent they didn't even bother to campaign against the women. "They thought they could rest on their laurels," Ms. Harper recounted. "The man that we ran against said, 'I don't see how you two would win. The party did not endorse you.' They thought we didn't have a chance, and that when people were in the voting booths, they would pull the lever down for them and they would be back in. But they were disappointed."

Since her election, she claims she has brought renewed vigor to her office. "I have done more things in the neighborhood," she boasted. "The streets are cleaned better since I have been the committeewoman. I just call City Hall. The men just didn't bother. They just weren't interested." Even within the party, Ms. Harper claims to have been more zealous than her predecessors. "We registered 1,300 people," she said proudly. "The men didn't bother to go out and get people registered. We are definitely doing a better job." Ruth Harper was subsequently elected vice-ward leader, and encouraged by her success now aims for a seat on the City Council or in the state legislature.

One of her colleagues in Philadelphia, Dr. Ethel Allen, went the same route, beating a politically flabby incumbent before winning her City Council seat as a Republican in a district normally voting five-to-one Democratic. A Roman Catholic physician who bills herself as Philadelphia's fat Shirley Chisholm, Dr. Allen is fond of saying that the "only thing rarer than a black Republican is a White African elephant." Dr. Allen attributes her victory to heeding the advice of her mother, who cautioned her that anything worth saying could be said in two sentences. Succinctly put, Dr. Allen's speech read: "Whatever Mr. McIntyre [her opponent] has not done, I will do. And whatever he has done, I'll do better."

Most of those who agree with the theory of tackling only marginal incumbents join the rest of the movement in its policy of running candidates against representatives who have impeded the progress of women's issues. Doris Quinn, an active member of the caucus from Missouri, has announced her candidacy against the legislator in her state who has fought the ERA. Karen De Crow talked about her state caucus going over the voting records and margin of victory of each member of the New York State Assembly and Senate with an eye toward 1974. "If the guy has a lousy record on ERA, child care, abortion and so on, and also won by a narrow margin, we're going to get somebody to defeat him." she said. "Some of those seats are really winnable. What I'm really getting going for '74 is that this kind of careful analysis be made in every state to, in effect, take over the legislatures—or at least make a start at it."

Whether they tackle weak districts or strong, women have demonstrated to the party and to the community that they can master the skills necessary to win elections. Encouraged by the early returns, many plan future campaigns for higher office. "I just rode by the White House the other day," remarked a rather hard-nosed woman politician from New York with a gleam in her eye. Women now realize that taking the plunge into what at first seems like icy water is well worth their while, even if they lose initially. "Politics is like anything else," said Martha Griffiths. "You've got to be known. Very few people win the first time around . . . for anything."

The new breed of political woman does not consider election to the school board or to the state legislature her final resting place but aspires to higher office in the same way an ambitious man might view his career. With the thrust of her support coming from the women's movement or from an organization of her own creation, she cannot be claimed as a creature of the party and in her career development stands out as markedly different from her fellow party regulars. Indeed, she may often challenge the party on policies she considers unfair or dishonest without experiencing the kind of punishment and retribution inflicted on party mavericks in the past. Although Sarah Weddington bypassed the party machinery to become elected, the party did not isolate her in the legislature; in fact, as a sign of changing times, she even managed to get assignments on the committees she had requested.[12] She now makes an effort to attend all the party's functions, but since the party gave her no help in her campaign, it knows better than to make too many claims on her time or on her votes.

Unlike other candidates who owe their office to the party, many women enjoy the luxury of championing unpopular causes without being quashed as quickly as their more obligated colleagues. Gwen Cherry told of attempting to eliminate filing fees for Florida elections, a move regarded as heretical by both political parties, which rely on these fees for income. Their wrath failed to convince her to withdraw her bill; she felt strongly that these fees discriminated against poor candidates. She also argued at the credentials committee that the slate presented by her state's party organization was not representative of the people of the state of Florida. "They said, 'How could a good Democrat keep doing this?'" she recalled. "I have been putting some heat on them [the state organization] for some time as far as blacks and women are concerned. . . . Blacks and women have been shut out. Youths have been shut out, too. And a black youth that is female has really been shut out."

But few women who have succeeded in politics question the party system; they would rather work within its confines, where they know how much more effective they will ultimately be once they've mastered the established channels. "We're getting back to the old virtues of loyalty and service," concluded Representative Audrey Beck, a committed feminist and active party member who also organized a group of eight women in the Connecticut Assembly to work for women's issues. "You can't win on ideas alone. You've got to have a function in the party.[13] I realize that not everyone is as ideological as I am. People have to realize that I'm working hard for reelection and for the party."

Evaluating the effect of running women and supporting them through the caucus, Nikki Beare summed up what she felt would be the impact of the women's political movement in the next few years: "In the next four or five years, the Women's Caucus is going to be one of the nation's most powerful organizations. Much more so than the NAACP. It's going to be powerful because power is election, and many of our NOW members and our caucus members will be elected. They will be powerful in terms of being there and making something happen. Their voice will be heard because they pushed that button. And that's where it's at. Pushing that button."

Chapter VIII

Making Policy, Not Coffee: Women and Clout in Kevin White's Administration

Move more into what men are doing. Don't settle for women's activities and women's things. . . . Any woman who wanted to could come over and take over a precinct, just like that and we would welcome her.

> —JOIE PREVOST, dispenser of
> patronage at Boston's
> City Hall

The women I've hired are good administrators. They are disciplined . . . they are competitive without being abrasive. . . . Women are less prone to get involved in the pettiness of politics—because they don't have that tendency to "hang" with the boys at night and carry on personality conflicts.

> —MAYOR KEVIN WHITE
> of Boston

City Hall is the government closest to the people, most sensitive to criticism, most visible and vulnerable. Nevertheless, most city governments continue to display a general indifference to women in politics, responding to pressures by appointing only a few highly visible women, or in some cases, none at all. The leaders of local block associations, for example, were the highest-ranking women politicians Newark's Mayor Kenneth Gibson could think of, when asked to name influential women in city government.

Several other mayors have attempted to promote women despite their claim of low political payoff from such appointments. In San Francisco Mayor Joseph Alioto acknowledged, "There is an unconscious prejudice against women"; nonetheless, he appointed a woman as director of the Port of San Francisco and vowed to appoint a woman police commissioner. Mayor Peter Flaherty of Pittsburgh appointed one woman among nine commissioners—Amy Bollinger, commissioner of labor—and he emphasized that she was "not a woman's-group appointee but rather an appointee of organized labor."

The brightest spot for women in city government appears in the unlikeliest of places, the "Last Hurrah," "Irish Mafia," Roman Catholic city of Boston, by reputation one of the most chauvinistic cultures in the country. There Kevin White, pursued by Louise Day Hicks, has, by instinct as well as conviction, appointed women to some of the most powerful governmental posts. Like political operatives in other governments, these women are expected to spend their evenings performing such mundane political duties as attending political dinners, organizing rallies, and tooling up political machines.

When a job seeker at Boston's City Hall asks, "Where's Joey? I want to see him. He's a good friend of mine," he is automatically suspect, because Joie—the patronage dispenser—is Joanna Prevost, the city's director of personnel, in charge of filling hundreds of job openings in all city agencies. In Kevin White's administration she is one of a small group of women who have been appointed to top-level positions, jobs with more power and influence than any other group of women has been known to hold anywhere else in the country. "Any male will tell you they're influential," said White proudly. Barbara Cameron, a former law partner of the mayor's, oversees the letting of all city contracts. Ann Lewis serves as one of the mayor's key aides, now specializing in his relationships with the state and national legislatures. Katherine Kane, a former state legislator, holds the directorship of the Office of the Bicentennial. And Geri Pleshaw, who has been active in both the women's political movement and in local politics, serves as a special assistant to the mayor.

"I have been in this job for five years, ever since Kevin White has been mayor," said Joanna Prevost, a former beauty queen (Miss Boston) and political organizer. Her appointment as patronage director dated back to well before the women's liberation movement, proof, she said, that White was acting not in response to pressure politics, but from an honest desire to give women a chance in government: "It was just that he felt I could do the job and he gave me the opportunity to see whether or not I could do it. . . . Most males have only lasted two years in this job, and I have been here five. . . . Now he says that I think I am the mayor. If somebody says, 'Does Joie know about it?' he says, 'Who's the mayor around here?' He gets a big kick out of it really. And it has worked out tremendously well."

To his credit, White broke with tradition in order to give women the chance to prove themselves in his administration, and in so doing was careful to choose women who were capable of sustaining their power, who could meet head on the interference White knew they would encounter. For many skeptics greeted White's innovations without enthusiasm, arching their eyebrows after learning of his appointment of a woman patronage director. To traditional-minded Boston politicians, the post of patronage director called most emphatically for a male, preferably cigar-smoking and poker-playing, someone willing to conduct his business in the shadows of political life. A women in this job produced nothing less than culture shock among many of White's colleagues. "I don't think you get any credit for bringing them [women] in," said White of his political confreres. "I don't think you get any loss, though. The only loss you get is parochial politics and I can take care of that. I have grown up in it, and you've got to pull that along. I have been pulling it along in this town for a long time."

Pulling in her own direction, Joie Prevost soon learned how hard she had to struggle to maintain her power, an effort, she says, that never ends for a woman holding this particular job—and an effort that marks the major difference between her performance in this post and a man's. She is forced to prove herself over and over again, each time a new commissioner enters the administration, whereas a man could sooner rest on his reputation. "Every bit of power that I now have—and I am said to have power—was fought for," she said. "And even now, every time a department head is changed and a new commissioner comes in, the power struggle begins once more. A department head naturally wants to run a department as he or she sees it. They don't want anybody interfering, and generally men, most men, aren't used to dealing with women in authority, and may resent it. And they don't know me from East Oshkosh. I pick up the phone and I say, 'Now, you have three assistant commissioners that are going to become available. And I have three candidates I would like you to interview. . . . I never say, 'These are the candidates you must take.' That's not the approach. The approach is this: When a vacancy occurs, particularly in non-civil-service departments, the department head must call me and give me the opening so that I can begin to send candidates. Now, you can say eighty percent of the time they take the candidates. But if they call me back and say, 'No, this isn't what I'm looking for, would you send someone else?' then I will send someone else. I don't run a ship where I cram someone down their throat."

Patronage is so highly centralized in Boston that Ms. Prevost enjoys substantially more power than most of her counterparts holding the title of personnel director in other cities.[1] If a commissioner wants to appoint his own candidate, he must send the candidate first to the personnel office to be screened and judged against the candidates Ms. Prevost has submitted. A conflict over a recent opening at the Youth Activities Commission illustrated the personnel director's control over other city officials in the area of hiring. The commission presented a candidate of its own to compete against two candidates sponsored by Ms. Prevost. "All right," she told them, "I'll be glad to see your candidate. But I want you to see mine." If she felt they had already prejudged the situation, in favoring their candidate over hers, she would say, "You're taking one of mine." Although department heads are allowed some leeway in the area of appointments within this system, Ms. Prevost's power ultimately prevails.

When disputes come to a head, as some are bound to do, added Ms. Prevost, the mayor is quick to support her position. "The mayor allows me to run my own ship," she said gratefully. "He really doesn't interfere. I don't think I have been to him three or four times with problems in the whole time I have been here. When it has come to a showdown, I am pretty darn sure I am right before I go in, because I don't enjoy being wrong. . . . And he has backed me up on each case."

The mayor, she continued, always backed her up without humiliating the department head, subtly persuading him to accept her in terms compatible with the department head's mental set. Mayor White understood the difficulties involved, she explained, and preferred a more evolutionary approach in educating men about women in policy-making roles.

"Once I was having a running battle with one commissioner who just wanted to hire everybody himself," she recalled, illustrating White's technique. After the feud had progressed for a while, White summoned the department head into his office and pleaded: "Look, do me a favor. Joie is a personal friend of mine. She golfs with my wife. I don't want to have to hear from my wife, and you know you can't win with women. So will you get along with her?" According to Joie Prevost, the commissioner threw back his head and laughed, and since then they have been the best of friends, never encountering another day's trouble.

Nothing could have been farther from the truth, however, than the mayor's story. Ms. Prevost explained that although she and the mayor's wife were friends, they were hardly golfing partners; besides which, "Kathryn White would never have interfered in a million years. In other words," she continued, "Kevin kind of fabricated that story to try to present it to this guy in such a way that he could accept it. . . . And it worked. It worked very well." It worked very well for White, too, since insubordination to Ms. Prevost threatens his own authority as well.

In Boston the job of personnel director combines political with administrative tasks, and refreshingly Ms. Prevost makes no bones about that fact. "I am the person that gets called at three o'clock in the afternoon and told to have four hundred people present the next day," she said. "And I have four hundred people present the next day," no doubt recruited from the hundreds of grateful recipients of city jobs. She also gives speeches for the mayor at political functions, campaigns for him, and conducts a wide variety of additional political activities. "Last night I entertained the Greek consul," she said by way of explanation. "I represent the mayor at all Greek affairs. I make all my speeches in Greek, and I am really enjoying it."

Ms. Prevost's background in politics provided the training ground for her current political roles. The first female president of the Greater Boston Young Democrats, she was successful in increasing the club's membership from 75 members to 1,000 in less than a year's time. She campaigned for Kevin White, worked for Endicott Peabody when he was governor, and was lauded in *Mademoiselle* magazine as the "Most Active Young Girl in Massachusetts Politics in the early 1960's."

Although she started out as a model, Joie Prevost quickly recognized her own talents for group organization. Like the other women around Mayor White, she made the decision early in her career not to get involved exclusively with women's groups, a calculation highly instrumental in determining her future success in politics. Ms. Prevost and her colleagues reached this decision independently, but they all shared the common experience of having worked with both sexes by actively participating in party politics. Getting accustomed to professional contact with men as well as with women, they all agreed, left them better prepared for the political roles they now occupy. "I don't deal in women's activities," stressed Ms. Prevost. "Frankly, there is nothing more nauseating to me than those little afternoon teas with women—it is just not my cup of tea. I like mixed company. I like women and I like men, and my activities center more around men than women."

In the long run there are advantages to being a woman in a patronage office, concludes Ms. Prevost, who feels that men suffer more abuse in her job. "Although I have been abused from time to time, I'm sure the abuse has been cut down because I am a woman." When she does get abused, she knows she can handle the situation with dispatch. "I had a man push me once," she recalled with a wide smile. "He was a shrimp and I am so tall," it was really no contest. Luckily for Ms. Prevost, most dissatisfied job seekers do not resort to physical violence. There were some, she recalled, who have fainted in her office, made threatening phone calls, sent ominous letters, and used vile language. Those who angered her most, though, were the ones who tried to influence her through flattery, unaware that a former beauty queen's head is not easily turned by this tactic. "In the beginning, I was 'dearie' and 'sweetie' and 'aren't-you-gorgeous.' 'She can be conned easily, so let's tell her all the nice things we can think of to tell her and we can get anything we want' was the feeling everyone had. Well, I think they soon found out that I cared too much about the city and much too much about Kevin White and probably myself and the job I was going to do. So that ended. The wooing, five years later, has totally stopped. They still might say, 'If I could have a woman like you working for me'—that kind of thing. But the flattery—what I considered phony flattery—that stopped."

Life as a beauty queen turns out to be an ideal background for career women politicians.[2] Former beauty queens have already experienced careers in which recognition and adulation are commonplace, giving them a self-sufficiency of ego not enjoyed by other politicians, particularly women, many of whom must overcome great insecurity before entering and succeeding in politics. They are also the beneficiaries of a telegenic age, in which their appearance is yet another advantage in the scramble for recognition.

The press called Ms. Prevost the Mayor's Czarina, the Dragon Lady, the High Priestess of Patronage; even the mayor himself called her Madame DeFarge. She laughs good-naturedly at all this, however, whether or not it is directed at her in fun. "If I can maintain sanity in this job five years later, it is only because I have been able to maintain some sense of humor," she explained, boasting that her office has always enjoyed good publicity, and there has never been a scandal while she headed it. This is an impressive record in view of the fact that in one year's time she processed and hired almost 1,500 employees: 800 in the Emergency Employment Act, plus 500 to 600 others in regular city jobs,[3] including all summer positions. She also developed and directed a senior aides program, in which older people were employed for four hours a day, five days a week in jobs providing services for other senior citizens.

As if to counter any negative impressions of patronage, Joie

Prevost described how she maintained her office's professionalism at the same time she met the mayor's political obligations. "Now, I do conduct a recruitment effort. I do have professional résumés. I do give tests for secretarial positions and so forth. Patronage today isn't just sticking an unqualified person in a job. It is sticking a qualified person in a job, someone perhaps you owe something to, but the cronyism is gone. It is not enough to be political. You must both be political and do a good job. If you can't do both, then we love you dearly and will help you get work elsewhere, but there is nothing for you in the city."

Maintaining power in such a highly centralized patronage system rests on Ms. Prevost's ability to establish hegemony over her staff and over the nebulous elites in the party, whose patronage needs must be satisfied. In overseeing the hiring for the entire city she maintains an elaborate intelligence network, whose intricacies she must master. "I have records of everything that exists, every personnel action that transpires in the city. We don't allow independent hiring in the departments. It is a good thing to do it this way because the departments get the benefit of getting the best person for the job. I know the places to send people. I know every job."

Her intelligence capacity extends also to ideological factors, knowing where to place people to avoid conflict. "I know whether the first-line supervisor is a bigot or whether he is a liberal. I know whether they want a woman or a man. Most of it is here," she continued, tapping her head, "because I have just got to know the people and the situations that exist."

Her power extends into the party organization, where she influences appointments. "A position became available recently," she recalled, "which hasn't yet been filled. It was an opening for Democratic state committeeman, because the senator is going to be named as a judge." Suddenly the people involved in making the choice began calling Ms. Prevost, to consult her about the final choice. "The biggest people involved in the system were calling saying, 'Please, can we go out to dinner? Can we talk about it?' figuring that I was the one to call the shot on it. They were really wooing me. The calls were made to me, and cleared and checked with me. . . . What I am saying is that I have not only a role here [in Kevin White's administration] but a role in the party and a voice in the party and certainly an awareness by the people who are involved in this that we are going to have a great deal to say."

Another political operative who wields considerable clout in Boston's City Hall is Ann Lewis, the mayor's special assistant in charge of legislative relations. She meets weekly with department heads to talk about what's coming up on the legislative calendar and who is going to represent the city's position. In contrast to the city's two lobbyists who work out of the State House at more traditional lobbying activities—building relationships with legislators, doing personal favors for them and the like—Ann Lewis coordinates their activities with the city's, and attempts to translate these efforts into substantive terms. On one day, for example, Ms. Lewis set up a luncheon meeting with the mayor and key members of the legislature's transportation and budget committees. Over sandwiches and coffee in the plush, paneled conference room at the new City Hall, Mayor White eloquently presented his case for increasing the city's taxable property along its coastline. A feminist and active member of the National Women's Political Caucus, Ms. Lewis took pains to include a newly elected state legislator, a bright young attorney from Newton, Lois Pines, recently elected to office on a feminist platform.

Like Joie Prevost and her other colleagues, Ann Lewis asserts the intensely political nature of her job, openly detailing the realities of the relationship between political and administrative functions. Having campaigned for Mayor White in the past, she now maintains contact with Democrats throughout the country, including those on the National Committee. She also wields some job patronage, finding jobs for people with whom she deals—a task considerably expedited by her friendship with Joie Prevost.

Ann Lewis also handles the mayor's involvement with state legislative elections, to ensure that the maximum number of people elected will be sympathetic to the mayor. She offered an example: "There is a special Senate election in East Boston coming up. Do we have a candidate? . . . My argument is if we do not at this point have a strong candidate, I need that vote in the House more than I do in the Senate. It is to our interest, therefore, if we are neutral on the candidacy, to delay the special election. He [White] got a commitment from the president of the Senate and he tells me we can do that—hold the election later in the year. That gives us time to use the votes in the House."

To enlist more cooperation in the House, she continued, she would then proceed to maximize the interim period by playing competing forces off against each other. In this particular election two candidates interested in running for the Senate surfaced from the lower House, each of whom would benefit considerably from the mayor's support and endorsement. "We can call them both in," continued Ms. Lewis, "and say, 'Hey, the election is not until September. We are going to watch what you do in July.'"

Ann Lewis navigates yet another course in her role as political-intelligence operative: keeping buoyant egos afloat in a sea of detail. She keeps the lines of communication open and nurtures an ongoing relationship with the top members of the Democratic National Committee: "I call to ask them to tell Chairman Strauss that Joe Mahoney was in the hospital. I talk to a friend of mine who works in the chairman's office and I say, "You ought to send him something.'" The national committee informs her, in turn, that one of the Massachusetts national committeewomen is about to be appointed to a commission, and would Ms. Lewis please clear it with the mayor. On the local level she offered the example that she might "suggest to the mayor that he tell a certain representative who has been friendly toward us that he did a nice job on a certain bill, so that he felt he had been adequately appreciated." She also participated in the Congressional campaigns of Representative Thomas P. "Tip" O'Neill, the Majority Leader, and Joe Moakley, the newly elected Representative from Boston's 9th Congressional District. "Tip is the best friend we've got in Washington, and we need all the friends we can get. He has been very good to the city. It is important that we take part in something that is important to him." On the state level, too, Ann Lewis has advocated vigorous participation, and herself acted as voter-registration director for the state during the McGovern campaign. "I think it is important for the mayor to be involved in politics at all levels. Therefore, I went in and worked in the presidential campaign on voter registration. We did fairly well."

The official who clears all city contracts is also a woman, Barbara Cameron by name, the only woman in the country in this unique position of political power. Although the mayor is required by law to sign all contracts, they clear through Ms. Cameron first, giving her enormous discretionary power to decide which contracts go through and which do not. "I don't have the time to digest that much," explained the mayor as he outlined the scope of her power. "Barbara, I trust implicitly, I trust her loyalty. Her loyalty is unquestioned."

Unlike the other women, enthusiastic about spreading the message of women's role in White's administration, Barbara Cameron declined to be interviewed, offering no explanation for her refusal. "It's shyness, believe it or not," said White. "I don't think she meant to be rude. She didn't want to do it, and I respect that. I said if she was uptight about it, forget it. I have a few people around here who are genuinely reticent and shy. They have never given interviews."

Others around City Hall explained her reluctance differently. Said one, "Barbara is really tops, and able and capable and has no problems with just being Barbara Cameron. Which is why she just doesn't want to be involved in being interviewed as a woman"—a common response from many successful women, reluctant to be identified with other women's struggle for equality.

White seemed genuinely taken by surprise talking about the women in his administration; he is at a loss at first to explain why he alone among the nation's mayors has given women roles of substance and power in his administration. A thoughtful, progressive and articulate man, White's efforts on women's behalf seemed motivated by a genuine appreciation of their talents, and not from a desire to win women's votes. If this were the case, these women would have been assigned to more visible offices, and one or two appointments would have served the purpose. Do White's women administrators defuse the supporters of Louise Day Hicks (his opponent in the last mayoralty campaign)? Most definitely not, argued White, who reasoned that women voting for Louise Day Hicks were attracted by her stance on the school busing issue, and not by any feminist feelings on their part.

Prefacing his reflections on women in power with the disclaimer that he lacked "canned answers" on the subject, Mayor White outlined what he considered the unique advantages resulting from his own experience in hiring and promoting women into positions of such immense political responsibility. The quality shared by all his women appointees that sprang immediately to mind, said White, was a loyalty to him that was superior, on balance, to that of the men who had worked for him. "Surprisingly enough," said White, "women are less prone to get involved in the pettiness of politics—because they don't have that tendency to 'hang' with the boys at night and carry on personality conflicts. They are so absorbed in their jobs that I never really worry about them being caught up in anything besides their loyalty to me or their philosophical commitment to what they are doing." Loyalty to him, added White, should not be interpreted as subservience. "We argue for long hours, and they all hold tenaciously to their own points of view."

Certain of their loyalty, White feels secure enough to allow his women aides to work for other candidates' campaigns on the state and national levels: Katherine Kane worked for McGovern; Joie Prevost for Muskie; and Ann Lewis for Muskie and McGovern. Well known for national aspirations of his own, White also knew his workers would promote his interests wherever they worked and that their activities would enhance and expand his personal political base beyond the confines of Boston city politics.

Is the fact that these women have proved less ambitious than men in terms of running for office themselves the real reason they are more loyal to White than men in comparable positions have proved to be? Are they less prone to plot against White and go off and run for mayor themselves? That's a good question, replied White, and one he hadn't thought of in that light before. All would make superior candidates in their own right; and perhaps after White progresses to the next stage of his political career, some will run for office themselves.

Demolishing yet another stereotype, Mayor White hypothesized that in certain ways he found women more competitive than men. "I think you find that they are trying harder because of this position," he conjectured. "They're competitive without being abrasive. You get some good talent. The women I've hired are good administrators. They are disciplined. . . . Politics is a profession that breeds comradeship, camaraderie. The girls are industrious. There isn't a sense of that with them.

"Again, it is discipline," he continued. "I think that a woman has . . . a tendency to keep her eye on the issue or the ball or the question and keep it moving. Seldom are they distracted. Now, I suppose if we had a room full of women, we would all get distracted. But they are not in a room, and they do not get distracted from the issues." As his face crinkled into a broad smile, White specified that none of these attributes applied to his wife, "who I wouldn't hire for two minutes, yet she is the only one I would ever want to be married to."

According to Ann Lewis, one of the reasons Mayor White enjoys such wide latitude regarding women in his administration rests with the unique personality of his wife: "Kathryn White is superb. She is the best political wife I have ever seen. She does anything you ask her to do, and she does it very well, and when the campaign is over, she just walks away from it. Campaign wives tend—if they were that good in the campaign—to want to help govern. She is interested in doing more traditional things."

In spite of their progress in his administration there are limits to the power White has given women. By his own admission he affirmed that women had never occupied high positions in his campaign organization. "I never found a woman to run my campaign," he said candidly, "but I wouldn't be averse to it if I found the talent." Joie Prevost, according to one of her colleagues, has attempted at various times to take more of an active part in White's campaigns but has not as yet succeeded in entering his inner circle of campaign advisers. In his multiple roles White presides over several concentric inner circles, one of which—his highly personal and political circle—has never been penetrated by women. Some of the women interviewed referred, though without bitterness, to their exclusion from this group. Perhaps those very qualities of anticronyism and loyalty, valued so highly by White, clash with the other prerequisites of political success, namely, group identification and cohesion.

As a political figure who prides himself on being progressive, White revels in the knowledge that he has reversed some long-standing political traditions. When another mayor succeeds him, he theorized, "He may get rid of Joie, but it will not be beyond the realm of possibility that he will staff a woman in that job or in one related to it, if he finds someone good. He might not have done it if I hadn't."

White also considered appointing women to commissionerships traditionally held by men, and talked seriously of a woman as traffic commissioner. Recruiting women for consumer affairs posts lacked imagination, he reflected; the practice had become old hat at this point. "Lindsay put Bess Meyerson in consumer affairs. I wasn't going to do that. I thought one place a woman might fit, believe it or not, was in the Traffic Commission. That is a job that needs a person with a sense of public relations. Most of these jobs do not demand expertise. They demand a capacity to administer and a good mind."

In spite of his own enlightenment on women in government White thought San Francisco Mayor Joseph Alioto's idea of appointing a woman police commissioner was beyond the art of the possible. "Police is a process of education," he argued. "You can go too far. But I don't say that twenty years from now that is either a laughable or inconceivable idea. The difference is that these girls [White's aides] have my power, and they can use it more effectively because it comes directly from me, and I support it and I buttress it. The police commissioner is off by himself."

White analyzed his own unusual feelings about professional women in terms of the strong influence exerted on him by his mother. "My own mother," he reminisced, "was not a political woman, but she understood politics. She convinced me a long time ago, long before this lib thing came along, subtly and intellectually, that women are as strong as men, mentally and physically. Sometimes I think that they can more than compete with them. Maybe it isn't so much my liberalism as it is the quality of the people. I think people like Kathy and Joie are good. Joie is hard and tough without being unfair." Added White, "The only thing I feared for them was that they might lose the feminine quality, and they have not done that. There are distinctions between men and women and I value those distinctions. Remember, I grew up in the fifties."

The women in White's administration share characteristics that set them apart from less political women. To the outsider the most striking of these is their readiness to submerge themselves totally in their political careers, often at the expense of their personal lives. They experience the same conflicts with which other career women grapple, but when the coin is tossed, it comes down firmly on the professional side. Joie Prevost, for example, who is unmarried, has the edge on her colleagues in terms of mobility. "Married women don't have the dedication to time," concluded Ms. Prevost. "They can't. They have children, husbands. They have to be home in the evenings. It does hamper them. I am here in the evenings." Nonetheless, it is still difficult for Ms. Prevost, who says she is often conflicted, especially when forced to choose between spending her evenings with her boyfriend or at a political function. He is also in politics, she explained, but unlike her, he is "a political introvert, who doesn't enjoy going to things particularly." This forces Ms. Prevost, by her own admission a "political extrovert," into choosing whether to suppress her professional ambitions or to continue to conduct her professional life in her accustomed style. Somehow, she reflected, she has managed to retain her own identity, while managing to keep her personal life intact, even though it meant spending some evenings without male company. "Tonight, for example," she said wistfully, "is a time when he could be coming along and he just out and out refused to. There are a lot of female things that I sacrifice to do this. . . . Sometimes the transition of roles is very difficult. To be King Kong's mother all day long, and then become female again in the evening. That becomes a problem —switching roles."

The other women with families also sacrifice a great deal for their political careers. Ann Lewis, a divorcée with three children, has opted to give up some measure of home life as the price for a stimulating political career. "I know I'm not home very much," she said, "but the thing I like to do best is demanding." Nevertheless, Ann Lewis has managed, in her characteristically efficient way, to compensate by involving her children in her political life. Susan Jane, her ten-year-old, distinguished herself in school as "the only kid who brought up the Supreme Court decision on abortion and the mayor's fight with the City Council in current events.

"These are the things they understand," said Ms. Lewis. "They go to rallies, they can go to meetings." Another daughter, Patty, age fifteen, has worked on campaigns during the summer and would have been promoted volunteer coordinator had not her mother stepped in and said no, on the grounds that she wasn't yet ready for that role. Her third daughter, Beth, age thirteen, is not at all enthusiastic about politics, she laughed, and "thinks it's like having a mother who's in the roller derby. She treats me as though it was sort of a childish thing. She tells me that I don't get enough sleep or enough to eat and sort of pats me on the head and says, 'Did you have a good time?' But she really doesn't take it very seriously."

Ann Lewis laughs when she describes how her children help her keep things in perspective. On the way home from the airport one night, returning from meetings with party leaders in Washington, she stopped at a pet store to pick up her daughter's pet snake. As she rode home in the taxi, with the snake curled up in its box on the seat beside her and the day's events still fresh in her mind, the contrast brought her quickly back to reality.

All of these women take this kind of life-style for granted, aware that in order to be taken seriously, they must work harder, try harder, and subject their personal lives to the schedules to which men in politics have always adhered without complaint. Geri Pleshaw, a special aide to Mayor White, recalled campaigning in the governor's race right before her first child was born. "I remember the campaign manager giving me a list of people to call and he said, 'When are you due to go to the hospital?' And I said, 'In two weeks.' And he said, 'Make sure you get those calls made before you go.' . . . When the baby was a few months old, I was right back in the campaign."

In order to drive their own wedge into the locker room, the women in Mayor White's administration have developed an ability to cope directly with difficult situations. Ann Lewis talked about the periodic external pressures created by the locker-room atmosphere of politics, pressures that create more problems in Boston, where sexual attitudes are more conservative. She recalled attending a political meeting, seated behind a man who, not seeing her, exploded, "I don't know what we are going to do about that fucking thing." And he turned around and said, "Jesus Christ, Ann, I forgot you were in the room." He was so shocked, Ms. Lewis said, that he "literally rose up out of the couch." Later on that evening, when he apologized to her again, she decided to tackle the situation. "You know," she told him, gently, "I know all those words. I'm going to say them all at once now and break the taboo once and for all."

One conviction shared by the women who work for Kevin White is that the political system is open to women who, like themselves, are willing to work hard. They grant it is much harder for a woman to break into the system, but they argue this is more than compensated for by the large group of talented women in society, many of whom could fill roles similar to theirs if they were willing to take the proper routes to political power.

"Move more into what the men are doing," Joie Prevost urges women. "Don't settle for women's activities and women's things." She grew very angry as she described how she and her colleagues, recently combing some list to evaluate their best precinct captains, suddenly realized there weren't more than a handful who were women. "Now any woman who wanted to could come over and take over a precinct, just like that, and we would welcome her," stressed Ms. Prevost. "I think women are really missing the boat because politics is one of the most exciting careers a woman could choose. I think men, too, miss the boat by not giving more women an opportunity to serve in this type capacity. It has worked out awfully well in Boston, and Boston is a very, very political town, very much so."

Ann Lewis agreed that there were no obstacles to women running precincts, although she felt that as women rose higher, more obstacles arose. "It is very difficult to be taken seriously as a woman," she said. "In fact there is no question, and we deceive ourselves if we think differently. We have to work harder. Men are much less likely to accept a woman, but once you have done it, then the fact that you are a woman doesn't really matter. You have broken through and you have the professional credentials."

All of these women possess the right credentials, which they have developed into political success. Backed by the mayor and by their own belief in themselves, they are now able to negotiate on an equal basis with the male-dominated political machine and with other city administrators. And most important, they are exercising real political power—the power over jobs, intelligence, communications, and contracts—not figurehead posts or phony arts-and-letters or garden-club appointments, an opportunity few political leaders have given women.

Chapter IX

Femopolitics: Women's Liberation and the 53 Percent

There was no hostility to the fact that I was a woman. I remember truck drivers leaning out of their trucks and saying, "I think it's great . . . it's fantastic that a woman is running." . . . I found mothers taking their daughters up to meet me. . . . They wanted their daughters to have a different conception of the possibilities for them.

—Representative
Elizabeth Holtzman

The majority of women today tend to look to other women to represent their sex in political offices. . . . There appears to be a large untapped source of available "women power" that political candidates are neglecting in their campaigns.

—The 1972 Virginia Slims American Women's Opinion Poll, conducted by Louis Harris and associates

Feminism and Successful Politics

"As she wheeled her flatbed truck around the giant Jim Bridger power-plant construction site in southwestern Wyoming, twenty-two-year-old Debbie Vase of Rock Springs let out a scornful laugh at the mention of women's liberation.

"She is one of about twenty women among the 2,600 workers

employed on the project. A member of the Teamsters Union, she is qualified to drive anything from a semi-trailer rig to a pickup truck and has done a lot of cement-truck driving. She has been driving . . . at the Bridger site for almost a year and really sees nothing out of the ordinary in what she is doing.

"'I don't need women's lib to get a job,' she said confidently. 'All that stuff is just a little too much. There are other gals out here. One is even a labor foreman. It's not that hard.'"[1]

Ms. Vase is typical of many women who have broken into previously all-male professions who feel that they owe nothing to the women's movement. Not only does she fail to credit the women's movement for its role in advancing her professional status and earning power, but she ridicules it as well, almost as if in her anxiety to integrate into the male world, she wholeheartedly adopts its value system as well. These women are like the assimilated children of first-generation Americans who are slightly ashamed of their parentage. "I'm not one of those women's libbers" is heard as often from stevedores as from company presidents, whom Caroline Bird describes so acidly as the "Loophole Women,"[2] women who have managed to achieve top positions, yet negate the pervasive problems of discrimination that preclude many of their sisters from enjoying the same success.[3] Others refer to this attitude as the "Queen Bee" syndrome.

In the light of all this media-reinforced self-hatred, it is all the more remarkable that so many successful women in politics have remained so outspoken in their identification with feminism. "For some reason 'women's lib' is a real snarl word, while 'women's rights' is a real purr word," laments Representative Pat Schroeder, a candidate who stood firmly behind "women's lib," while she attempted to educate the public about its real meaning.

"Women ask, 'Are you one of those women's libbers?' I say, "Will you tell me what that means? Does it mean equal pay for equal work? Does it mean giving women the opportunity of choice within their profession?' I finally get a grudging acceptance from them. I can't understand what there is about the feminist movement that has produced this reaction. Every part of the movement—equal pay, etc.—they're in agreement with."

Most women now running for office share Pat Schroeder's view and identify to some degree with the women's movement. Finding the public responsive, they include feminist planks in their platforms and offer their experience in women's causes and in women's groups as background for public service. Most women in the Maryland legislature, for example, had worked for the League of Women Voters. Before running for office, Gwen Cherry, the Florida state legislator, had served as legal counsel to NOW, litigating many sex-discrimination cases for them in the Miami area. In one of her more well-known but unsuccessful cases she challenged National Airlines' "Fly Me" ads, in which stewardesses with aircraft named after them tantalized the public with the flagrantly sexual suggestion, "I'm Sandra, Fly Me to Miami."

Defying the conventional wisdom, many candidates have emerged victorious from campaigns with distinct feminist appeals. Elaine Gordon won an assembly seat in Hallandale, Florida, an area with many senior citizens of Jewish and Catholic background, while staunchly defending feminism and her background in the women's rights movement throughout her campaign. "When the older women and older men would confront me . . . and ask me how I stood on women's lib, I said, 'I am a leader in the women's liberation movement.' They would say, 'How do you stand on the Equal Rights Amendment?' and I said, 'I supported it.' Their response was, 'Great.' Men and women alike would say, 'What we need is another woman up there. I'm so proud we can get behind a woman like you.'"

Many other candidates with distinct feminist inclinations also found their elections unaffected regardless of region, by the pejorative connotations of "women's lib." To name a few: Barbara Mikulski, Baltimore; Sarah Weddington, Texas; Pat Schroeder, Colorado; and Bella Abzug, New York.

Despite their early successes, women candidates embracing feminism are careful to include other issues in their campaign packages. Sarah Weddington campaigned on a wide range of issues including consumer affairs, public employees benefits, public education, good government and ecology. She says she did not stress abortion reform as her single most important issue but generally mentioned it in her speeches and did not back away from the issue when questioners confronted her with it. By not emphasizing the issue, she managed to defuse a rather formidable group of opponents from the antiabortion forces, who did not realize who she was until nearly the end of her campaign. At that point, she recalled, there was an attempt to organize an opposition based on that issue, but it was generated too late to endanger her campaign.

Few predicted how successful Bella Abzug would be as a candidate from the most extreme end of the feminist political spectrum; indeed, feminism provided Ms. Abzug with a substantial political base and added a crucial dimension to her candidacy. "I'm a leader of the women's movement," she reminds her constituents at campaign time. "I'm a leader of the abortion movement and I reflect it in the political arena more than any other woman in politics. I have a national abortion-rights bill. I fought for child care. . . . I projected the only bills that have been projected on changing the credit laws to provide for equal treatment for women. . . . I projected the Women's Equality Day, which finally passed both houses, although it didn't carry my name." Even in New York, where the women's movement is badly split, Ms. Abzug's feminism paid political dividends, as women of all ages came to her aid to work for her in her second Congressional race.

But not all women politicians felt as secure with women's liberation as Elaine Gordon, Pat Schroeder, or Bella Abzug; many found themselves in the untenable position of fighting for women's rights while disclaiming too close an identity with "women's lib." Some women candidates seemed almost afraid to reeducate the public about the real meaning of women's liberation, to the dismay of Gloria Steinem, who reflected on recent electoral victories: "The women played up the issues," she said, "but they did not all feel able to say 'women's liberation.' . . . Many set out on purpose to deodorize—to make accurate—the term. They would not—when they got the inevitable 'you're not one of those women's libbers'—argue: 'Yes, I am.'" Martha McKay of North Carolina, for example, claimed credit for eliminating the expression "women's lib" from her own political environment, convincing the press and her fellow politicians to discontinue their widespread use of the phrase.

In close touch themselves with public opinion, women politicians fear the electoral consequences of the public's divided image of women's liberation. They know that to many voters "women's lib" spells disruption: disruption in courtship patterns, in family life, in employment, in dress, and in an infinite number of treasured American folkways. The newest product of a media age, the women's movement has both benefited and suffered from a communications apparatus that has dwelled on its most dramatic features while neglecting goals more acceptable to the general public.

Nevertheless, women candidates and women activists have made great strides in communicating the real meaning of the women's movement to the public; projecting women's liberation as a movement for equality between the sexes within a framework of basic humanist goals.

Other women, still uncertain of the effect of the movement on their careers, stop short of militant feminism even though their sympathies lie in that direction. Shirley Chisholm, for example, has always been outspoken on women's issues and on the sexism she has confronted in her own career, yet she specifically rejected a solely feminist candidacy on the grounds that this would restrict her future. Referring to her campaign for President, she said, "One of my biggest problems was that my campaign was used as a symbolic gesture. . . . My primary objective was to have people respect me as a real, viable candidate. . . . I specifically rejected the feminist candidacy, as I did a black candidacy or an antiwar candidacy.[4] I chose to run for the nomination of one of the major national parties. I did this because I feel that the time for tokenism and symbolic gesture is past. Women need to plunge into the world of politics and battle it out toe-to-toe on the same ground as their male counterparts. If they do not do this, they will not succeed as a Presidential candidate, or in any other campaign for political office."

At the same time, however, Ms. Chisholm has always spoken out on women's issues, and on her own identification with feminism. In a statement given wide circulation she challenged her own constituency with the remark that she had suffered more discrimination as a woman than as a black; and in a recent book recounting her experience running for President, Representative Chisholm went further, and attacked the sexism inflicted on her by black male politicians who resisted her candidacy on the grounds that she was a woman. At a convention in Chicago, she wrote, she overheard a brother's stage whisper broadcast in her direction: "There she is—that little black matriarch who goes around messing things up."[5] In contrast she found women supportive and encouraging, particularly women from the ranks of the feminist movement. In Houston she affirmed how sisterhood had helped her Presidential candidacy, lauding the "fantastic support of some of the leading feminists. . . . Betty Friedan and Gloria Steinem . . . who went out and did a job, not in terms of rhetoric, but in terms of commitment. . . . [they] worked as hard as they knew how."[6]

Clout at Infinity: Broadening the Bases of Support

With an eye on expanding their electoral potential, women leaders are now actively seeking out groups of women still resistant to "women's lib" but receptive to "women's rights." To reach these women they have broadened the range of women's issues, in effect twinning political ambition with the more philosophical goal of deepening the impact of women on politics. As a result many women previously apathetic about politics are becoming politicized, their resources funneled into candidates and groups who hold out the promise of change.

Geri Pleshaw, Mayor Kevin White's liaison to women's groups, travels the Boston area attempting to raise the political consciousness of women from more traditional, "anti-women's-lib" areas. An attractive young women in her early thirties, Ms. Pleshaw uses a low-key approach at her speeches and workshops; she is more interested in helping women understand the issues than she is in proselytizing them.

In the town of Quincy, where she lives, she worked with many women from blue-collar families whose husbands were employed by the local shipyard. Although these women were unlikely to join groups like NOW or the NWPC, they still expressed a great deal of anxiety on what Ms. Pleshaw regarded as women's issues. Many women, for example, expressed their fears about what they were going to do with themselves once their children were grown. "The kids are going to be grown in a couple of years," one woman told her. "How can I go out and work? I used to teach, and now I am thirty-six years old. I have been away from it for twelve years." (Focusing national attention on this particular women's issue, Mayor Joseph Alioto of San Francisco announced that society had an obligation to create employment for the women who had raised its children.[7] This followed the dramatic disappearance of his wife, who explained, on her return, that she had acted to punish her husband for leaving her alone for such long periods of time.)

Other Quincy women complained to Ms. Pleshaw about the town's school lunch program, a deceptively simple issue with important implications. The town leaders originally planned the program only for lower-class families. They operated on the archaic assumption that only lower-class women would be out working. Women from other socioeconomic classes argued angrily that they, too, needed the benefits of a school lunch program so that they could work, or plan to work, without worrying about who was going to feed their children lunch.

To help women understand the issues affecting their immediate destinies, Geri Pleshaw holds workshops for a wide range of women's groups running the gamut from the YWCA to the Women's Resource Center (a militant feminist group). She sees them as part of a new constituency, adding new dimensions to the women's political movement in her area. Many women, she finds, are still conflicted about their roles either as working or nonworking women. "What I try to do," she explained, "is to give them a perspective of the women's movement that relates to the home. . . . The women appreciate the learning they are doing in a nonfrightening atmosphere. We have monthly programs now, films, rap sessions and political workshops." One workshop on child care was particularly successful, she felt, in sensitizing more women to the needs of day care, whether or not they still needed day care for their children. "They got a better understanding of who needs child care," she recalled, and they became more sympathetic toward those most in need of day care. "I don't need it because I stay home," she quoted one woman saying at the end of the workshop, "but there are so many women who can't afford that luxury. And they want a good place for their children—not just at a neighbor's."

The working mother of a young child herself, Ms. Pleshaw identifies with the conflicts women face on the issue of women's liberation, taking a very supportive view of these problems in her workshops. "I sort of defend their conflict," she said. "I tell them there is nothing wrong with feeling this pull, this burden of feeling guilty, of having to justify which responsibilities take preference. That's a choice a man never really has to make, or doesn't have to make in quite the same way.

"I always use economics in my appeals," she continued. "Women are very aware of being economically dependent, and they are very aware of the divorce situation. . . . Their friends are getting divorced. The high school graduate feels very concerned about not having any skills. And she knows this. And when you start talking about these kinds of problems, she can identify with them and she is more likely to become sympathetic with other women. She will probably not become very radical, but she knows what you are talking about."

From establishing a sympathetic understanding of women's issues, Ms. Pleshaw progresses logically toward teaching women how these conflicts can be resolved politically. Women who want to work or who need to work, she argues, will be even more conflicted because of the strains imposed on them of getting child care at a cost they can afford. Well-run child care needs the financial commitment of the state; otherwise it will outprice many women who can not afford to take advantage of it. This commitment has never been achieved, primarily because women have not yet organized powerfully around that issue. President Nixon's veto of the day-care bill—on the grounds that it would foster a communal way of life—met with little organized resistance; indeed, many argued that his veto message would not have been as strong had he faced significant opposition.

With patience, understanding and a willingness to involve

herself in the slow process of reaching out, Geri Pleshaw has translated the women's movement into terms that more conservative women are able to accept. "The groups I talk to, you understand, aren't feminists, so it is a very slow thing. But part of the appeal, I think, is in not being very radical, and in sort of looking respectable."

The goal is power: teaching women how to increase their input on public policy. "What I do is vocalize their fears for them," she said, "and sort of make them look at these fears, then tie them to the political process. Today, for example, I was talking to this woman and she said, 'You know, these men can't make decisions for us.' And I said, 'Well, here is the thing you do. You live in a small town, so everyone knows everyone. When appointments come up, all you need is a group of women—and you don't need an awful lot. And you say, 'Look, we want women on this board and on that board—and in a small town you know the boards run the town—and you want fifty percent representation, and not one woman to be the secretary to send out the cards for the meetings and stuff. Don't settle for that. It is not that hard in a small town.'"

One unlikely group politicized by leaders of the National Women's Political Caucus were women delegates at the Republican national convention in 1972, many of whom openly voiced their opposition to women's liberation. Identifying women's liberation with the "big screamers" at the Democratic national convention held a few weeks earlier, they resisted any connection with either the movement or with their Democratic counterparts. Confronting their hostility, Doris Meissner, former executive director of the NWPC, invited women delegates to a luncheon held in a suite generously donated by Common Cause. Much younger than most of the delegates, Ms. Meissner graciously invited her guests to be seated after they had picked up their box lunches, assuming that in the absence of chairs, they would sit on the floor. A gross miscalculation, laughed Ms. Meissner. These women were shocked at the very idea of sitting on the floor. "They all stood for half an hour, wearing their jacket dresses, and just looked at me," she recalled. "It was clear they were all very hostile, and they were coming up to just see what this was all about. They'd heard about things like this before; they weren't going to be like those Democratic women who were big screamers, and several of them said it."

But Ms. Meissner, an intense and articulate young woman now working as a White House "fellow" in the Justice Department, stood her ground and kept talking to the group until finally a national committeewoman from Arizona raised her hand. "Now, wait a minute," she scolded the group. "They know what they're talking about. I know that I've always been included in party affairs, but it doesn't matter what numbers we are at this convention. Women have always been involved in the Republican party. It is not a problem. The real question is influence. I know myself that even though I'm a national committeewoman, I don't have the kind of influence that I really ought to have."

At that point, related Ms. Meissner, the tide of opinion shifted, as other women began to relate their own experiences and feelings. When the meeting broke up, the atmosphere had changed; much of the hostility had melted away, as the delegates, still standing, and the caucus members shared their common experiences in politics. Encouraged by their success, the caucus invited the Republican women back for lunch the following day, when a smaller but more committed group appeared. According to Ms. Meissner, the women were more candid the second day, expressing their anger at the ways in which women had been discriminated against in politics, as well as their concern with certain planks in the White House platform. "They brought up issues like credit discimination," recalled Ms. Meissner, "suffered by the delegates, many of whom were divorcées and had attempted to get credit on their own. 'I couldn't get a BankAmericard. Isn't that ridiculous?' said one woman. 'I've always paid my bills.'

"And they slowly began to radicalize," said Ms. Meissner. "I'd call that radicalizing. It's kind of amazing how it happened, but if we'd gone in there with a very issue-oriented, women's liberation kind of pitch, there's no way. . . . You always have to have the spearheading effect of the Betty Friedans and the Gloria Steinems, but in terms of a one-to-one relationship you've got to start breaking down those barriers."

And slowly the barriers are crumbling, as women approach

other women outside the well-known movement groups. In Memphis the women's caucus members work closely with the YWCA to reach women they could not otherwise recruit to their ranks. Mary Robinson and Pat Vanderschaaf of the Memphis WPC were asked by the local YWCA to help them find new ways for women to be effective. Gathering women of all political persuasions together, they formed a group called the New Women's Political Experiment, which, they say, has been very successful in bringing diverse groups of women into the same orbit. They had attempted the same kind of thing two years before, but it did not work; few women were attracted to it, and fewer still were willing to give it the time and work necessary to get it off the ground. "When the experiment started," said Mary Robinson, "I guess we felt desperate, like we had no voice; nobody listened. And the YWCA is such a benign, innocent thing that we can get more things done with the YWCA doing it. We can get people to come to lunch that wouldn't have touched us if we hadn't held it in their building." As an afterthought, she mentioned that as an indication of how seriously their project was taken, the local press reported it in the regular news section instead of on the society page where "women's news" traditionally appeared.

Based on the number of invitations she receives to address their groups, Representative Margaret Heckler has reported a sharp increase in the interest of older, more conservative women in the women's movement. They have been somewhat radicalized, she says, by their daughters; they now view the women's movement in terms of their daughter's opportunities, even if they themselves are perfectly content as housewives and seek no professional advancement of their own. "Their support can be reached," said Representative Heckler of these women. "My whole approach is to try to have the broadest scope of input on every issue, particularly on women's issues." Emphasizing that she would go anywhere to rally support for women's issues, she added that she works most closely with middle-of-the-road women's groups: the Business and Professional Women, the Federation of Women's Clubs and the Republican Women's Federation.

Many groups are "tuning in to equality" according to feminist

Betty Friedan, who noted that the YWCA, the Girl Scouts, and the League of Women Voters were drawing closer to the women's political movement.[8] Although part of the "cutting edge" herself, Ms. Friedan now advocates a more moderate tone, urging the NWPC to work with groups grounded in a community-based solidity, rather than with groups she labels "the ideological wing," the "sex-class-warfare bunch," and the "infantile radicals." Avoiding the term "left-wing," she charged these groups with "messing up out of existence the New York State Women's Political Caucus," preventing what she considers legitimate women's issues from coming to the fore in the 1972 election. "Why have free abortion on demand," she asked angrily, "when we don't even have free medical care on demand?"

To redirect the movement along more centrist lines, Ms. Friedan has initiated several attacks on Gloria Steinem, whom she feels is a leading exponent of radicalism on women's issues. Whatever her personal reaction to Ms. Friedan's press conferences and public statements, Ms. Steinem chose not to answer Ms. Friedan's charges publicly, a wise, sensitive decision that has done much to prevent the movement from polarizing.

To their credit, the large women's groups, such as NOW and the NWPC, have expanded their issue base without splitting into discernible radical and conservative wings, bridging their differences without diluting their limited resources. On the major issues there is a wide span of agreement unifying women around political independence and increased influence. No longer frightened by the term "women's lib," more and more women now perceive the necessity to unite on such issues as equal pay for equal work, increased career opportunities for women, and the removal of obstacles preventing women from meaningful participation in politics. And although many would still not consider themselves women's liberationists, they find they can identify with the values and goals of the women's movement.

Sex as an Advantage in Politics

Women candidates are now finding their sex an advantage in politics, and its drawbacks substantially reduced in comparison with the past. "There was no hostility to the fact that I was a woman," said Representative Liz Holtzman, recalling her Congressional campaign in Brooklyn. "I remember truck drivers leaning out of their trucks and saying, 'I think it's great; I think it's fantastic that a woman is running.' People screamed the same thing out of supermarkets. Basically their attitude was extraordinarily positive. . . . you might think that because so many of them had been deprived of the kind of opportunity in their lives that I had that they might resent my running, but instead there was an enormous kind of projection about supporting me, and a terrific response. After the primary I found mothers taking their daughters up to meet me, mothers from lower-middle-class Irish and Italian families. They wanted their daughters to have a different conception of the possibilities for them."

The surge of support for women candidates owes much of its force to the Watergate scandals; in their wake women's chances are likely to continue to improve as the public's demand for honesty in government becomes translated into votes. Capitalizing on what she calls women's "higher credibility" with the voters, Harriet Cipriani hopes to promote as many women as she can into candidacies in the 1974 elections. Although their approach would have to be more subtle, Republicans would be wise to follow a similar course to mitigate the effects of a massive post-Watergate defeat.

Even before Watergate there was evidence that the public perceived women candidates as different from men. Representative Margaret Heckler, who ran for local office for the first time in 1962, remembered the disenchantment with politics was particularly acute during that period. Explaining why women have greater credibility with the voters in extraordinary times, she said, "When the public has a lack of confidence, and in some cases, great suspicion and abhorrence of people in politics, they are willing to look to someone they would not have originally considered as acceptable. With the voters I was considered trustworthy. They came to me; they believed in me and believed me. Being a woman, it was easier for me to establish these credentials because women had not been associated with 'the mess we were in'—the usual phrase."

Several years later, when she ran for Congress, Ms. Heckler experienced the same feminine advantage; to her surprise she and Senator Edward Brooke were the only two Republicans elected that year. "The governor"—she chuckled—"whose coattails I tried to clutch as vigorously as possible—while he tried to avoid my grasp just as actively—was defeated. Here I was clutching Volpe and he never got elected. I went to every single Italian supper. I have eaten more spaghetti—and I love it, too—I got the Italian vote, but I don't know what happened to John Volpe."

The public, she continued, tended to identify women with morality in government. "For whatever reason, we just have not had enough women to have amoral or immoral women in government. You might dislike that spotlight, but you can't point to a corrupt woman in government, and I hope that you never will. And I suspect that they are going to be very hard to find, because even in politics, women are very different from men."

Although Representative Heckler's observations are generally true, there have been some exceptions. Shirley Chisholm's Presidential campaign committee, for example, was accused by the General Accounting Office of mishandling funds. Her husband, Conrad Chisholm, was actually in charge of all receipts and spending, the GAO reported, although he was nowhere listed as a campaign official. In addition, the campaign committee submitted a final report claiming a $6,000 deficit, while the GAO found a surplus of more than $18,000. The GAO was unable to document her reports of campaign spending, but the Justice Department eventually absolved her of any wrongdoing.

As candidates, women are still sufficiently unusual to be more easily recognized than men. Boston's Katherine Kane recalled that her sex was a distinct advantage when running in a field of seven candidates for a seat in the state legislature. "People at least remembered that," she said, although the fact that she was also the only liberal in the race, she added, also helped her candidacy. Ms. Kane served two terms in the state Assembly before joining Mayor Kevin White's administration.

Once elected, women retain their high visibility. Each of the 16 women in Congress has the unique advantage of standing out among her 419 other colleagues and, if she chooses, can exploit this advantage to the benefit of her district and her career. If a Cabinet member meets fifty Congressmen and only one Congresswoman at any of the scores of dinners and receptions enjoyed by official Washington, there is a greater chance that he will remember the Congresswoman if she calls the following day concerning a project affecting her district.

"Female chauvinists" further advocate the superiority of women as candidates and officeholders, basing their case on the unique socialization process experienced by women, particularly career women. By juggling lives more complicated than the average man, they argue, women who combine careers and families demonstrate the ability to cope with many different roles and activities within a limited time frame. Exhorting a group of Boston women to run for office, Ronnie Eldridge made this point: "If you can run a household, market food, pick the children up from school, worry about who was going to take who to dancing lessons, have company for dinner . . . if you can cope with all that and keep some kind of semblance of order, then that's fantastic training for politics. That's the same kind of thing that's done in a campaign, and if you understand that experience, you'd be great in running for office."

The Politicization of Women: The Virginia Slims Poll

Although the party still discriminates against women, recent polls show a quiet revolution among the voters in their attitudes toward women. A study conducted by the Louis Harris polling firm found growing support for a woman candidate for President. A majority of those interviewed indicated they were ready to accept a female candidate for President, while 2 out of 3 voters felt the nation would be ready to elect a woman President in fifty years or sooner.[9]

The study also showed growing numbers of women responding to the efforts of what they termed "bona fide women's organizations," as well as clear-cut agreement among men and women that not only did "women exert more influence in politics than they are given credit for, but that the country would be better off if women had more to say about politics." The study's authors also felt there were important differences in intensity of concern between men and women, with women showing greater concern than men over the war in Vietnam, gun control, and the drug problem. In dealing with the drug problem there was also a significant difference between men and women; women opted for rehabilitation over imprisonment as a way of dealing with the drug problem, while more men than women selected stiff prison terms over medical and psychiatric treatment. A woman President, said a majority of respondents (58 percent), would be less likely to take the nation into war than a man.[10]

The data also debunked some widely held myths about the role of women in politics. The voters, more sophisticated than politicians believe, seem to dispute Dr. Edgar Berman's theories on the incapacity of women to reason logically; 3 out of 4 women, and 71 percent of the male population agree, "Women in public office can be equally logical and rational as men." The study also indicates a strong desire on the part of women to increase their participation in politics. Particularly in the East and in the West, as well as in the cities and the suburbs, high percentages of men and women favored greater female involvement in politics. "In almost identical proportions," concluded the report, "both men and women favor the formation, by leaders of the women's movement for equality, of 'new organizations to strengthen women's participation in politics.' . . . There is no doubt that greater involvement of women in the political processes of this country is desired by both sexes."[11]

Confounding the authors, a wide disparity appeared between the high levels of motivation women displayed toward politics on the one hand, and the low scores they attained in tests designed to show actual levels of participation on the other. Although there were almost as many women as men registered to vote, women were found to participate on more active levels of politics only a fraction of the time that men participated. Only 1 in 3 women has attended rallies for candidates running for political office, for example, compared with 38 percent of the male population; 1 in 4 women has contributed money in support of candidates compared with 34 percent of men. Only in the area of telephone canvassing did women surpass men—10 percent compared with 13 percent.

The political performance of women does not, therefore, adequately reflect their desire to participate in politics; a large pool of political resources remains to be tapped by political candidates. The groups expressing the most willingness to campaign are the same groups who most strongly favor changing their status in society: women in urban settings, younger women, well-educated women and black women. In view of this gap between performance and motivation, conclude the authors, "The candidates and the political parties are making poor use of the 'women power' available for campaigns."

Evidence shows that the gap is rapidly closing. Women candidates have emerged across the nation to campaign for women's rights and women's issues. They are supported by a growing national network of involved and dedicated women who are convinced that the solution to their social and economic problems lies in political activism in mainstream politics.

Chapter X

Conclusion:

The New Political Consciousness

> *I always tell the young people, "Look, while you're waiting for that other thing, that revolution of yours, pick up a piece of political power and do something."*
> —Representative Bella Abzug

> *We will have to stand up to a great deal. We will have to stand up to all kinds of threats. We will have to face the fact that we are challenging the power structure as it exists. But it is just possible that, having had patriarchy and racism for the past many thousands of years, we are on the verge of a new period of humanism.*
> —Gloria Steinem

The coming of age of women in politics coincided with the coming together of diverse political movements, abetted by several accidents of history, in the seventh decade of the twentieth century. It was a compound of women's liberation and Watergate, George McGovern and raised expectations, the peace movement and the sexual revolution, increased education and mounting frustrations. Taken together, they created a bond of sisterhood, stripped women of their political inhibitions, supplied some early victories, and created a "can do" spirit that became self-fulfilling. Women helped women—Republicans helped Democrats and vice versa—New Yorkers helped Chicagoans. It was a network. Of camaraderie. Advice. Talent. Know-how. Encouragement. And solace.

Within two years women had increased their representation in state legislatures by 50 percent, and although their representation remained numerically puny, they were clearly on the move. Women mayors won office in virtually every state in the Union. Women candidates for City Council had a disconcerting habit of leading their tickets, and women were taking aim at governors' mansions.

On Capitol Hill women's heightened political power is reflected in the increased number of women administrative assistants —chiefs of staff—to Senators and Representatives. "When I first came to the Senate in 1955, and groups of legislative assistants got together to go over legislation, very often I was the only woman there," recalled Frances Henderson, the $36,000-a-year administrative assistant to Senator Clifford P. Case, New Jersey Republican, and one of the most knowledgeable and influential Capitol Hill operatives. "Today, there are scores of women." Women now serve as administrative assistants to 73 members of the House, an increase of 21 in the last two years, and 10 Senators, an increase of 3.

"Similarly, the image of the lobbyist as a cigar smoker, a wisecracker, a glad-hander, a backslapper and, above all, a man, is being challenged by the Capitol's small but growing band of women lobbyists."[1] The number of women lobbyists on Capitol Hill has grown from fewer than half a dozen in 1963 to 28 today.

There are further signs of ferment. In the spring of 1974, 1,198 women were candidates for public office, including 13 candidates for governor. The most important were Ella Grasso, the front-runner in Connecticut; Sissy Farenthold, who had previously made a strong showing in Texas, but who lost in her second campaign to incumbent Dolph Briscoe; Betty Roberts, an Oregon state legislator; and Louise Gore, a Republican national committeeperson from Maryland.

Women candidates also took aim at the United States Senate: Barbara Gunderson, a former Republican National Committeeperson from South Dakota, sought to unseat George McGovern, and Paula Hawkins, a Florida state public-service commissioner, looked closely at the seat held by Senator Edward Gurney. In Maryland, Barbara Mikulski announced she would run for the Senate, as did Maya Miller in Nevada. In 1972, when 1,028 women ran for public office, 488 were victorious. The following year, 1973, the number of women in state legislatures had increased by 50 percent, bringing the total up to 7 percent. Off-year elections in 1973 also brought many women into county and municipal offices. In Massachusetts, where one of the most active Women's Political Caucuses is based, 66 women won local offices, including 36 school committee members, 26 City Council members, 2 assessors, 1 city clerk, and 1 collector.

They prevailed, in part because politics represents one of the few professions whose selection process is open to public scrutiny and public judgment. As such, its immediate potential for women's advancement far surpasses the worlds of commerce and industry, academia and the arts, where candidates are chosen *in camera* by those who have a vested interest in the perpetuation of the status quo. In government, moreover, the salary of women elected officials is exactly the same as their male counterparts—one of the few areas in which women are assured equal pay for equal work. The pay often provides an added incentive—the salary for county executive in some areas, for example, runs as high as $30,000 a year—for well-trained and highly educated women who are held back from comparable achievement in other professions.

For women no less than men the biggest political accident of the early 1970's was the discovery of the Republican break-in at the Democratic headquarters in the Watergate hotel in Washington during the 1972 Presidential campaign. Although ignored during 1972, to the chagrin of the Democratic Presidential candidate, the Watergate case preoccupied the nation and its politicians in the years that followed as the depth and breadth of White House duplicity slowly, painfully, but relentlessly came to light. The President's questionable income-tax payments, the enrichment of his property in San Clemente and Key Biscayne, his intervention in an antitrust suit involving ITT, his raising milk prices after the dairy industry had become a major campaign contributor, his unauthorized and illegal bombing of Cambodia—all unraveled before the eyes of an incredulous, outraged public.

As Congress debated impeachment, Congressmen discovered that they, too, had been tarnished by the scandal. Polls revealed public confidence in Congress had deteriorated to a disappointing 21 percent. A national distrust of politicians gripped the land. Senior Republicans in Congress retired in large numbers and observed, in the words of former Representative Howard W. Robison, who quit when he was dean of New York's Republican delegation, "It's going to be a hard year for incumbents."

A hard year for incumbents is automatically a good year for women. "Watergate has stepped up the influx of women candidates," Liz Carpenter noted. "Many who would not have run before were prompted to by Watergate." Women made a virtue of their political impoverishment, their ostracism from the seats of power, their lack of political IOU's. They had been spared the years of entangling alliances that ensnare most veteran male politicians and could exercise an independence undreamed of by men who had sold their souls to political machines, Assembly Speakers and Congressional committee chairmen. Nor were women saddled with political obligations imposed by fat-cat contributors, most of whom had assiduously avoided women; big labor and industry had remained equally aloof.

Another significant breakthrough for women in politics came with the change in their own outlook, the slow but inexorable reversal of what psychologist, and now president of Radcliffe College, Matina Horner identified as women's "will to fail." Centuries of second-class status had taken their toll in self-confidence, creating generations of women who felt that they and their sisters lacked the ability to assume the responsibility and decision-making powers exercised by men. In effect they had accepted and internalized the contempt in which they were held by male politicians, and by their own hand were their worst enemies.

But here, too, another political development speeded their liberation: the battle over the Equal Rights Amendment. Having passed the House and Senate, the amendment was sent for ratification to the state houses, and the women came to lobby, to argue, to suffer, to triumph—and to observe. And what they saw on the floor of the legislatures gave them a new perspective on their own political ability. The male politicians who had told them women lacked the experience, training and temperament for public office were by and large an unimpressive lot. Observing the state Senates in action, discoursing with state representatives, they discovered the mediocre quality of most legislators. They returned home, as they had from the conventions of 1972, shorn of inhibitions, convinced of their own suitability for state office.

It was a baptism by fire. The harsh realities of political life forced women to develop more successful coping mechanisms. To ensure her position with New York's political leaders, for example, Esther Newberg checked in to run Senator Edmund Muskie's Presidential campaign in New York State six months before a man in her position would have had to begin. "I had to go in a whole year before, in June, just so I could visit every county leader, get them used to me, and build up IOU's. A guy wouldn't have had to set this up till November." Even so, her efforts needed some help from Jack English, Muskie's national coordinator. Between the two of them they trained the county leaders to accept and work with a woman—an extraordinary exercise in behavior modification.

"In the beginning Meade [Esposito, Brooklyn Democratic county leader] wouldn't return my phone calls," recalled Ms. Newberg. "He would only speak to English or Muskie. Why talk to some girl who wears pants and what the hell has she ever done before? Working with him took collusion. Jack wouldn't return *his* phone calls. He would say, 'Look, Meade, about that meeting, Esther's got all the details, and I'm going to be in Ohio.' Meade was the most powerful and therefore the most important to get to. Eventually he worked with me, and so did the other county leaders."

As women began to perceive themselves as members of an oppressed caste, they increased their determination to make an impact on politics. This was true of Republicans as well as Democrats, rich women and poor. For the privileged woman the inability to obtain credit or a job or job advancement or to be taken seriously or, indeed, to be regarded as a person in her own right fueled the fires of discontent. Her impoverished sister is afflicted by all of these problems plus those imposed by poverty.

Identifying with the oppressed, women in politics have, as a group, come down heavily on the side of humanism. In Congress Pat Schroeder became an instant thorn in the side of F. Edward Hebert, Louisiana Democrat and chairman of the House Armed Services Committee, where she obtained a seat over his protests and scandalized the committee by voting for the Cambodia bombing halt. Liz Holtzman initiated a lawsuit that nearly ended the Cambodia bombing. Martha Griffiths led the fight for the Equal Rights Amendment. Edith Green fought for federal aid for higher education. Leonor K. Sullivan led the fight for consumer Protection. And Julia Butler Hanse championed a Congressional reform that led to reorganization of the House of Representatives to give greater powers to junior members at the expense of their senior colleagues.

The gloves-off approach is being used more and more by women politicians, with striking results. One of its most ardent advocates, Eleanor Holmes Norton, has managed—probably through these principles—to survive the upheavals of a new mayor and retain her position as the city's human rights commissioner. "Any all-male preserve has a certain ambience," she said, "and you've got to be willing to at least extract that part of it that enables you to function. If you allow men to get away with outdealing you—based on the male ambience—you're in real trouble. Because the fact is there are only a few ways to deal, and just because men have taken over those ways doesn't mean that women shouldn't also find a way to deal. At City Hall you've got to meet cats who will give you nothing because you are a woman. You know you've got to deal with [Jay] Kriegel [former aide to Mayor Lindsay] the way anybody else deals with him; you know, hang up on his ass if he messes with you."

Ms. Norton added that there was one woman in the mayor's inner circle, whom she regarded as very tough politically, who had the disconcerting habit of crying when the pressures became too great. "I regard that as a no-no," she said. "I think if you do that, you should excuse yourself. Although it may seem a perfectly natural thing to do, a man would regard it as a weapon," a sign of weakness women can ill afford at this point in their political development.

As increasing numbers of women enter public life, they will surely improve the status of women in private life. The attack on discriminatory public laws is merely the opening round of an attack on discrimination in the private sector, which has become more and more dependent on government—for contracts, grants, regulations, and general goodwill. One can expect the influx of women in government will lead to the opening of doors long closed, the removal of sex-related obstacles to women's advancement, and the insistence on more vigorous enforcement of legislation prohibiting sex discrimination.

In the final analysis the political process is open. It is possible for women of talent to begin at the precinct level and persevere to positions of influence and power. Politics, therefore, represents a unique opportunity to effect economic and social changes long sought by women, which will ultimately benefit men as well. In the years to come women's humanistic perspective points to a reordering of priorities, a process bound to continue at least until they have been integrated so thoroughly as to be politically inseparable from men. In the process they will improve not only their own status, but will alter the structure of politics and government, and thereby change the structure of society.

Appendix A

National ERA Ratification Council Membership

Advisory Committee, Women's Rights and Responsibilities, HEW
American Association of University Women
American Civil Liberties Union
American Home Economics Association
American Nurses Association
Citizens Advisory Council on Status of Women
Common Cause
Communications Workers of America, AFL-CIO
Counselor to the President for Women's Affairs
Democratic National Committee
District of Columbia State Federation of Women's Clubs
District of Columbia State Federation of Business and Professional Women's Clubs
Federally Employed Women
Federation of Organizations for Professional Women
General Federation of Women's Clubs
Intercollegiate Association of Women Students
Interstate Association of Commissions on Status of Women
League of Women Voters
Legislative Advisors to Senators Birch Bayh and Marlow W. Cook and Representatives Donald M. Fraser and Martha W. Griffiths
National Association of Women Deans and Counselors
National Association of Women Lawyers
National Council of Jewish Women
National Education Association
National Federation of Business and Professional Women's Clubs
National Organization for Women

National Woman's Party
National Women's Political Caucus
Network Staff (Catholic Nuns)
Past Chairwoman, Task Force on Women's Rights and Responsibilities
Past President, National Federation Republican Women's Clubs
Republican National Committee
Staff Assistant to the President for Women Power Recruitment
United Automobile, Aerospace and Agricultural Implements Workers of America, UAW
United Church Women
Washington Forum
Women's Bureau, U.S. Department of Labor
Women's Equity Action League (WEAL)
Women United
Zonta International

Appendix B

Anne Wexler's Memo to the National Women's Political Caucus on ERA

Notes for NWPC

I would like to see the caucus take a systematic approach toward the '74 elections. If unable to look at all twenty unratified states, a sampling where (a) caucus is strong (at least 200 members) and (b) where effort will give most fruitful results in terms of the ERA.

The approach I am suggesting would simply augment current ERA efforts.

1. State caucuses would collect data on legislative districts and legislative incumbents which would be used as criteria for the selection of a group of potentially fertile districts.

2. The caucus could then go about the business of finding a good female candidate, pledged to the ERA, who can run with the support of the caucus, ERA people and active help of NOW political arm, if requested.

3. Some of the criteria which should be considered in the selection of districts:

   a. Previous vote on ERA

   b. Previous public position on ERA

   c. Previous vote/position on approximately five sensitive issues. Assume those would vary from state to state, but would probably include taxes, environment, consumer issues, etc. It would be best to avoid such issues as busing, zoning, and abortion.

   d. Plurality total votes cast in '70 election

e. Political party

f. Own political party's percent of registered voters in district

g. Sex

h. Number of women previously elected from this district

i. District "ethnology," i.e., percent of black, white, Italians, Poles, Irish, etc.

j. Additional personal data, e.g., occupation, marital status, ages, number of terms, etc., where available

k. Other information deemed pertinent

Following criteria selection, then "weight" should be assigned to each criterion (e.g., if threshold or cutoff value of 5 is decided, then if ERA is major criterion, then 5.01 weight would be assigned to negative ERA vote, to assure that field is narrowed to negative ERAer's first).

These weights should be finally determined by state people, within guidelines from steering committee.

The caucus must concern itself with replacement of mediocre legislators as well as noteworthies. Not only will their strength (number of votes) be maximized in state legislatures, but they will be doing the country a service by eliminating some of these Amvet-Jaycee lawyers responsible for the deplorable state of state governments. And vis-à-vis feminist goals, much of the pertinent legislation (education, marriage/divorce, abortion, employment) is settled on state level, so state governments are where it's at.

Passing the Equal Rights Amendment—A Plan for Action

The following plan will provide the basics for the development of an effective Equal Rights Amendment initiative in your state. It is a two-part program which first requires the collection of data by defining the status of the amendment, and then a three-year program for passage.

PART I   Data Collection and Information

Before a coalition can even begin to be effective its members will have to know the following:

1. If the amendment has passed, is there a possibility of a rescission effort?
2. What is the condition of the existing ERA coalition—making an honest assessment of strengths and weaknesses, conflicts and problems?
3. The opposition—who are they, how do they operate, what can be learned from them?
4. What does the legislature look like? Assess by district and vote counts. Who is for ERA, and how can they help? Who is against, and why? Who are the supporters of the legislators in opposition, and who can change their minds? How does the group deal with the opposing legislators?
5. How is the state organized for passage?
6. What is the strength of your constituencies?
7. What about the press?

PART II

Before setting up the necessary task forces to do the job, the coalition should take a good hard look at itself and what changes, both internally and externally, it will have to make. Have you considered any of the following?

- If there is no statewide office, where can one be set up?
- Should you set up satellite offices around the state, as a show of force, as well as convenience?
- Setting up the steering committee to include at least one man. "Men for ERA," see below.
- Set up a timetable and accountability procedure.

TASK FORCES

The following list of task forces represents some possibilities for organizing a coalition in a state.

ORGANIZATIONAL TASK FORCE

1. Responsible for the growth of the coalition.
2. Confirm the endorsements of all local groups and affiliates of all national organizations who have supported the ERA.

3. Work for endorsements from groups who have not endorsed the ERA, especially labor unions.
4. Seek endorsements of local officials, i.e., governor or mayor.
5. Identify coordinators in each district of the state (state could be divided into HR or State Senate Districts) who will broaden the base at the local level. They in turn would develop a unit of workers by giving people very specific instructions and setting achievable goals. The district leaders would in turn report to members of the coalition task force.
6. "Men for ERA"—one sub-task force should be set up for male supporters of the amendment. One man should be in charge of this effort whose main responsibility is to recruit endorsements of prominent men and men's organizations.

OPPOSITION TASK FORCE

1. In charge of constant monitoring of opposition literature, speeches, and all other activities, including meetings where arguments can be publicly countered.
2. Furnish prompt responses to opposition attempts to misstate the case through designated spokespersons and coordination with public-information task force.

LEGISLATIVE TASK FORCE

1. In charge of analysis of legislators by district.
2. Report on legislators' individual attitudes and recommendations on how best to answer their questions and concerns.
3. Assessment of votes—monthly, weekly daily vote counts and changes to be communicated to district workers through coalition task force.
4. Identify districts where grass-roots activity is necessary, where hostile press exists or where letters to editor should be initiated, and work with public-information task force to that end.
5. Appoint and brief lobbyists.
6. Responsible for speakers at hearings and should work with public-information task force to bring attendance to hearings.

7. Collect information on legislators who may be vulnerable in 1974.

PUBLIC-INFORMATION TASK FORCE

1. Should serve as a clearinghouse for all information on ERA.
2. Develop a system of response to individual legislators dealing with their specific questions on ERA, as the information is fed to or by the task force on legislators and legislation.
3. Work with state and local press. First, gather data on positions of all news, TV, radio media and obtain names of reporters sympathetic to our position. Then work on unsympathetic media.
4. Develop a speakers' bureau.
5. Disseminate public information on hearings and votes.
6. Develop a mailing list.
7. Development of printing of literature and materials.
8. Set up volunteer newspaper-clipping service by district which monitors opponent and proponent press.

FUND RAISING

1. Responsible for raising funds within the state. This includes organizing benefits, either parties or speaking engagements or organizing a direct-mail campaign.
2. Can also work on approaching wealthy individuals for contributions or solicit contributions from groups.

With the constant interaction of these task forces no effort is wasted and every effort is directed where it should go. The daily tracking of the task forces can provide the following results:

- The lobbyists know who to talk to and on what issues.
- Changes in votes are reported and proper action results.
- Letters and phone calls go to the right people on the right issues in the right districts.
- The right newspapers get the right letters to the editor from the most effective individuals and organizations.
- The opposition is pinpointed and answered.

- Those who want to work can be put to work.
- A presence is created in the state and in districts where it is important to do so.
- People and organizations who have specific talents can use them most effectively and accumulate experience, know-how, writing press relations, printing, office space, telephoning, etc.

Appendix C*

Original Labor Endorsers of ERA

1. Air Line Pilots Association
2. Amalgamated Clothing Workers
3. American Federation of Teachers
4. Automobile Aerospace, and Agricultural Implement Workers of America, International Union (UAW)
5. Barbers, Hairdressers, and Cosmetologists International Union of America
6. Brewery, Floor, Cereal, Soft Drink and Distillery Workers, International Union of
7. Cement, Lime and Gypsum Workers International Union
8. Chemical Workers Union, International
9. Communications Workers of America
10. Electrical, Radio and Machine Workers, International Union of
11. Electrical Workers, International Brotherhood of
12. Granite Cutters International Association of America
13. International Union Department, AFL-CIO
14. International Brotherhood of Teamsters
15. International Brotherhood of Painters and Allied Trades
16. International Union of Electrical Workers
17. Leather Workers International Union of America
18. The Newspaper Guild
19. National Education Association
20. National Professional Employees International Union
21. United Steelworkers

*List courtesy of NOW legislative office.

Appendix D

"You Can Do It"

REMARKS OF CONGRESSWOMAN PATRICIA SCHROEDER
at the National Women's Political Caucus
Rice Hotel, Houston, Texas
February 9, 1973, 9:30 A.M.

Senator Robert Kennedy once said of his brother John after the President's assassination, "If there is a lesson from his life and death, it is that in this world of ours we can no longer be satisfied with being mere spectators, critics on the sidelines."

And surely that must be the continuing message for all of us here today. Women especially can no longer be mere spectators of the political process, critics on the sidelines, but active participants, playing an important and vital role out on the field.

By your presence here today, each of you is demonstrating her interest in the political process. Many of you have no doubt taken active roles in community and civic organizations, political activities and campaigns, or business and professional activities. You can, do the job—but first, you have to *get* the job. For those of you, and I hope there are many, who may be contemplating a run for office—whether it be party, city, state, judicial, or federal—let me offer a few suggestions from my own experience.

First: Assess critically your own qualifications. It is probably fair to say—although certainly unfair in practice—that a woman running for public office should be "overqualified." Having been chairwoman of your church's women's club may not carry the same clout as being program chairman of the local Rotary Club.

It is interesting to note that all five of this year's new Congresswomen are lawyers. Perhaps this is because, as lawyers, we have necessarily been thrust into an adverse, and often

259

competitive, role with members of the male establishment. Furthermore, we have come into constant contact with many of the problems that face our communities, and worked on possible legislative solutions.

Second: Examine carefully the real base of your support. The support of one's family, close friends, and associates is indispensable. But what contacts or qualifications do you have that will enable you to gain the confidence and backing of other groups and allies? In my own case an extensive labor-law background was valuable in helping eventually obtain both organizational and financial support from many labor unions. Teaching contacts with three major colleges in Denver were also important. Finally, it is essential to take the pulse, and constantly stroke the brows of many of the key party leaders and workers in your area. Many of these veterans of the political wars often will make astute judgments about prospective candidates. Every candidate honestly believes he or she is in fact *the* best candidate. If none of the pros agree, best reexamine your position.

Third: Build credibility. Because you are a woman, you will constantly confront the attitude that you are not "a serious candidate." At our county nominating convention it is customary for candidates to have booths, give away courtesy coffee, distribute literature, placard the walls with posters, etc. I had a basic feeling of aversion to that sort of thing; but we decided it was probably more important that I do some of the traditional things, simply because I was the untraditional candidate.

Because you are a woman you may have the ability to gain more than your fair share of press and media coverage, because you are the different candidate. But the other side of the coin is that you will often be more severely cross-examined on your views and statements by newspeople than is the average male candidate.

Fourth: Develop a strong "grass-roots" organization. You will find that there are great reservoirs of dedicated, talented women who will really work for another woman. This is especially true of many older, retired women and many younger gals, such as students and working girls.

You will probably have a very hard time raising money. My husband often said that the money "is controlled by male-chauvinist pigs." Organization and union money is controlled by men, and they will usually have little confidence in the chances of a woman candidate. Hence, the bigger and better volunteer group you can muster, the better chance you will have of putting your scarce dollars into essential items like printed materials and media time.

Fifth: Use innovative and hard-hitting media. Because a woman candidate is "different," don't be afraid to run a different kind of campaign, utilizing original and different media techniques and content. Let me give you one example: the standard political brochure. You know what I am talking about—the picture of the candidate with family, with coat over the shoulder, in front of the Capitol, etc., with the standard one-liners: "X is honest; X is against pollution; X is for fiscal responsibility." We were able to achieve real impact—and also ruffle some feathers—with colorful mini-posters.

And finally, *Sixth: Be issue-oriented.* Running for public office is too time-consuming and too expensive to embark on such a venture merely for the experience or for the ego satisfaction. If you run, take a stand. Get out front on the issues that concern you, your family, your community, and the nation. The risk, of course, is great; but so are the rewards.

And again, being a woman has both its advantages and disadvantages. I think a woman can more easily take a strong position on the war, on gun control, or education, than perhaps can a man. Isn't a mother going to be against wholesale bombing, for tougher gun control, for better schools? However, you must also guard against being pushed into unreasonable or irresponsible extreme positions by your erstwhile supporters. I was the only major candidate running in Denver last fall who would attend and speak at an abortion panel hearing held at a local college. But I was criticized by some women there when I tried to emphasize my support for birth control and family-planning programs, rather than an "abortion on demand" policy. It is all too easy to become a "Kamikaze candidate"—crashing and burning on one or two emotionally packed issues.

So, it can be done. Women can run. And win. "You can do it!" I hope there will be questions later, and I look forward to talking with many of you individually later on today. Thank you.

Appendix E

Tips On Running For Public Office—From the Office of Women's Activities, Democratic National Committee, Washington, D.C.

This "how to" is designed to give you a few hints on how to succeed in politics by really trying hard. Although the emphasis is on running for the state legislature, with certain changes it can be applied to any public office. It's not a set of hard-and-fast rules. It's not the last word. It can best be called a set of guidelines to encourage you to make a try.

I. Stage One—Preliminaries

1. *Requirements:* In order to comply with state election laws, find out what they are. Obtain a copy of the state requirements. Study the law and be sure you meet the qualifications for the office you want.
2. *Filing:* A candidate must file her intentions with the city or town clerk and, where applicable, pay a filing fee. This must be done before a specific date and time. Check with the local election committee for rules applying to you.
3. *Contact:* If you have not done so already, notify the Democratic State Committee of your candidacy and when you would be available to appear with the major candidates when they are in your area. You may or may not seek the endorsement of your state committee, but in any case you should notify them that you are a candidate.
4. *Goal:* As an official candidate of the Democratic party, your

goal is to win the election. That's easier said than done. Example: If you have 15,000 people in your district (varying from state to state, district to district) and half of them are registered voters, you will need about 4,000 votes to win.

5. *Approach:* The direct approach to the voter is the best system for gaining the needed majority. Meet as many of the voters as possible, tell each of them of your candidacy and convince them that you can do the best job for them as their representative.

Note: The pre-campaign work is mostly preparation. You should have the letters written, cards and posters printed and the state committee notified as soon as possible. Choose the techniques that are most suited to your personality, district and position. The following are suggested materials to be used during the next stage.

Photographs:	Have new photographs taken for use in publicity, on posters and literature.
Printed Cards:	Have a postcard-size card printed with your name, address, telephone number and biographical sketch on it, also a slogan about your campaign and the Democratic party. You may want to have your picture on the card.
Posters:	These could be about 15" x 24", suitable for placing in store windows, etc., and should have your name, address, telephone number and slogan—if you have one. This is a good place to use the new photo.
Mailings:	If you use this method, you can state your position on key issues in the state. You should try to mail one to each voter in the district. You may want to have a new letterhead printed with your name, address and campaign slogan or simply, "Democratic candidate for_____."

Stage Two—The Campaign

1. *House to House:* Visit every home in your district, preferably on evenings or weekends when you're sure most people are home. Tell the residents you're seeking election, that you need their votes and that you will be responsible to them to do whatever is possible to be their voice in government. Be pleasant, but avoid becoming involved in prolonged discussions. You have many other houses to visit. Here may be a time to use volunteers who enjoy house-to-house canvassing. Remind them to be pleasant, informative and leave a good impression of you, the candidate.

2. *Get out the Vote:* During these house calls, ask if there is anyone in the house or neighborhood who needs an absentee ballot or ride to the polls on election day. Also, there may be some members of the household who are not registered voters. Now would be a good time to explain the voting requirements for your community and to offer help in any way to get their names on the voting lists. Don't forget to keep a record of this information for later use.

3. *Circulation:* Attend or initiate political rallies or social events in your town and attend statewide events when possible. Go to meetings of clubs and civic organizations to promote your candidacy.

4. *Innovations:* In one small town a successful Democratic candidate spent Saturday morning at the supermarket giving away coffee and literature on her campaign. She found scores of voters there only too happy to drink coffee, chat and vote for her on election day.

   In your town or district there may be a popular meeting place where you could appear regularly to campaign. Station yourself at employees' entrances to large stores or factories as people are going to work or at quitting time. Don't neglect the shut-in vote; visit convalescent and nursing homes, homes for the aged and other institutions where you can win friends and offer voting assistance.

5. *News Coverage:* Prepare a press release announcing your

candidacy and send it to the papers as soon as you file. (See model press release.) When sending the release to a newspaper, be sure you enclose a recent picture of yourself—a glossy print, head-and-shoulders type, any size.

If you write your own press releases during the campaign, be sure you include your name, address, and name of the office you are seeking on each one. You should be sure the releases have some news value, too. For instance, tell in the release that you spoke to a club or group of supporters and explained your position on an issue. Also, try to have some pictures taken of you meeting some voters, performing some civic service, opening campaign headquarters, etc., and send it to the newspaper editor in your area.

MODEL PRESS RELEASE

For release 10 A.M.
Monday, January 10, 1972

Mary Jones of 1715 Elm Street, Goodloe Heights, said today she will seek election to the state legislature as a Democrat. She will run in the 7th District. Ms. Jones filed her intentions this week with the Goodloe Heights town clerk.

(Here give three or four sentences of biographical data, clubs of which you are a member, any offices you have held, and any other information to help people recognize your talents for the office.

In the last paragraph, list schools you attended, your birthplace, occupation and hobbies, if any. List names of your parents, spouse, children and grandchildren if any.)

For further information call:
Mary Jones
363-3341

(Releases should be typewritten, double-spaced, on one side of the paper.)

6. *Advertising:* Weekly newspapers and local radio stations are the best and least expensive media for candidates to use. Local papers and radio-TV stations search for newsworthy items and appreciate your letting them know of future events. Remem-

ber that to the press future news is the best kind. Let the press know in plenty of time of your future activities and get free coverage.

Your mailings, hand cards, posters and house calls are, in effect, advertising techniques, but now and then it's necessary to place an ad in a newspaper, particularly if your opponent is doing it.

The important thing to remember about ads is that state law requires every ad to be signed either by the candidate or by her so-called fiscal agent. The agent can be a friend who has agreed to let her name be used in your campaign.

With radio ads, part of the message has to include the fiscal agent's name, too. Thus, an ad or commercial would say something like this:

> Vote for Mary Jones, the woman who will do her best to represent you. Remember, a vote for Mary Jones is a vote for continued progress in your state. Sponsored by the Mary Jones for Legislature Committee, Sally Smith, Chairwoman.

One successful candidate used ten-second radio spots recorded by each of her three children and her husband. This showed family support and at the same time repeated the name seven times in ten seconds:

> This is Betty Doe, asking you to vote for my mother, Jane Doe, for the state House of Representatives. This is a political announcement paid for by me, Betty Doe, and by my brothers, Jack Doe and Jim Doe, my father, John Doe, and my mother, Jane Doe.

If you plan to buy radio ads, contract for them a month or so in advance. This will assure you of a good time slot. An economical technique in advertising is to associate with other Democrats on the ballot and buy some ads that mention the entire slate. Also, why not try to collect a list of supporters in your town who will let their names be used in an ad? The ad could say that the following citizens of your voting district will support you. This has the bandwagon effect on voters who haven't made up their minds. This type of advertising is most effective in the last few days of the campaign.

7. *Financing:* No matter how large or small your campaign, it will take some funds. Costs will vary according to the size of your district, or the office you're seeking, but don't let financial worries keep you from running. (See "Money Makers, Old and New" for ideas on fund raising.)

Stage Three—The Election

1. *Get Voters to the Polls:* This requires the use of the telephone, newspaper, radio-TV ads and house calls even though you have been doing all of this during the campaign. Election day is the payoff! It will be the busiest day and night of the year for you. By the end of the afternoon you may find, by checking the voting list, that some of your supporters haven't shown up at the polls. Your staff can now begin calling these people, offering rides to the polls and, in some cases, going to their homes ready to escort them. Young Democrats seem to enjoy this personal contact and can be used during this hectic time.
2. *Poll Watching:* If there is more than one polling place in your district, have someone at each place watching the checklist. Ordinarily the Democratic party provides watchers at the polls. Provide each watcher with a checklist. These can be obtained before election day from the clerk's office. Use the list to check off known supporters as they vote. (Try to do this inconspicuously. Voters don't like to be watched by obvious poll watchers.)

EPILOGUE

ELECTION NIGHT: Now is the time to invite your faithful friends in to watch election returns—and to celebrate your victory.

SUPPOSE YOU DON'T WIN: Now is the time to start planning the next campaign—the one you *will* win.

II. *You Could Be a State Legislator*

How many people know who their U.S. Congressman is? Surprisingly few.

Then consider how many know who their representative in the *state* legislature is. Even fewer. (Just do a quick canvass in your area and you'll be amazed.)

Now consider this proposition: A Representative whose name isn't familiar to the voters could be easily displaced . . . by someone who *is* known to the voters. This could be the key for capturing Republican-held seats in your state legislature.

1. Analyze your legislative districts carefully. List those that are represented by Republicans. Then determine which are vulnerable. Look for these vulnerability symptoms:
    a) An incumbent who feels "safe" and never bothers to campaign
    b) An incumbent who is colorless or relatively unknown in the district
    c) An incumbent who has taken an unpopular stand on local issues
    d) An incumbent who has remained unchallenged although the political makeup of the population has changed
    e) A district where the voter turnout has been very low
2. A strong Democratic candidate could challenge these incumbents. The best candidate may be a woman who is well known for her political or community activities and who is respected and trusted. Women candidates are often more successful in winning bipartisan support than men.
3. That candidate could be *YOU*.

If you decide it could be you or one of your friends, the Democratic National Committee has a number of tools to help.

It Can Be Done!

It takes hard work and a plan—but it can be done. Here are some tips:

Have a plan. Have a carefully thought-through campaign plan and stick to it—unless, of course, it becomes obvious in the middle of its execution that you've made a mistake and it is the wrong plan for you. Understand what it is you are trying to do so that you can put the right priorities on your time and not be distracted by extraneous things. For instance, consider the size of the district; if it's small, plan to visit each house. Weigh your friends' offers to have coffees for you against reaching more people in the same amount of time by house-to-house canvassing. If it's a large district, it might call for different strategy, but don't lose sight of the importance of personal contact.

Organize. You don't have time to do everything yourself. Decide early to run so that you will have time to build a personal organization of people who will take responsibility for many of the details. Start with your friends, neighbors, and acquaintances. You'll be surprised at how many people think it's fun to be part of a political campaign.

Prepare. The secret to getting and keeping workers is to have specific jobs ready for them to do at all times. This means preparation. Have a carefully prepared instruction sheet which explains the purpose of the chore, suggested techniques, and where appropriate, provide the necessary details.

Follow-up. Somebody must keep a record of who is responsible for what, and make periodic checks to see that each job is completed on schedule.

A Success Story

Here is how one Democrat did it. The first Democrat ever elected to the state legislature from her Republican district.

Her district had about 11,000 citizens (5,601 registered voters). Since it was a Republican district, she had to persuade the voters that party affiliation was not the only factor to be considered when choosing a Representative and, therefore, ran a strictly personal campaign.

She tried to visit the home of every voter. If not one was there, she left a printed card (carrying her photograph) on which she added a note in her own handwriting, including her phone number. Between the primary and November she spent almost every day, including weekends, canvassing. She felt that this was the most efficient use of her time and energy and that it was the *kind* of contact necessary to get her known in the district. She made no effort to get speaking engagements, but did give a few speeches if they didn't interfere with her canvassing schedule. In other words, her number-one priority was to personally visit every household in her district before the end of October and this she did!

Her friends did many things for her: typed 3" x 5" cards for every registered voter and sorted them by street address; hand-addressed envelopes; wrote personal notes to acquaintances on her behalf; made posters for election day; participated in all the traditional election day poll watching to check on who voted and telephoning those who hadn't by noon.

It worked! She won a two-to-one victory in a predominantly Republican district. And it was her first campaign.

Her advice: "Do it! Win or lose, it's a great experience."

How-To Materials Available

The following sample materials are available for distribution in limited quantities from the Office of Women's Activities. Any of these samples will be sent to you on request. Since these are mostly one- or two-page information sheets, we encourage you to reproduce them in any form that best suits your organization's needs.

On Clubs
  Democratic Women's Clubs
  How to Organize a Democrat-
    ic Club
  Sample Constitution and By-
    laws
  Tips for Club Presidents
  How to Run a Membership
    Drive

On Volunteers
How to Get and Keep Volunteers
How to Use Campaign Volunteers

On Campaign Techniques
Tips for a Winning Campaign
Women as Campaigners
Put Your Campaign on Wheels
Tips for a Candidate's Husband
Tips for a Candidate's Wife

On Social Events
Coffee Hours for Candidates
Tips for the Coffee Hour Hostess
How to Set Up a Conference
How to Plan a Luncheon or Dinner

On Fund Raising
Money Makers, Old and New
Fund Raising with Gimmicks and Gadgets

On Organization
Finding Democrats by Telephone—A Registration Program
How to Build Precinct Strength
What's in a Canvasser's Kit
County Political Countdown
How to Have Livelier Meetings
Election Day Victory Plan

On Publicity and Public Relations
  How to Draw a Crowd
  Tips for Speakers
  So You're Going to Have a
    Speaker
  How to Get Out a Newsletter
  When You're on Camera
  How to Get Good Radio, TV
    and Press Coverage for Vis-
    iting VIP's

Miscellaneous
  Political Brainstorming
  From Fair Booth to Election
    Booth
  Home Headquarters—Some-
    thing New for Your Candi-
    date
  Tips on Running for Public
    Office
  Making the Most of Your
    Headquarters

We welcome your comments on any of this material and your suggestions about new material needed. If your group has worked up any literature that is especially useful, or developed a highly successful program that you would like to share with other Democrats across the country, be sure to let us know. The most useful ideas come from those who are working in the field.

Office of Women's Activities
DEMOCRATIC NATIONAL COMMITTEE
1625 Massachusetts Ave., N.W.
Washington, D.C. 20036

Notes

INTRODUCTION

1 Ronald Sullivan, New York *Times*, September 25, 1972, p. 78.
2 New York *Times*, November 26, 1972, p. 40.
3 Bill Lawrence, *Six Presidents, Too Many Wars* (New York, Saturday Review Press, 1972), p. 228.
4 Joe Napolitan, *The Election Game* (Garden City, N.Y., Doubleday, 1972), p. 89.
5 Richard Reeves, "Reel Politics," *New York* (June 26, 1972), p. 49.
6 Robin Morgan, ed., *Sisterhood Is Powerful* (New York, Vintage Books, 1970), p. xxxiii.

CHAPTER I

1 To ensure that the McGovern reforms materialized into political reality, Women's Education for Delegate Selection (WEDS) was formed as an arm of the bipartisan National Women's Political Caucus. WEDS masterminded the selection of women delegates in many states by thorough and painstaking efforts on a state-by-state basis to educate and influence women to run as delegates. The group also sought to promote women into positions of influence within the convention by bringing pressure to bear on the party's national committee in cases involving those states violating the sex-discrimination guidelines ("as equally divided among men and women as possible") in appointing members of the convention's platform, credentials and rules committees.

Following WEDS' complaint to the national committee's general counsel, Joseph Califano, Jr., action was taken against Florida, Georgia and Maryland for discriminating in the appointment of members to the convention's committees. *Congressional Quarterly News Service*, Washington, D.C. (June 14, 1972), pp. 1–3.

2 With Shirley Chisholm also a contender for the Presidential nomination, many women faced a difficult choice: Should they support a man who was excellent on women's issues who had a chance of winning, or should they give their resources to a woman whose candidacy held great symbolic value for them but little chance of success?

3 Major representatives negotiating for the feminist political movement at the convention were Gloria Steinem, Betty Friedan, and Bella Abzug. As an elected Democratic Congresswoman, Bella Abzug bridged both camps, although at the convention she fell in more often with the ranks of feminist leaders.

4 Some have argued that sexism was not the reason in this case, citing the similar ousting of Republican National Chairman Dean Burch after the defeat of Barry Goldwater in 1964. Dean Burch, however, was named shortly afterward to a high post on the Federal Communications Commission; Jean Westwood received no such consolation prize.

5 Anne Wexler disputed the cochairperson promise. "The original commitment was that McGovern was committed to O'Brien as chairman. Period. The rest was negotiable," she reported.

6 Washington *Post,* July 13, 1972, p. 1.

7 New York City's Commissioner of Human Rights.

8 Washington *Post,* July 13, 1972, p. 1.

9 Germaine Greer, "McGovern, the Big Tease," *Harper's* (October, 1972), pp. 56–71.

10 Nan Robertson, New York *Times,* July 15, 1972, p. 1.

11 Theodore H. White, *The Making of the President 1972* (New York, Atheneum, 1972), p. 186.

12 And, indeed, the choice did come up. On the South Carolina vote Martha McKay voted with the women, against instructions from Terry Sanford's people, who wanted South Carolina left alone because they'd had some votes for themselves in the original delegation.

13 White, *op. cit.,* p. 168.

14 *Ibid.*

15 Nan Robertson, New York *Times,* July 5, 1972, p. 13.

16 *Ibid.*

CHAPTER II

1 New York *Times,* February 20, 1972, p. 91.
2 *Congressional Quarterly Weekly Report,* April 22, 1972, p. 883.
3 *Ibid.*
4 Figures computed from a variety of sources, including *State Elected Officials and the Legislatures* (supplement to *Book of the States*), Council of State Governments, Washington, D.C., 1973.
5 Figures from Harriet Cipriani, director of the Office of Women's Activities, Democratic National Committee, Washington, D.C., 1973.
6 Figures extrapolated from the following sources: Salaries and Compensation of Legislators and State Administrative Officials: Annual Salaries (Tabular Summary), courtesy of the Council of States, Washington, D.C. 1973, supplement to the *Book of the States* 1972–3; from *State Elective Officials and the Legislatures 1973, op. cit.;* and from figures provided by the National Women's Political Caucus, Washington, D.C.
7 After publication of her famous book *The Feminine Mystique* (New York, Norton, 1963), which became one of the best-known tracts of the women's liberation movement.
8 Ms. Boggs' husband, Majority Leader Hale Boggs, was lost on an airplane trip in Alaska. According to Louisiana law, Ms. Boggs was technically not declared a widow at the time of her election.
9 Martin Gruberg, *Women in American Politics* (Oshkosh, Wis., Academia Press, 1968), p. 122.
10 Like most widows' successions, Ms. Smith still had to run in a special election called in June, 1940, and later that year in the general election. See Hope Chamberlin, *A Minority of Members: Women in the U.S. Congress, 1917–72* (New York, Praeger, 1973), pp. 141–43.
11 Some smaller unions, such as the Carpenters Union, supported Ms. Griffiths; larger organizations, the AFL-CIO and the UAW, for example, did not.
12 In the meantime, Williams had appointed her to a short-term

vacancy on the Criminal Court, where she served for ten months, hearing matters involving colleagues of labor leader James Hoffa. None of the other judges, she says, wanted to adjudicate these cases.

13 *Congressional Quarterly Weekly Report,* April 22, 1972, p. 883.

14 Prior to this, there is some evidence indicating that the Democratic party recognized its tendency nationwide to relegate women to lower service roles in the political party and in 1964 issued a campaign manual urging that women be considered for more than traditional woman's activities. One party worker is quoted as saying that the party would have to advance good volunteers if it wanted to keep them: "If you ask her to stuff envelopes . . . she'll quit. That's what she's been doing for the Cancer Drive or the PTA." See Martin Gruberg, *op. cit.,* p. 53.

15 Ann B. Matasar and Mary Cornelia Porter, *The Role and Status of Women in the Daley Organization.* Paper delivered at the 1972 annual meeting of the American Political Science Association, Washington, D.C., pp. 1–30.

16 Doris Gold, "Women and Voluntarism," in Vivian Gornick and Barbara Moran, *Woman in Sexist Society* (New York, Basic Books, 1971), pp. 384–400.

17 Martin and Susan Tolchin, *To the Victor—Political Patronage from the Clubhouse to the White House* (New York, Random House, 1971), Chap. 4, pp. 131–86.

18 League officers and board members are prevented from working for political candidates.

CHAPTER III

1 One hundred and fifty women made up the book's sample, including Congresswomen, assemblywomen, state senators, City Council representatives, political appointees in the executive branches of state and federal government, White House aides, Congressional aides, mayoral aides, defeated candidates from all levels of political office; activists from a wide variety of interest groups, among them, the National Women's Political Caucus and its state affiliates, the National Organization for Women, the League of Women Voters, the

Daughters of the American Revolution, the Radical Feminists; and representatives from both the Democratic and Republican party hierarchies. Men were also interviewed for the study.

2 Fred Greenstein, *Children and Politics,* rev. ed. (New Haven, Yale University Press, 1965), p. 127. Women political scientists have begun to question the data on which such conclusions in the literature on voting behavior and political participation are based. See Susan C. Bourque and Jean Grossholtz, "Politics as an Unnatural Practice: Political Science Looks at Female Participation," an incisive, unpublished paper presented at the American Political Science convention in New Orleans, 1973.

3 For a brilliant exposition of the role played by the culture in subordinating women, see Simone de Beauvoir, *The Second Sex* (New York, Bantam, 1965), particularly Parts I–IV. She draws from the teachings of history, religion and Biblical literature to show how few heroines there are for women to emulate or admire. Almost all myths and folklore revolve around the exploits of men; only women who have achieved sainthood are accorded the same reverence. Women in mythology tended to be freaks, while men provided the heroism. In religion the heroes are almost all male: God the father is male, as are Christ, the Pope, the prophets, most ministers and rabbis, and all priests. (In September, 1972, the Vatican handed down a decision upholding the church's tradition barring women from the priesthood.) Queen Esther, a rare heroine in Biblical history, saved the Jews by kneeling before Ahasuerus, the king—a heroine cast in the role of supplicant.

4 Attacking his "phallocentric bias," Dr. Natalie Shainess argues that Freud's view of women has given rise to what she terms a slave mentality among women: submissive on the surface, concealing a seething resentment beneath. This finds its apex, she says, in Oriental culture, where the surface submissiveness of women contrasts sharply with their inner strength and rage. "A Psychiatrist's View: Images of Woman—Past and Present, Overt and Obscured," in Robin Morgan, ed., *Sisterhood Is Powerful* (New York, Vintage Books, 1970), pp. 230–45. For an interesting commentary on the effects of the Communist revolution on Chinese women, see Joseph Kraft's article, "The

New Maoist Woman," in *Cosmopolitan* (May, 1973), pp. 175–78.

5 Maurice Duverger, *The Political Role of Women* (Paris, UNESCO), p. 129.

6 Edmund Constantini and Kenneth H. Craik, "Women as Politicians: The Social Background, Personality, and Political Careers of Female Party Leaders," *Journal of Social Issues*, Vol. 28, No. 2 (1972), p. 218.

7 Kirsten Amundsen, *The Silenced Majority* (Englewood Cliffs, N.J., Prentice-Hall, 1971), p. 84; and Hope Chamberlin, *A Minority of Members: Women in the U.S. Congress, 1917–72* (New York, Praeger, 1973), pp. 313–15.

8 Bella Abzug, speech delivered before the National Women's Political Caucus convention in Houston, Texas, February 9, 1973.

9 Keeping women apart from social and political control in this way is traced by de Beauvoir to a tradition common among primitive cultures of ascribing an aura of religious purity to women. Citing anthropologist Claude Lévi-Strauss, she describes the identification with the earth accorded to women by primitive societies. Related to the myth of the Earth Mother, women were regarded as fertility symbols and often given the role of tilling the soil as part of this belief system. Some tribes thought pregnant women in the fields would make the crops more abundant. Imbuing women with a mystical, almost godlike quality invested them with other-worldly powers, while men retained solid control over social and political authority in the real world. The patterns persisted, even though in modern culture women are not believed to hold supernatural powers. De Beauvoir, *op. cit.*, p. 65.

10 Leo Kanowitz cites a series of laws prescribing sex-based differences in the minimum marriageable-age requirements in which females are allowed to marry without parental consent two to three years earlier than males. "Only eleven states prescribe the same minimum age for marriage for males and females, where parental consent is not required. The remaining thirty-nine states permit girls to be married from

two to three years earlier than boys, the most frequent arrangements being a twenty-one-year minimum for boys and eighteen for girls." The rationale for these laws, according to Kanowitz, is based on certain assumptions, e.g., that "early marriage impedes preparation for meaningful extra-family activities," therefore, "society has decreed that males should not be permitted this digression from life's important business at too early an age"; on the other hand, "the married state is the only proper goal of womanhood," justifying the legal presumptions for allowing women to marry earlier. See *Women and the Law: The Unfinished Revolution* (Albuquerque, N.M., University of New Mexico Press, 1969), pp. 10–11.

11 Along with Assemblyman Albert Blumenthal, a reform Democrat from New York City's Upper West Side, who championed the reform bill despite several defeats before its passage. Assemblywoman Constance Cook from Ithaca, New York, was also an effective worker for abortion reform and was particularly instrumental in saving the bill from repeal. The Supreme Court ultimately removed the issue of abortion reform from the state legislatures, affirming women's freedom of choice in this area.

12 An interesting conflict has presented itself within this issue area. While women have fought for the right to regard pregnancy as a natural and healthy part of a woman's life, they also feel they have the right to receive medical benefits for hospitalization and financial compensation for time lost in the process of giving birth. To gain these benefits, in the language of most medical plans, pregnancy must be reformulated, to be regarded as an "illness," which, of course, it is not.

13 Hope Chamberlin, *op. cit.*, pp. 264–65.

14 For further discussion of this problem, see Judy Syfers, "I Want a Wife," *Ms.* (Spring, 1972), p. 56; and in the same issue, Jane O'Reilly, "The Housewife's Moment of Truth," pp. 54–59, and Susan Edmiston, "How to Write Your Own Marriage Contract," pp. 66–72.

CHAPTER IV

1 His argument drew credibility from a monograph published

by the Office of Legislative Research, Connecticut General Assembly, called *The Potential Impact of the Proposed Equal Rights Amendment on Connecticut Statutes,* March 7, 1973, which examined in detail the laws endangered by the passage of the ERA. Under "protective" labor laws, for example, the report cited three types of labor legislation that might be affected by the passage of the ERA: (1) laws that confer a benefit on women, such as minimum-wage laws, mandatory rest periods, or required seats for rest periods; (2) laws that exclude women from certain occupations or exclude women from employment before and after childbirth; and (3) laws that restrict the hours or conditions of employment for women. Instead of taking privileges and protections away from women, the report points out, proponents of the bill believe that privileges and protections benefiting women should be extended to men. If a woman is allowed a rest period, a man covered by the same legislation ought to be allowed the same rest period. (This is known as the benefit-burden formula.) The report also covered more than ten separate areas of laws affected by the ERA, including domestic relations, elections law, property law, health and welfare, labor, retirement, disability and death benefits, and military law.

2 It was first introduced in Congress in 1923 at the behest of the National Women's Party, three years after the passage of the Women's Suffrage amendment. The amendment was written by Alice Paul, who founded the militant Congressional Union for Women's Suffrage in 1913, which later became the Women's Party. The amendment was introduced by Senator Charles Curtis, who was later Vice President under Herbert Hoover, and Representative Daniel R. Anthony, a nephew of Susan B. Anthony.

3 Nick Thimmesch, "The Sexual Equality Amendment," *New York Times Magazine* (June 24, 1973), p. 8.

4 *Ibid.*

5 Outlined in her book *A Choice Not an Echo,* widely distributed during the 1964 Presidential campaign.

6 Eileen Shanahan, New York *Times,* January 15, 1973, p. 12.

7 See Appendix A for a complete list of ERA's supporters.

8 The ERA Action Committee, a core group, is composed of Elizabeth Chittick, National Chairwoman, National Woman's Party; Pat Keefer, Legislative Officer, Common Cause; Jan McMichael, Staff Director, National Women's Political Caucus; Leslie Dunn, Staff Director, Legislative Action, League of Women Voters; Marguerite Rawalt, Washington Forum; Elizabeth Espinoza, President, D.C. State Federation Business and Professional Women's Clubs, Inc.; Lucille Shriver, Director, National Federation Business and Professional Women's Clubs, Inc.; and Dr. Irene Murphy, from the Center for Women's Policy Studies. Mary Gereau, from the NEA, chairs the group, which holds its meetings at NEA's headquarters in Washington.

9 Eileen Shanahan, New York *Times,* May 29, 1973, p. 38.

10 States that had not ratified at that time but were scheduled to meet in 1974 were North Carolina, Mississippi, Virginia, Georgia, Illinois, Indiana, Arizona, Montana, Oklahoma, Louisiana, Missouri, Ohio, South Carolina, Maine and Florida. Since then, Ohio, Maine and Montana have ratified the amendment.

11 See Appendix B for a copy of this memo.

12 Eileen Shanahan, New York *Times,* January 15, 1973, p. 1.

13 The full amendment reads as follows: (1) Equality of Rights under the law shall not be denied or abridged by the United States or by any state on account of sex. (2) The Congress shall have the power to enforce, by appropriate legislation, the provisions of this article. (3) This amendment shall take effect two years after the date of ratification.

14 Interview on *Firing Line,* an interview show hosted by William F. Buckley and broadcast on public television stations. Published in pamphlet form by Southern Educational Communications Association, Columbia, S.C., 1973. The show was televised on April 1, 1973.

15 The court decisions were slim pickings, however, leading the Citizens Advisory Council to conclude in 1970 that "during the past half-century, women have been largely unsuccessful in seeking judicial relief from sex discrimination in cases challenging the constitutionality of discriminatory laws under

these provisions." See *Women in 1970,* March, 1971, p. 11. For further discussion of women's rights and the law, see Leo Kanowitz, *Women and the Law: The Unfinished Revolution* (Albuquerque, N.M., University of New Mexico Press, 1969).

16 Common Cause, "Questions and Answers on the Proposed 27th Amendment to the Constitution, Now Before the States for Ratification," Washington, 1973.

17 *Ibid.*

18 Barbara Brown, Thomas I. Emerson, Gail Falk, and Ann Freedman, *Yale Law Journal,* Vol. 80, 1971, p. 943.

19 Citizens Advisory Council on the Status of Women, "The Equal Rights Amendment and Alimony and Child Support Laws," Department of Labor, Washington, D.C., January, 1972, pp. 2–3.

20 *McGuire* v. *McGuire,* 157 Neb. 226, 59 N.W. 2d 336 (1953).

21 Barbara Brown, Thomas I. Emerson, Gail Falk and Ann Freedman, *Yale Law Journal,* Vol. 80, 1971, p. 943.

22 Citizens Advisory Council, *op. cit.,* pp. 4–5. The report they cite was conducted by the American Bar Association, the Support Committee of the Family Law Section, 1965, monograph no. 1. The authors, Ms. Una Rita Quenstedt and Col. Carl E. Winkler, surveyed 575 domestic-relations-court judges, friends of the court and commissioners of domestic relations.

23 *Webber* v. *Webber,* 33 C. 2d 153, 199 P. 2d 943 (1948).

24 Citizens Advisory Council, *op. cit.,* p. 7.

25 Indicating the priorities are set by male-oriented research, as in most areas of scholarly inquiry.

26 *Ibid.*

27 Letter dated February 5, 1973.

28 Such as the United Auto Workers, the American Newspaper Guild, the Communications Workers of America, the International Brotherhood of Painters and Allied Trades, the International Brotherhood of Teamsters, and several state affiliates of the AFL-CIO. See Appendix C for a complete list of the unions supporting ERA.

29 In the opinion of Myra K. Wolfgang, vice-president of the Hotel and Restaurant Employees and Bartenders Internation-

al Union, AFL-CIO. Quoted in Office of Legislative Research, Connecticut General Assembly, *op. cit.*, p. 28.

30 She also headed the Woman's Bureau during the Kennedy administration. Before that she worked as a lobbyist for the Amalgamated Clothing Workers Union. Now she serves as a consumer affairs executive for Giant Foods.

31 Statement of Andrew J. Biemiller, director, Department of Legislation, American Federation of Labor and Congress of Industrial Organizations. Before Subcommittee No. 1 of the House Committee on the Judiciary on H.J. Res. 208. The Equal Rights Amendment and H.R. 916. The Women's Equality Act, p. 1.

CHAPTER V

1 *The Congressional Record,* Vol. 119, No. 86, 93d Congress, p. 4356.

2 *Ibid.*

3 Last year the major proponents of the bill included the American Association of University Women, American Nurses Association, Church Women United, Day Care and Child Development Council, Interstate Association of Commissions on the Status of Women, National Association for the Advancement of Colored People, National Council of Jewish Women, National Council of Negro Women, National Federation of Business and Professional Women's Clubs, National Organization for Women, National Women's Political Caucus, Women's Equity Action League, Women's Lobby, Women's Service Club of Boston and YWCA National Board. Other groups supporting the bill included Amalgamated Clothing Workers, Amalgamated Meat Cutters Union, American Ethical Union, AFL-CIO, AFSCME, American Humanist Association, American Veterans Committee, Americans for Democratic Action, Environmental Action, Friends Committee on National Legislation, Household Technicians of America, ILGWU, Leadership Conference on Civil Rights, Migrant Legal Action Program, NAACP, National Conference of Catholic Laity, National Consumers League, National Council of Churches, National Council of Senior Citizens,

NEA, National Farmers Union, National Student Lobby, National Welfare Rights Association, National Urban League, Unitarian Universalist Association, UAW, United Church of Christ, Council for Christian Social Action, U.S. Catholic Conference.

4 These groups included the Methodist women ("great and well organized," according to the women who worked with them), Church Women United, the Newspaper Guild, the American Association of University Women, the American Nurses Association, and the American Home Economics Association.

5 *The Congressional Record, loc. cit.,* p. 4358.

6 *Ibid.*

7 *Ibid.,* p. 4363.

8 *Ibid.*

9 Report of the National Commission on Consumer Finance, December, 1972, p. 152.

10 *Ibid.*

11 *Ibid.,* p. 153.

12 *The Congressional Record,* October 17, 1973, 0–6600.

13 U.S. Department of Labor, Women's Bureau, Facts About Women's Absenteeism and Labor Turnover, August, 1969.

14 Home Mortgage Delinquency and Foreclosure. John B. Herzog and James S. Early, National Bureau of Economic Research, New York, 1970.

15 U.S. Department of Labor, "Work Life Expectancy and Training Needs of Women," *Manpower Report No. 12* (May, 1967), p. 4.

16 Elizabeth Waldman and Kathryn Gover, "Marital and Family Characteristics of the Labor Force," *Monthly Labor Review* (April, 1972), p. 19.

17 Elizabeth Waldman, *Monthly Labor Review* (May, 1970), p. 19.

18 Chart, p. 46, *Monthly Labor Review* (March, 1971).

19 U.S. Bureau of Census, Current Population Reports, Series P–23, No. 36, "Fertility Indicators: 1970," p. 36.

20 Washington *Post,* March 5, 1972, p. D6.

CHAPTER VI

1 The emphasis was hers. Press release, February 16, 1972.

2 A wealthy former actress who ran against Representative Koch.

3 Advertisement in New York *Times,* November 4, 1972.

4 New York City suffered a split in its political caucus, between the original group, already enfranchised as the New York Women's Political Caucus, and the group accorded real legitimacy—renamed the Manhattan Women's Political Caucus.

5 Debate with William F. Ryan, New York *Times,* June 9, 1972.

6 Debate with Priscilla Ryan, New York *Times,* November 1, 1972.

7 Although she appeared to draw considerable support among Congressmen. A fund raiser given for her by Washington columnist Milton Viorst drew thirty Congressmen ready to contribute to her campaign.

8 Even though his aid behind the scenes was so vigorous, Representative Abzug played down the mayor's support publicly since his popularity among New Yorkers was uncertain at that time.

9 The 20th C.D. stretches from Greenwich Village up Manhattan's West Side, through Washington Heights and into the Riverdale section of the Bronx.

10 Interestingly, two other elections in which widows ran for their husbands' Congressional seats during the same time period failed to produce the same response from feminists. Like Ms. Ryan, neither of these women (Lindy Boggs and Carliss Collins)—each of whom won her election—was strongly identified with the women's movement.

11 Speech by Congresswoman Bella S. Abzug to the National Women's Political Caucus, July 10, 1971, Statler Hilton Hotel. Ms. Abzug was one of the founders, along with Ms. Steinem and Ms. Friedan, of the NWPC.

12 A New York *Times* headline, referring to the county committee election, which ran a month before the general election read: RYAN-ABZUG RACE IS RATED A TOSSUP. New York *Times,* October 1, 1972, p. 1.

13 The district lines are created by the legislature—the Republican-controlled legislature in Albany. The Democratic leader-

ship, however, works closely with the Republican leadership (indeed, some Republican and Democratic leaders are business partners), and together they parceled out seats to those who cooperated with them, and removed those who did not—despite all the rhetoric to the contrary.

14 HR 967, A Resolution to Impeach Richard Nixon. A petition to Carl Albert, Speaker of the House.

15 At the first debate at the New York *Times,* June 9, 1972, between herself and the late William Fitts Ryan. Transcript.

16 Michael Barone, Grant Ujifusa and Douglas Matthews, *The Almanac of American Politics* (Boston, Gambit, 1974), p. 696.

17 A statement liberally quoted by the Ryan forces during the campaign. Mark J. Green, James M. Fallows, and David R. Zwick, *Who Runs Congress?* (New York, Bantam Books, published jointly with Grossman Publishers, 1972). (The Ralph Nader Congress Project.)

18 Richard Madden, "Ms. Abzug Finding Mr.'s Rule House," New York *Times,* October 11, 1971, p. 37.

19 In New York, July 10, 1971.

20 Shirley Chisholm, *The Good Fight* (New York, Harper & Row, 1973), p. 74.

CHAPTER VII

1 From a speech to the National Women's Political Caucus, February 9, 1973.

2 In early figures collected by the National Women's Political Caucus in November, 1973, at least ten women had declared their intention to run for office the following year.

3 Lead time is also an important factor in the campaigns of well-known and highly visible candidates. Joseph Napolitan pinpoints most of the blame for the narrow defeat of Hubert Humphrey's Presidential campaign in 1968 to the fact that as Humphrey's political consultant, he was allotted only two months' lead time. See *The Election Game* (New York, Doubleday, 1972).

4 See the testimony of Sissy Farenthold on behalf of the NWPC before the Senate Rules Committee, Subcommittee on Privileges and Elections, September, 1973. One of only two

women scheduled to testify, Ms. Farenthold urged reform of the present system of campaign financing: "We believe that lack of money is the major reason why so few women seek public office and why so few of those who do are successful." National Women's Political Caucus, *Newsletter*, VII, p. 1.

5 At a press conference called in Washington by the National Women's Political Caucus. Ms. Farenthold is chairperson of the NWPC. Washington *Post*, Mary Russell, February 14, 1974, p. A2.

6 The NWPC, a bipartisan group, does not contribute to political candidates. The finances are used for staff salaries, office expenses, running conferences, and a speakers' bureau. Operating on a small budget, its expenditures for 1972 totaled $74,586.19, exceeding its income of $70,863.68. Its expenditures for 1971 totaled $16,471.85, from an income of $18,576.00. Figures from Doris Meissner, former executive director of the NWPC.

7 Martin Gruberg, *Women in American Politics—An Assessment and Sourcebook* (New York, Academia Press, 1968), p. 65.

8 Women candidates have achieved marked success running from college towns or districts encompassing colleges or universities. Thanks to the advent of the eighteen-year-old vote, their numbers may increase in these areas. To name a few: Sarah Weddington, whose district included the University of Texas at Austin; Constance Cook, an outspoken champion of abortion reform, elected from Ithaca (Cornell University); Audrey Beck, a state Assemblywoman from Storrs, Connecticut (University of Connecticut, where her husband teaches political science); Barbara Ackerman, the mayor of Cambridge (Harvard University); and Pat Sheehan, the mayor of New Brunswick (Rutgers University). East Brunswick has also elected a woman mayor, Jean Walling. Pat Schroeder's district included the University of Denver.

9 From remarks of Congresswoman Pat Schroeder at the National Women's Political Caucus First Annual Convention, entitled "You Can Do It," advising women how to run for office. Houston, February 9, 1973. See Appendix D for full text. The Office of Women's Activities of the Democratic

National Committee has also developed a program designed to help women run for office. See Appendix E, "Tips on Running for Public Office."

10 Other contributors include the Irwin-Sweeney-Miller Foundation, Joint Foundation Support, and Cudahy Fund.

11 Unlike many other party organizations requiring representation of both sexes in a committee district, in Philadelphia a district may be represented by two members of the same sex.

12 Criminal Jurisprudence, Appropriations and Insurance.

13 As she does. Ms. Beck is editor of the party's weekly newspaper and president of her county Democratic club.

CHAPTER VIII

1 Indeed, the title personnel director was changed from patronage director. In New York, for example, the personnel director is subordinate to the patronage dispenser, traditionally the deputy mayor or one of the mayor's personal aides.

2 Former New York City Consumer Affairs Commissioner Bess Meyerson—former winner of the Miss America title—succeeded, through the force of her own personality, in imprinting consumer protection on the public consciousness for the first time in the city's history.

3 The numbers vary each year, according to Ms. Prevost, depending on the changes in needs, the instituting of new departments and programs, the cutting back of others, etc.

CHAPTER IX

1 New York *Times,* December 9, 1973, p. 55.

2 Caroline Bird, *Born Female* (New York, McKay, 1969).

3 But many women are nonetheless breaking into the business world thanks to the great strides the women's movement has been able to achieve. "Women are at last moving into the pipeline of American business," reported Marilyn Bender in the New York *Times,* January 20, 1974, pp. 1, 43, "largely as a result of government pressure and militant feminism." Ms. Bender cited women across the country who have moved into professional and lower managerial jobs, such as corporate staff lawyer, auto factory foreman, computer marketing manager,

as well as executive positions in what were previously all-male preserves, such as brokerage and banking, and corporate financial jobs. These changes were brought about by concrete actions on the part of women who resented the limits society imposed on their career development. Suits were filed with the Equal Employment Opportunity Commission (EEOC), which in turn instituted suits against the companies allegedly practicing sex discrimination. One successful suit forced AT&T to agree to award $38 million in back pay and increases to its women and minority male employees. Now that the federal government has indicated that it intends to enforce Title VII of the 1964 Civil Rights Act, banning sex discrimination, other companies and institutions have begun efforts to recruit and promote women.

4 Perhaps a veiled reference to Bella Abzug.

5 Shirley Chisholm, *The Good Fight* (New York, Harper & Row, 1973), p. 32. See also *Unbought and Unbossed,* her political autobiography (Boston, Houghton Mifflin, 1970).

6 At the annual meeting of the National Women's Political Caucus, February 9, 1973.

7 At a news conference televised on February 7, 1974 (CBS News).

8 From remarks made at a panel on "Women and Politics" at the Northeast Political Science Association's annual meeting, Buck Hill Falls, Pa., November 9, 1973.

9 The pollsters modified this upbeat conclusion to their data showing figures indicating that 2 out of 5 women still feel the Presidency should be reserved for a man. This, the pollsters say, suggests that "women might well suffer from a collective inferiority complex, which must be overcome before women can attain high political offices." See Louis Harris and Associates, "A Survey of the Attitudes of Women on their Roles in Politics and the Economy" (The 1972 Virginia Slims American Women's Opinion Poll, monograph, 1972), pp. 35–38.

On voting behavior of women, see also Carolyn Setlow and Gloria Steinem, "Why Women Voted for Richard Nixon," *Ms.* (March, 1973), p. 66.

Still another study conducted by the Eagleton Institute in

1974 examined the attitudes of New Jersey voters; their conclusions were even more optimistic than the Harris poll. Their data showed that 91 percent of the sample would support a woman running for local office or for a state legislature; 90 percent would support a woman running for Congress; 82 percent would support a woman running for governor; and 63 percent would back a woman running for President. See *Congressional Quarterly, Weekly Report,* Vol. XXXII, No. 15 (April 13, 1974), p. 941.

10 Prior research, although now somewhat dated, also suggests differences between men and women in their issue positions. "Women are less willing to support policies they perceive as warlike or 'aggressive'—policies ranging from universal military training to capital punishment," wrote Fred Greenstein, a political scientist. "Women have been shown more likely to support sumptuary legislation—for example, restrictions on alcohol consumption and gambling. Women also seem to be less tolerant of political and religious nonconformity." He also cites an early Roper poll—showing much more female concern with two 1952 campaign issues, the Korean War and allegations of government corruption—which appeared in Louis Harris' *Is There a Republican Majority?* (New York, Harper, 1954). See Fred Greenstein, *Children and Politics,* rev. ed. (New Haven, Yale University Press, 1965), pp. 106–7. Additional research on this subject mentioned by Greenstein includes the following: Harold F. Gosnell, *Democracy: The Threshold of Freedom* (New York, Ronald Press, 1948), Chap. 4; Maurice Duverger, *The Political Role of Women* (Paris, UNESCO, 1955); Robert E. Lane, *Political Life* (Glencoe, The Free Press, 1959), pp. 209–16; H. Cantril and M. Strunk, *Public Opinion 1935–1946* (Princeton, Princeton University Press, 1951); and Angus Campbell and others, *The Voter Decides* (Evanston, Illinois, Row, Peterson, 1954).

11 Harris et. al., *op. cit,* p. 9.

CHAPTER X

1 Judy Klemesrud, New York *Times,* November 14, 1973, p. 50.

Selected Bibliography

Books

Abzug, Bella, *Ms. Abzug Goes to Washington*. New York, Saturday Review Press, 1972.

Altbach, Edith H., ed., *From Feminism to Liberation*. Cambridge, Mass., Schenkman Publishing Co., 1971.

Amundsen, Kirsten, *The Silenced Majority: Women in American Democracy*. Englewood Cliffs, N.J., Prentice-Hall, 1971.

Barone, Michael, Ujifusa, Grant, and Matthews, Douglas, *The Almanac of American Politics*. Boston, Gambit, 1974.

Beard, Mary, *Women as a Force in History*. New York, Macmillan, 1946.

Bernard, Jessie, *Women and the Public Interest*. Chicago, Aldine, 1971.

Bird, Caroline, *Born Female*. New York, McKay, 1969.

Boston Women's Health Collective, *Our Bodies, Ourselves*. New York, Simon & Schuster, 1973.

Bullough, Vern L., and Bullough, Bonnie, *The Subordinate Sex*. Urbana, Ill., University of Illinois Press, 1973.

Campbell, Angus, and others, *The Voter Decides*. Evanston, Ill., Row, Peterson, 1954.

Cantril, Hadley, and Strunk, Mildred, *Public Opinion 1935–1946*. Princeton, Princeton University Press, 1951.

Catt, Carrie, and Shuler, Nettie, *Woman Suffrage and Politics: The Inner Story of the Suffrage Movement*. Seattle, University of Washington Press, 1969.

Chamberlin, Hope, *A Minority of Members: Women in the U.S. Congress*. New York, Praeger, 1973.

Chesler, Phyllis, *Women and Madness*. Garden City, N.Y., Doubleday, 1972.

Chisholm, Shirley, *The Good Fight*. New York, Harper & Row, 1973.

———, *Unbought and Unbossed*. Boston, Houghton Mifflin, 1970.

293

De Beauvoir, Simone, *The Second Sex.* New York, Knopf, 1953.

De Crow, Karen. *The Young Woman's Guide to Liberation.* New York, Pegasus, 1971.

Decter, Midge. *The New Chastity and Other Arguments Against Women's Liberation.* New York, Coward, McCann & Geoghegan, 1972.

Duverger, Maurice, *The Political Role of Women.* Paris, UNESCO, 1955.

Epstein, Cynthia, *Woman's Place: Options and Limits in Profesional Careers.* Berkeley, University of California Press, 1970.

Firestone, Shulamith, *The Dialectic of Sex: The Case for Feminist Revolution.* New York, William Morrow, 1970.

Flexner, Eleanor, *Century of Struggle: The Women's Rights Movement in the United States.* Cambridge, Mass., Belknap Press of Harvard University, 1959.

Frankfort, Ellen, *Vaginal Politics.* New York, Quadrangle, 1972.

Friedan, Betty, *The Feminine Mystique.* New York, Norton, 1963. (Tenth Anniversary Edition, Norton, with new introduction and epilogue, 1974.)

Garskof, Michele, *Roles Women Play: Readings Toward Women's Liberation.* Belmont, Calif., Brooks/Cole, 1971.

Gornick, Vivian, and Moran, Barbara, *Woman in Sexist Society.* New York, Basic Books, 1971.

Green, Mark J., Fallows, James M., and Zwick, David R., *Who Runs Congress?* (The Ralph Nader Congress Project.) New York, Bantam Books, 1972.

Greenstein, Fred, *Children and Politics,* rev. ed. New Haven, Yale University Press, 1965.

Greer, Germaine, *The Female Eunuch.* New York, McGraw-Hill, 1971.

Grimes, Alan Pendleton, *The Puritan Ethic and Woman Suffrage.* New York, Oxford University Press, 1967.

Grimstad, Kirsten, and Rennie, Susan, eds., *The New Woman's Survival Catalog.* New York, Coward, McCann & Geoghegan, 1973.

Gruberg, Martin, *Women in American Politics: An Assessment and Sourcebook.* Oshkosh, Wisconsin, Academia Press, 1968.

Hecker, Eugene Arthur, *A Short History of Women's Rights from the*

Days of Augustus to the Present Time. New York and London, G. P. Putnam's Sons, 1910.

Hole, Judith, and Levine, Ellen, *Rebirth of Feminism.* New York, Quadrangle, 1971.

Horney, Karen, *Feminine Psychology.* New York, Norton, 1967.

Huber, Joan, *Changing Woman in a Changing Society.* Chicago, University of Chicago Press, 1973.

Janeway, Elizabeth, *Man's World, Woman's Place.* New York, William Morrow, 1971.

Jenness, Linda, ed., *Feminism and Socialism.* New York, Pathfinder Press, 1972.

Kanowitz, Leo, *Sex Roles in Law and Society: Cases and Materials.* Albuquerque, University of New Mexico Press, 1973.

———, *Women and the Law: The Unfinished Revolution.* Albuquerque, University of New Mexico Press, 1969.

Kirkpatrick, Jeane, *Political Woman.* New York, Basic Books, 1974.

Koedt, Anne, Levine, Ellen, and Rapone, Anita, eds., *Radical Feminism.* New York, Quadrangle, 1973.

Komisar, Lucy, *The New Feminism.* New York, Warner Paperback, 1972.

Kraditor, Aileen S., *The Ideas of the Woman Suffrage Movement 1890–1920.* New York, Columbia University Press, 1965.

———, *Up from the Pedestal: Selected Writings in the History of American Feminism.* Chicago: Quadrangle, 1968.

Ladner, Joyce, *Tomorrow's Tomorrow: The Black Woman.* Garden City, N.Y., Doubleday, 1971.

Lamson, Peggy, *Few Are Chosen: American Women in Political Life Today.* Boston, Houghton Mifflin, 1970.

Lane, Robert, *Political Life.* Glencoe, The Free Press, 1959.

Lash, Joseph, *Eleanor and Franklin.* New York, Norton, 1971.

———, *Eleanor: The Years Alone.* New York, Norton, 1973.

Lawrence, Bill, *Six Presidents, Too Many Wars.* New York, Saturday Review Press, 1972.

Lemons, J. Stanley, *The Woman Citizen: Social Feminism in the 1920's.* Urbana, Ill., University of Illinois Press, 1973.

Lifton, Robert Jay, ed. *The Woman in America.* Boston, Beacon Press, 1964.

Lund, Caroline, and Stone, Betsey, *Women and the Equal Rights Amendment.* New York, Pathfinder Press, 1970.

Maccoby, Eleanor, ed., *The Development of Sex Differences.* Stanford, Stanford University Press, 1966.

Mailer, Norman, *The Prisoner of Sex.* Boston, Little, Brown, 1971.

Martin, Wendy, ed., *American Sisterhood: Writings of the Feminist Movement from Colonial Times to the Present.* New York, Harper & Row, 1972.

Marx, Karl, and others, *The Woman Question: Selections from the Writings of Karl Marx, Frederick Engels, V. I. Lenin, and Joseph Stalin.* New York, International Publishers, 1970.

McAllester, Susan, ed., *A Case for Equity: Women in English Departments.* Urbana, Ill., National Council of Teachers of English, 1971.

Mill, John Stuart, and Mill, Harriet Taylor, *Essays on Sex Equality,* ed. and with an intro. by Alice Rossi. Chicago, University of Chicago Press, 1970.

Mill, John Stuart, *The Subjection of Women.* New York, Appleton, 1870.

Millett, Kate, *Sexual Politics.* Garden City, N.Y., Doubleday, 1970.

Mitchell, Juliet, *Woman's Estate.* New York, Pantheon, 1971.

Morgan, David, *Suffragists and Democrats: The Politics of Woman Suffrage in America.* East Lansing, Michigan State Press, 1971.

Morgan, Robin, ed., *Sisterhood Is Powerful: An Anthology of Writings from the Women's Liberation Movement.* New York, Random House, 1970.

Murphy, Irene, *Public Policy on the Status of Women: Agenda and Strategy for the Seventies.* Lexington, Mass., Lexington Books, 1973.

Napolitan, Joseph, *The Election Game.* Garden City, N.Y., Doubleday, 1972.

Notes from the Second Year: Women's Liberation. Major Writings of the *Radical Feminist.* Box AA, Old Chelsea Station, New York, N.Y. 10011. *Notes from the Third Year* also published, 1971–1973.

O'Neill, William, *Everyone Was Brave: The Rise and Fall of Feminism in America.* Chicago, Quadrangle Books, 1969.

———, ed., *The Woman Movement: Feminism in the United States and England.* Chicago, Quadrangle Books, 1969.

Reed, Evelyn, *Problems of Women's Liberation: A Marxist Approach.* New York, Pathfinder Press, 1971.

Reeves, Nancy, *Womankind Beyond the Stereotypes.* Chicago, Aldine, 1971.

Reische, Diana L., ed., *Women and Society.* New York, H.W. Wilson Co., 1972.

Riegel, Robert Edgar, *American Feminists.* Lawrence, University of Kansas Press, 1963.

Rossi, Alice, ed. and with introductory essays, *The Feminist Papers: From Adams to de Beauvoir.* New York, Bantam, 1973.

Roszak, Betty, and Roszak, Theodore, *Masculine/Feminine: Readings in the Sexual Mythology and the Liberation of Women.* New York, Harper & Row, 1969.

Rowbotham, Sheila. *Women, Resistance and Revolution: A History of Women and Revolution in the Modern World.* New York, Pantheon, 1973.

Sanders, Marion K., *The Lady and The Vote.* Boston, Houghton Mifflin, 1956.

Schneir, Miriam, ed., *Feminism: The Essential Writings.* New York, Vintage, 1972.

Scott, Anne F., *The Southern Lady: From Pedestal to Politics, 1830–1930.* Chicago, University of Chicago Press, 1970.

Seaman, Barbara, *Free and Female: The Sex Life of the Contemporary Female.* New York, Coward, McCann & Geoghegan, 1972.

Shaw, George Bernard, *The Intelligent Woman's Guide to Socialism, Capitalism, Sovietism and Fascism.* New York, Vintage, 1972.

Smith, Margaret Chase, *Declaration of Conscience.* Garden City, N.Y., Doubleday, 1972.

Smith, Page, *Daughters of the Promised Land.* Boston, Little Brown, 1968.

Sochen, June, ed., *The New Feminism in Twentieth-Century America.* Lexington Books, 1971.

Tanner, Leslie, ed., *Voices from Women's Liberation.* New York, Signet, 1970.

Thompson, Mary Lou, ed., *Voices of the New Feminism.* Boston, Beacon Press, 1970.

Tolchin, Martin, and Tolchin, Susan, *To the Victor—Political Patronage from the Clubhouse to the White House.* New York,

Random House, 1971.

Watkins, Mel, and David, Jay, eds., *Black Woman: Portraits in Fact and Fiction.* New York, William Morrow, 1970.

White, Theodore, *The Making of the President 1972.* New York, Atheneum, 1973.

Wollstonecraft, Mary, *Vindication of the Rights of Woman.* New York, Source Book Press, 1971. (Unabridged republication of the 1792 London edition.)

The Women's Movement, Editorial Research Reports, *Congressional Quarterly.* Washington, D.C., 1973.

Women's Struggle for Social and Political Equality in the United States. 6 vols. Source Library of the Women's Movement, 1970.

Wortis, Helen, and Rabinowitz, Clara, eds., *The Women's Movement: Social and Psychological Perspectives.* New York, Halsted Press, 1972.

Articles, Periodicals, Monographs, Dissertations, Bibliographies and Newspapers

Banthin, Joanna, "The New York State Women's Political Caucus—A Case Study in Organizational Behavior." Unpublished PhD dissertation, University of Michigan, 1973.

Biemiller, Andrew J., "Statement Before Subcommittee No. 1 of the House Committee on the Judiciary on H.J. Res. 208. The Equal Rights Amendment and H.R. 916." 1971.

Bird, Caroline, "The Case for a Woman President." *New Woman* (April/May, 1972), pp. 32–35.

"Bode *v.* National Democratic Party: Apportionment of Delegates to National Political Conventions." *Harvard Law Review,* Vol. 85 (May, 1972), pp. 1460–77.

Bourque, Susan C., and Grossholtz, Jean, "Politics as an Unnatural Practice: Political Science Looks at Female Participation." Unpublished paper presented at the American Political Science Association convention, New Orleans, 1973.

Boyd, Ramsay, "Women and Politics in the U.S. and Canada." *Annals of the American Academy of Political and Social Science,* Vol. 375 (January, 1968), pp. 52–57.

Brown, Barbara, and others, "The Equal Rights Amendment: A

Constitutional Basis for Equal Rights for Women." *Yale Law Journal,* Vol. 80 (April, 1971), pp. 871–985.

Burstein, Patricia, and Cimons, Marlene, "Women Candidates Who Won." *Ms.,* Vol. 1, No. 9 (March, 1973), pp. 68–71.

"Campaign '72: Women's Struggle for a Larger Role." *Congressional Quarterly Weekly Report,* Vol. 30 (April 22, 1972), pp. 883–85.

Common Cause, "Questions and Answers on the Proposed 27th Amendment to the Constitution, Now Before the States for Ratification." Washington, D.C.

Congressional Record. Vol. 119, No. 86, 93rd Congress. (Debate over whether to include domestics in the pending minimum wage bill.).

Constantini, Edmund, and Craik, Kenneth, "Women as Politicians: The Social Background, Personality, and Political Careers of Female Party Leaders." *Journal of Social Issues,* Vol. 28, No. 2 (1972), pp. 217–36.

Costello, Mary, "Women Voters." *Editorial Research Reports* (October 11, 1972), pp. 767–84.

Cox, Harvey, "Eight Theses on Female Liberation." *Christianity and Crisis,* Vol. 31 (October 4, 1971), pp. 199–202.

Democratic National Committee, Office of Women's Activities. 1971, 1972 and 1973 nationwide figures on elected women at all levels of political office.

Didion, Joan, "The Women's Movement," *New York Times Book Review* (July 30, 1972), sec. 7, p. 1.

Edmiston, Susan, "How to Write Your Own Marriage Contract." *Ms.* preview issue (Spring, 1972), pp. 66–72.

Ephron, Nora, "Women," *Esquire,* Vol. 78, No. 5 (November, 1972), p. 10.

"Equal Rights: Amendment Passed over Ervin Opposition." *Congressional Quarterly Weekly Report,* Vol. 30 (March 25, 1972), pp. 692–95.

"The Equal Rights Amendment." Transcription of the debate between Ann Scott and Phyllis Schlafly on "Firing Line," television program hosted by William F. Buckley. Published by the Southern Educational Communications Association, 1973.

"The Equal Rights Amendment and the Military." *Yale Law Review,* Vol. 82 (June, 1973), pp.1533–37.

Fasteau, Brenda F., and Lobel, Bonnie, "Rating the Candidates." *Ms.* (Spring, 1972), pp. 74–84.

Frappollo, Elizabeth, "The Ticket that Might Have Been: Vice President Farenthold." *Ms.*, Vol. 1, No. 7 (January, 1973), pp. 74–76.

Friedan, Betty, "Up from the Kitchen Floor." *New York Times Magazine* (March 4, 1973), p. 8.

Gehlen, Frieda, "Women in Congress." *Transaction* (October, 1969), pp. 36–40.

Greenstein, Fred, "Sex-Related Political Differences in Childhood." *Journal of Politics* (May, 1961), pp. 353–72.

Greer, Germaine, "McGovern, The Big Tease." *Harper's* (October, 1972), pp. 56–71.

Hacker, Helen, "Women as a Minority Group." *Social Forces,* No. 3 (1951), p. 7.

Harris, Louis, and associates, "A Survey of the Attitudes of Women on their Roles in Politics and the Economy." The 1972 Virginia Slims American Women's Opinion Poll, monograph.

Herzog, John, and Earley, James, "Home Mortgage Delinquency and Foreclosure." National Bureau of Economic Research monograph, New York, 1970.

Horner, Matina S., "Toward an Understanding of Achievement: Related Conflicts in Women." *Journal of Social Issues,* Vol. 28, No. 2 (1972), pp. 157–76.

Israel, Lee, "Helen Gahagan Douglas." *Ms.*, Vol. II, No. 4 (October, 1973), pp. 55–59.

Jennings, M. Kent, and Thomas, Norman, "Men and Women in Party Elites: Social Roles and Political Resources." *Midwest Journal of Political Science,* Vol. 12 (November, 1968), pp. 469–92.

Johnson, Dorothy E., "Organized Women as Lobbyists in the 1920's." *Capitol Studies,* Vol. 1 (Spring, 1972), pp. 41–58.

Kerr, Virginia, and Sudow, Ellen, "Call to Action: A Legislative Agenda for the 93rd Congress." *Ms.*, Vol. 1, No. 7 (January, 1973), pp. 81–85.

Krichman, Albert, *The Women's Rights Movement in the United States 1848–1970*—a bibliography and sourcebook. Metuchen, N.J., Scarecrow Press, 1972.

Lerner, Gerda, "The Feminists: A Second Look." *Columbia Forum,* Vol. 13 (Fall, 1970), pp. 24–40.

Levenson, Rosaline, *Women in Government and Politics: A Bibliography of American and Foreign Sources.* Council of Planning Librarians, 1973, 80 pages.

Levitt, Morris, *Women's Role in American Politics.* Council of Planning Librarians. A bibliography, 1973.

Lynn, Naomi B., and Flora, Cornelia B., "Motherhood and Political Participation: The Changing Sense of Self." *Journal of Political and Military Sociology,* Vol. 1 (Spring, 1973), pp. 91–103.

McDonald, Donald, "The Liberation of Women." *The Center Magazine* (May/June, 1972), pp. 25–44.

McDowell, Margaret B., "The New Rhetoric of Woman Power." *Midwest Quarterly,* Vol. 12 (winter, 1971), pp. 187–98.

McFadden, Judith Nies, "Women's Liberation on Capitol Hill." *Progressive,* Vol. 34 (December, 1970), pp. 22–25.

Marcus, Barbara, "The Year of the Women Candidates." *Ms.,* Vol. 1, No. 3 (September, 1972), pp. 64–69.

Matasar, Ann B., and Porter, Mary Cornelia, "The Role and Status of Women in the Daley Organization." Paper delivered at the American Political Science Association convention, Washington, D.C., 1972.

Means, Irgunn Nordeval, "Political Recruitment of Women in Norway." *Western Political Quarterly,* Vol. 25 (September, 1972), pp. 491–521.

National Women's Political Caucus *Newsletter,* 1972–1974.

O'Reilly, Jane, "The Housewife's Moment of Truth." *Ms.,* preview issue (Spring, 1972), pp. 54–59.

Orth, Maureen, "The Great American Child-Care Disgrace." *Ms.,* Vol. 1, No. 11 (May, 1973), pp. 88–90.

Rosenberg, Marie Barovic, "Political Efficacy and Sex Role: Case Study of Congresswomen Edith Green and Julia Butler Hansen." Paper delivered at the American Political Science Association convention, Washington, D.C., 1972.

Rosenberg, Marie Barovic, with Matasar, Ann, and Lynn, Naomi, "Research Guide for Undergraduates in Women's Studies." General Learning Corporation, 1974.

Rosenberg, Marie Barovic, with Bergstrom, Len, "Women in

Society: A Critical Review of the Literature with a Selected Annotated Bibliography." Sage Publications, 1974.

Shaffer, Helen, "Status of Women," *Editorial Research Reports,* Vol. 2, No. 5 (August 5, 1970), pp. 565–85.

Schuman, Pat, and Detlefsen, Gay, "Sisterhood Is Serious—An Annotated Bibliography." *Library Journal,* Vol. 96 (September, 1971), pp. 2587–94.

Seifer, Nancy, "Barbara Mikulski and the Blue-Collar Woman." *Ms.,* Vol. 2, No. 5 (November, 1973), pp. 70–74.

Setlow, Carolyn, and Steinem, Gloria, "Why Women Voted for Richard Nixon." *Ms.,* Vol. 1, No. 9 (March, 1973), p. 66.

"Sex Discrimination and Equal Protection: Do We Need A Constitutional Amendment?" *Harvard Law Review,* Vol. 84 (April, 1971), pp. 1499–1524.

Steinem, Gloria, "Coming of Age with McGovern." *Ms.,* Vol. 1, No. 4 (October, 1972), pp. 39–43.

———, "The Ticket that Might Have Been: President Chisholm." *Ms.,* Vol. 1, No. 7 (January, 1973), pp. 72–74.

Steinem, Gloria, and others, "Special Section: Running for Office . . . How to Campaign on the Issues, Lobby for Your Interests and Reform Your Party and the System Itself." *Ms.,* Vol. 2, No. 10 (April, 1974), pp. 61–68.

Syfers, Judy, "I Want a Wife." *Ms.,* preview issue (Spring, 1972), p. 56.

Thimmesch, Nick, "The Sexual Equality Amendment." *New York Times Magazine* (June 24, 1973), p. 8.

Tolchin, Susan, and Tolchin, Martin, "Getting Clout." *Esquire,* Vol. 80, No. 1 (July, 1973), pp. 112–15.

Transaction (November/December, 1970), issue on women.

Waldman, Elizabeth, and Gover, Kathryn, "Marital and Family Characteristics of the Labor Force." *Monthly Labor Review* (April, 1972).

Werner, Emmy, "Women in Congress: 1917–1964." *Western Political Quarterly,* Vol. 19 (March, 1966), pp. 16–30.

———, "Women in the State Legislatures." *Western Political Quarterly,* Vol. 21 (March, 1968), pp. 40–50.

Whaley, Sara Stauffer, "American Women in National Political

Life," a bibliographical essay. *Women's Studies Abstracts.* Vol. 1 (spring, 1972).

"Women in Politics," report from a conference held by the Center for the American Woman and Politics, Rutgers University, New Brunswick, N.J., 1973.

"Women in Public Service." Republican National Committee monograph, Washington, D.C.

"Women State Legislators: Report from a Conference." New Brunswick, Center for the American Woman and Politics, Eagleton Institute, 1973.

Women's Studies Abstracts, a quarterly publication that abstracts materials on women, as well as listing articles and books relevant to women's studies. PO Box 1, Rush, N.Y.

Public Documents

"The Equal Rights Amendment and Alimony and Child Support Laws." Citizen's Advisory Council on the Status of Women, Department of Labor, Washington, D.C., January, 1972.

"Women in 1970." Citizens Advisory Council on the Status of Women, monograph. See also, "Women in 1971," and "Women in 1972." Department of Labor, Washington, D.C., 1971, 1972 and 1973, respectively.

National Commission on Consumer Finance, Testimony of Hearings on Sex Discrimination. December, 1972.

"The Potential Impact of the Proposed Equal Rights Amendment on Connecticut Statutes." Office of Legislative Research, Connecticut General Assembly monograph, March 7, 1973.

"Fertility Indicators: 1970." United States Bureau of the Census *Current Population Reports,* Series P–23, No. 36, p. 36.

"Facts About Women's Absenteeism and Labor Turnover." United States Department of Labor, Woman's Bureau, August, 1969.

"Work Life Expectancy and Training Needs of Women." United States Department of Labor *Manpower Report,* No. 12, May, 1967.

"Equal Rights for Men and Women 1971: Hearings, March

24–April 5, 1971, on H.J. Res. 35, 208, and related bills, proposing an amendment to the Constitution of the United States relative to Equal Rights for Men and Women, and H.R. 916 and related bills concerning the recommendations of the presidential Task Force on Women's Rights and Responsibilities." United States House of Representatives, Committee on the Judiciary, Subcommittee No. 4. 92d Congress, 1st Session.

"The Equal Rights Amendment hearings, May 5–7, 1970, on S.J. res. 61, to amend the Constitution so as to provide equal rights for men and women." United States Senate, Committee on the Judiciary, Subcommittee on Constitutional Amendments, 91st Congress, 2nd Session.

"Equal Rights 1970: hearings September 9–15, 1970, on S.J. res. 61 and S.J. res. 231, proposing an amendment to the Constitution of the United States relative to equal rights for men and women." United States Senate, Committee on the Judiciary, 91st Congress, 2nd Session.

"A Matter of Simple Justice." United States. President's Commission on the Status of Women, 1970.

Index